Forever England

Reflections on Race, Masculinity and Empire

Jonathan Rutherford

Lawrence & Wishart
LONDON

Lawrence & Wishart Limited
99a Wallis Road
London E9 5LN

First published 1997

British Library Cataloguing in Publication data.
A catalogue record for this book is available from the
British Library.

ISBN 0 85315 828 2

Photoset in North Wales by
Derek Doyle & Associates, Mold, Flintshire.
Printed and bound in Great Britain by
Redwood Books, Trowbridge.

CONTENTS

If I should die, think only this of me;
    That there's some corner of a foreign field
That is forever England.
                    (*The Soldier*, Rupert Brooke, 1914)

1
INTRODUCTION

> I have been dogged for years, from as far back as I can remember, by the impulse to return to a place where I have never been – an imaginary and actual island ... sometimes the shore shines and is bright with miraculous possibilities, sometimes it is the manifestation of my most secret fears ... the chance has come to return to this island and I will take it only because it is no longer my story.
>
> (Iain Sinclair, *Down River*)

We are living in an age of migration, change and uncertainty. Our unease about the places and spaces we inhabit has been reinforced by the contemporary shifting of racial, class and sexual boundaries. I have never migrated, I am not a traveller, I have always stayed close to home, but I share this preoccupation with displacement. It is to do with a dislocated sense of class belonging and the ambivalences that are a part of my masculine identity. It is also to do with the historical uncertainties of my white, English ethnicity. I was prompted to start thinking about my own ethnic identity by the contemporary generation of black and Asian English intellectuals – Paul Gilroy, Stuart Hall, Kobena Mercer, Isaac Julien, Lola Young, Pratibha Parmar – who were thinking reflexively and historically about race, gender and ethnicity. My involvement in radical politics on the left had taught me to disavow the racial exclusivity of white ethnicity, but never to analyse or try and understand it. Being white was a vague, amorphous concept to get hold off; it wasn't a colour, it was invisible. And who wanted the risible, sometimes ugly, baggage of Englishness? Everything which signified Englishness – the embarrassing legacy of racial supremacy and empire, the union jack waving crowds, the royalty, the rhetoric about Britain's standing in the world – suggested a conservative deference to nostalgia.

The problem with intellectually disowning white English ethnicity was that the left never got around to working out what it was, and what our own emotional connections to it were. We left that door wide open for the New Right and its language of family values and patriotism. We ignored our own feelings about home and belonging, disavowing our troubled preoccupations with our origins, security and family as regressive personal failings we had to overcome. Such anxieties were treacherous because they unearthed unspoken personal feelings which did not accord with our apparent openness to difference and otherness. It was a self-deception which could only be sustained by avoiding a range of awkward questions about our relationship to white English ethnicity. The purpose of this book is to address some of the awkward questions; to begin a discussion about the relationship between masculinity, whiteness and English ethnicity in the context of a cultural history of race, imperialism and colonialism. In particular to explore the intimate connections between home and family, and the culture of English ethnicity.

Recent years have seen an increasing preoccupation with white English ethnicity. The work of black English scholars, the ferment in the Conservative Party surrounding Britain's entry into the ERM, and New Labour's plans for constitutional reform have focused attention on the dominant ethnicity of the British Union. England was once the driving force behind the empire and colonialism and it is the white English who have found their loss the hardest to come to terms with. The central premise of *Forever England* is that an historic epoch is drawing to a close. Since the seventeenth century and the puritan revolution, English nationalism and the emergence of Britishness have been integrally linked to the rise of the English middle classes as an economic and political power. This historical force was accompanied by a puritan's sense of mission: 'Here we find for the first time a people aroused and stirred in its innermost depths, feeling upon its shoulders the mission of history.'[1] It is this sense of mission which provided an emotional, religious and cultural impetus behind England's expansion overseas and the growth of empire. This national/class formation both shaped, and was shaped by, the gendered order of the middle class family. With the end of empire, and the changing patterns of family life which began in the 1960s, the connections between the middle classes and the dominant expressions of English ethnicity have been weakened. This book will focus on one aspect of this history: the relationships of white, middle-class English men to family life, to fatherhood and to women, and their link to the vicissitudes of white English ethnicity.

The relationship of masculinity to English ethnicity begins in the

6

intimacies of the family. The first essay 'Our Dead Bodies' identifies the late nineteenth century as an historical conjuncture in which the gendered relations of the middle class family and the social demands of the New Imperialism gave rise to an hegemonic ideal of English manliness whose vestiges survive today. A central dynamic in the creation of this imperial manliness was men's childhood relationships with their mothers. Motherhood was the ideological centre of the Victorian bourgeois ideal of the family. Mothers were endowed with a sacred mission to raise their children and provide a haven for their husbands away from the corrupting world of money and business. In spite of this idealisation women commanded domestic power, and their control in the home was seen as a potential threat to male dominance. Motherhood came under intense scrutiny. Women were subjected to a variety of taboos and regulatory practices which sought to protect the conjugal rights of their husband and safeguard their sons from feminine influence. It was this patriarchal institution of motherhood and the fraught relationship of boys to it, which contributed to the making of a late Victorian masculinity characterised by narcissism, emotional immaturity and a preoccupation with self-sacrifice: qualities that found a popular expression in the first years of the twentieth century in the figure of Peter Pan – the Englishman as the eternal adolescent.

The historical significance of this family order can be seen in the three short biographies of Rupert Brooke, T.E Lawrence and Enoch Powell. The primary impetus behind their commitments to Empire and England lay in their ambivalent relationships with their mothers. There is a fine line between writing critically about the patriarchal institution of motherhood and its effects on men's lives, and the misogynist blaming of women and mothers for the travails of men. The problem of speaking about mothers in the context of a mother blaming culture begins with the language available. I have used Freud's psychoanalysis to explore the relationship of mothers and sons. But I have used it with a degree of scepticism. Freud's theoretical framework and categories tend to reproduce as much as analyse the gendered antimonies of the conventional, mid nineteenth century bourgeois family. His writing on female sexuality and his theory of the oedipus complex pay scant regard to the role of motherhood in psychological development. And what he does have to say reveals his complicity with his society's simultaneous demonisation and idealisation of motherhood. My aim has not been to pathologise the mothers of Rupert Brooke, T.E Lawrence and Enoch Powell. Rather it has been to describe the effect on men of growing up in a patriarchal family institution in which love and relationships are a scarce resource controlled by mothers and in which fathers are either absent or – emotionally speaking – ineffectual and marginal figures.

Imperialism was a central element in the making of modern Englishness. But during the Edwardian era there was a reaction against Government's preoccupation with 'abroad'. The experiences of moral uncertainty, anxiety about social unrest and increasing doubt about the efficacy of Empire, led to the emergence of an anti-imperialist English nationalism amongst growing sections of the Liberal middle classes. This was principally expressed in images of a Southern, English Arcadia and an idealising of rural life and nature. The second essay 'Under an English Heaven', on the life of the poet Rupert Brooke, offers a striking example of the relationship between pastoralism, patriotism and male sexuality. Brooke's Fabian politics, his 'Neo-paganism' and his connections to the Bloomsbury circle, made him an exemplary of anti-Victorianism. But his intense sexual confusion and subsequent breakdown transformed his early enthusiasm for decadence and liberal tolerance into an anti-semitism and an outspoken misogyny. His death in 1915 at the age of 27, aboard a troopship bound for Gallipoli, marked the beginning of his myth. The legend of Rupert Brooke as 'a young Apollo, golden-haired' became a homoerotic and nostalgic motif of England and Englishness during the interwar years and beyond.

If Rupert Brooke symbolised England and its Arcadian past, the legend of T.E Lawrence symbolised England's Empire and its future. The third essay 'An odd gnome, half cad – with a touch of genius', provides a portrait of the man and his legend. Like Brooke, Lawrence was a product of Victorian sexual prudery. His imperial exploits were driven by a desire to escape his family, and by a homoerotic attachment to a particular Arab boy. Lawrence suppressed his homosexuality by adopting a masochistic penitence. The privations of the desert provided him with the ascetic life he craved and after the war he sought monastic exile and anonymity in the RAF. His life ended in 1935 in a motorbike accident at a moment in European history when the imperial mission of its principal nations had peaked and had begun its turn back toward its neglected heartland of Europe in the form of Fascism and Nazism. While Lawrence had not been seized by the ideology of Fascism, his denial of his body and sexuality and his longing to be no more than a 'cog of a machine' had been an exemplary practice of self surrender to a cause greater than himself. His legend was used to propagandise England's imperial mission in the world. But the example of his life proved only that imperial manliness was bankrupt and that England's imperial mission was at an end.

This was the reality which would shatter the romantic imperialism of Enoch Powell. The Second World War marked the rise of US hegemony and the beginning of the end of the British empire. Enoch Powell, serving as a young intelligence officer, and eager to assist in the safeguarding of Britain's east Asian empire from American ambitions, secured himself a transfer to India. In one of the several Pauline conversions he was to experience during his life, he fell in love with the British Raj. But history and the 'winds of change' were to rob Powell of empire and thwart his own imperial mission. 'Powell's Island Story' is about one man's attempt to regenerate an English nationalism out of the detritus of Britain's postwar decline. More than any other public figure he gave vent to a feeling of profound and irreconcilable loss; of Empire, of personal identity, of ethnic belonging. It was a loss he sought to resolve in his poetry, his religion and his political life. His sentimental evocation of an Old England provided him with a sense of belonging but it was a myth which required enemies to confirm its existence. Powell's increasingly paranoid invective against 'enemies within' identified New Commonwealth immigrants and the liberal intellegentsia as the main threat to his idyll. He was disowned by the Conservative Party hierarchy for his embittered language of racial antagonism in his 1968 'Rivers of Blood' speech. Nonetheless his politics shaped future Conservative governments' legislation on citizenship and immigration control. Powell's monetarism and his attack on One Nation Toryism prefigured the rise of the New Right and through the 1990s he retained an influence on the right wing of the Conservative Party.

In 1995, Tony Blair laid claim to the Tory politics of One Nation. At the Labour Party conference in Brighton he spoke of the British as 'Decent people. Good people. Patriotic people ... these are "our people" ... It is a new Britain. One Britain: the people united by shared values and shared aims.' His populist rhetoric of one nation promoted a cultural homogeneity which ignored the plurality of ethnic identities which make up British culture. Blair's celebration of a national collectivity at the expense of an ethnic pluralism is symptomatic of a broader liberal retreat from the issues of race and race relations. The final essay, 'Mr Nice and Mr Nasty', argues that there has been a liberal failure of nerve around race which has allowed the right to construct a new language of white abdication from race relations, shifting the responsibility for racial discrimination on to black culture. This reaction to black people and to racial difference is connected to the backlash against feminism. The changing position of men in the family, the high levels of divorce and the exclusion of men from traditional forms of fatherhood, has led to a disillusion with the ideal of sexual equality. In turn there has been a white middle-class withdrawal from engagement with black people. The essay focuses on the relationship of white men to black men, a relationship which is a potent source of white racial antagonism and fear, and which is closely connected to men's uncertainties about their role in family life and their gender identities.

There is no conclusion to this book, no singular analysis and no answers. Its purpose is to raise questions – which I hope it does – and so provide some direction through the difficult territory of race and gender.

Notes

1. Hans Kohn (1940), 'The Genesis and Character of English Nationalism', *The Journal of the History of Ideas*, Vol. 1, No.1.

2

'OUR DEAD BODIES' MOTHERS, SONS AND IMPERIALISM

Take the tourist trail across central London. Begin at Victoria Station and work your way through Belgravia to Hyde Park, down to Buckingham Palace and then along The Mall to Waterloo Place. The public face of our national culture is overwhelmingly imperial and royal; grandiose and triumphal commemorations of military victories, self-sacrifice and violent death. There are no monuments dedicated to civic culture or intellectual life, there are no statues of philosophers or writers as there are scattered throughout Paris. It is only when you reach Waterloo Place that you will find a few statues of men not directly related to militarism or war. They are the explorers, the other face of empire. They too were celebrated in premature death: Franklin, who lost his life in the search for the North West Passage, and Robert Falcon Scott who died in his bid to reach the South Pole. At the base of Scott's statue is an inscription, taken from a letter he addressed to the British public, written in the last hours of his life. He apologises for his failure, he knows he is going to die, but bows to the will of providence. 'Had we lived,' he wrote, 'I should have had a tale to tell of the hardihood, endurance and courage of my companions which would have stirred the heart of every Englishman. These rough notes and our dead bodies must tell the tale.' The year was 1911. The long Victorian age was soon to end with the outbreak of the First World War. But it seems, walking across central London, as if it were still with us. All the dead bodies are still speaking from their graves, their tale of self-sacrifice and heroism fuelling the belief that England is the greatest nation on earth and the Englishman its most noble warrior.

White, English masculinity is in deep confusion over its history and identity. The legacy of Victorian public life and civic virtue has been reduced to detritus by the deregulated free market, but we still cling to its imperial myths; preserving in stone and memory its homoerotic, martial fantasies of an English manliness which once bestrode the globe. The mystique of this omniscient manliness still provides an illusory comfort in the contemporary maelstrom of modernity, with its insecurities of work and the vicissitudes of contemporary masculinities. The imaginary Englishman with his stiff upper lip and masterly control over world affairs was invented during another era of uncertainty, in the years between 1870 and the outbreak of the First World War. This period saw the appearance of hundreds of boys' adventure stories, eulogising Britain's empire builders.[1] Life for the fictitious imperial hero was a series of opportunities to exercise his prowess and demonstrate his supremacy over foreigners and the working classes. Nothing he encountered was beyond his knowledge, there were no surprises and no mysteries. Whatever the odds stacked against him, he was imbued with a boundless optimism. His was a world in which the white, male body radiated Teutonic splendour. Hundreds of thousands of boys could lose themselves in daydreams of heroic endeavour, projecting themselves out to far-flung corners of the empire without any fear of being lost or abandoned. Yet there is a frisson of unease in these insistent representations of heroic endeavour. In a 'final letter to his wife before he died, Scott wrote about his concern for his son's manliness; 'Above all, he must guard and you must guard him against indolence. Make him a strenuous man. I had to force myself into being strenuous, as you know – had always an inclination to be idle'.[2] He ends his letter 'What lots and lots I could tell you of this journey. How much better has it been than lounging in too great a comfort at home.' The strenuous exertions of the imperial hero, his refusal to contemplate, to think or to pause, suggest that his adventures involved a compulsion to escape the idleness and comfort of domesticity. Perhaps all those heroic dead bodies harbour a secret. Perhaps the icy wastes of the Antarctic proved easier to confront than a deeper fear, closer to home.

Manliness, Games and the Imperial Mission

This chapter is not an attempt at a definitive history of white, middle-class English masculinities. It seeks to identify and outline a number of specific sensibilities of men's emotional and sexual lives in the nineteenth and early twentieth centuries – sensibilities related to women and to race, which were shaped by the history of empire, family life, class and ethnicity; these continue to resonate today in the late 1990s and I shall return to them in the final chapter. I want to begin with the representations of imperial manliness inspired by an earlier moment in the history of the British empire. In 1849, the Punjab in the North West of India had been brought under colonial rule by John Nicholson and the two brothers John and Henry Lawrence. Their bloodthirsty exploits won enthusiastic support from the public and their highly individualistic style of administration became known as the 'Punjab creed'. Nicholson established the reputation of this creed, riding cross-country at the head of a band of Pathan tribesman, enforcing his own brand of terroristic law and order. Countless adventure stories were inspired by the image of a lone, dashing Englishman dispensing justice, wisdom and righteous retribution upon his brown subjects. In his *Life Memoir* (1899), Robert Cust, an assistant to John Lawrence, offered a nostalgic paean to those frontier days:

> the rough-and-ready Justice: the words of sympathy and good fellow-ship: the living alone among the people without soldiers and policemen: the Court held under the green mangoe-trees in the presence of hundreds: the *right* man hanged *on the spot*, where he committed the murder.[3]

Flogging, imprisonment and summary executions were endowed with a moral and religious virtue. The 'Punjab creed' was a duty bequeathed to Englishmen by God: 'Night and day,' wrote Cust, 'I reflect on what I can do for the people of India'.[4] Men like Cust were motivated by the evangelical Christianity which had swept through the early Victorian middle classes. Its biblical sense of mission hearkened back to the seventeenth century's Calvinist belief in a providential national destiny. Imperialism became a divine mission and transformed the expanding empire into a vast parish awaiting social and spiritual reform. In its promise of a transfigured life and its emphasis on leadership through example, evangelicism imposed a rigorous moral code of manliness on its imperial prodigies.

The great exponent of this moral manliness was Dr. Thomas Arnold, the headmaster of Rugby School. In his later years he reiterated its principles: 'And what I have often said before I repeat now: what we must look for here is, 1st religious and moral principles; 2ndly gentle-manly conduct; thirdly intellectual ability'.[5] Moral earnestness was like

13

a military duty: 'You should feel like officers in the army or navy, whose want of moral courage would, indeed, be thought cowardice.' Despite its unforgiving tones, moral manliness did not exclude the 'feminine' traits of feelings and concern. Tears were not to be ashamed of, and a father's close involvement with his children was encouraged. The manly code of early Victorian evangelicism was in many respects anti-masculine, androgynous and asexual. Leadership was instigated by personality and integrity, not force of arms; the exemplary man was obeyed because he was loved and respected, not because he was feared. The British Empire adopted this ideal and shrouded its economic might and Gatling guns in Arthurian style legends of virtuous, knightly Englishmen; the primary requisite for imperial rule was the strength of their characters. By the early years of the twentieth century the colonial governance of the 'Punjab creed' had become the official imperial policy of indirect rule. Despite the decline of evangelicism in the 1860s, a secularised version of its divine mission gave rise to 'the dreamers of Empire'; men 'who see the Holy Grail shining high and bright above the god called Moloch, or Mob, or Money.'[6]

By the 1860s Arnold's codes of moral earnestness and individual godliness were being transformed into the cult of athleticism and team spirit. The rising popularity of imperialism, and the influence of social Darwinism cultivated a manliness no longer dependent upon soul-searching, but upon subordination to the national ideal and an enthusiasm for being 'normal'. Edward Thring, headmaster of Uppingham (1853–1888), progressive educationalist and founder of the Headmaster's Conference, linked the new ideal of manliness with the public schools:

> The learning to be responsible and independent, to bear pain, to play the game, to drop rank, and wealth, and home luxury, is a priceless boon. I think myself that it is this which has made the English such an adventurous race; and that with all their faults... the public schools are the cause of this 'manliness'.[7]

One of the most eloquent and persistent ideologues of imperialist education was the Reverend J.E.C. Welldon, the headmaster of Harrow School:

> It can be said with truth of the English schools and universities that year after year, generation after generation, century after century, they send

forth men not without faults, not without limitations of knowledge or culture... but men of vigour, tact, courage and integrity, men who are brave and chivalrous and true.'[8]

The public schools sought to inculcate four qualities in their boys: sport – 'It is the instinct of sport which has played a great part in creating the British Empire'; readiness – 'It means courage, it means self-reliance, it means the power of seizing opportunities, it means resource'; character – 'It is the supreme ruling quality of Englishmen'; and lastly religion – deep down in the hearts of Englishmen was 'the fear of God'. Appreciation of intellectual life and academic work were not high on Welldon's list of priorities: 'These boys are not remarkably clever or remarkably cultivated, but if you take any one of them and put him down in difficult circumstances and tell him to make the best of them, the chances are he will not greatly fail.'[9] The 1863 report of the Public School Commission had heralded the ascendancy of the public schools into national life. By the turn of the century their ideologues had won over the middle classes, and sizeable parts of the more respectable working classes. The language of the public schools became the language of a national culture and its empire. Their ideals of manliness were the national ideal.

The public schools became the 'nurseries of empire' and the central focus of upper-class and upper-middle-class boyhood.[10] The school slang, the petty hierarchies of blazers, caps and colours, the symbolic rituals and sensibilities of the prep and public schools, constituted a form of life. As much as the family, they provided the emotional ties of childhood. *In loco parentis*, where matron replaced mother and housemaster replaced father, they discouraged the boys' continuing needs for the intimacies and comfort of home. Parental love was superseded by intense romantic bonds between boys, which often endured for a lifetime. While these relationships created an affective language of belonging amongst the upper middle classes, the homophobia of the schools precipitated sexual ambivalence, frustration and a predisposition to sexual brutality. Bullying and social exclusion were rife and demanded that 'a fellow' have nothing odd about him. The self-doubt and introspection of the early Victorians were viewed as weak-minded and 'muffish', their concern for the intellectual life, effete. In a system of rigid hierarchies and ritualistic codes of status and duty, survival demanded conformity to those with power, not a display of individuality. What mattered was a boy's willingness to submit himself to the strictures of the public school order and prove his good character. In this spartan environment the language of 'pulling together' and the almost religious espousal of loyalty to house and school formed the micro-language of loyalty to race and nation.

Games-playing became the emblem of this regime, and its athlete the touchstone of imperial manliness. The cult of games and its promotion of team spirit moulded boys into the vocabularies and discourses of nation and empire. Tom Brown in *Tom Brown's School Days* was an early devotee this late Victorian obsession. Tom, Arthur and the young Master are watching a game of cricket:

> 'But it's more than a game. Its an institution,' said Tom.
>
> 'Yes,' said Arthur, 'the birthright of British boys old and young, as *habeas corpus* and trial by jury are of British men.'
>
> 'The discipline and reliance on one another which it teaches is so valuable, I think,' went on the master. 'It ought to be such an unselfish game. It merges the individual in the eleven; he doesn't play that he may win, but that his side may.'[11]

Games encouraged physical courage and self-reliance in a context which subordinated the self to the team. They were a collective practice of asceticism intent on transforming the feminine bodies of young boys into the hardened musculature of imperial warriors. To the new breed of public school headmasters, physical exertion was a spiritually cleansing catharsis; the sports field the ideal antidote for degeneracy and decadence. Hely Hutchinson Almond, the headmaster of Loretto School and a sparto-christian fanatic, declared that compulsory games were for 'spoiled, coddled, overfed, novel-reading, dreamy, anaemic boys.'[12] This culture of will power was the antithesis of Arnold's moral manliness. It marked the victory of the anti-intellectual, normal boy over the exceptional boy who thinks for himself. The poet of the public schools, Henry Newbolt acknowledged that the single-minded pursuit of physical prowess made for a narrow education. On the other hand, he supported it. 'Its great merit was that it made men, and not sneaks or bookworms, and that its direct objects were character and efficiency.'[13]

While the imperial minded headmasters and their ideologues practised their rhetoric of anti-individualism and team spirit, they were careful to cultivate their own version of the evangelicist inspired exceptional English boy. He was a figure who excelled in conformity. The public schoolboy ran the British Empire as soldier and administrator, teacher and missionary, and he became a virtual archetype of the Victorian world view: 'The pluck, the energy, the perseverance, the good temper, the self-control, the discipline, the co-operation, the *esprit de corps*, which merit success in cricket or football, are the very qualities which win the day in peace or war.'[14] The boy's journals *Boy's Own Paper* (1879) and *Union Jack* (1880), which enjoyed a mass market, cross-class appeal, eulogised the empire's public school rulers as the highest form of life and men to aspire to. By exercising pluck and a taste for adventure, lower-middle and middle-class boys could elevate themselves to a similar station, not in the interests of personal gain, but in service to their race and nation. Developing character offered a path to the Victorian ideal of the gentleman. And as Philip Mason has pointed out, 'Being a gentleman had then, by the second half of the nineteenth century, become almost a religion.'[15]

John Robert Seeley, the regius professor of modern history at Cambridge, reinvented the evangelist message for the late Victorian age. In *The Expansion of England*, written in 1883, he argued that the moral principle of British history was the imperial expansion of the English state:

> the history of England ought to end with something that might be called a moral. . . it ought to exhibit the general tendency of English affairs in such a way as to set us thinking about the future and divining the destiny which is reserved for us.[16]

Empire had reached the height of its popularity during the Unionist administration of Disraeli (1895–1902) but by then, the underlyimng reality was a society no longer certain of its national destiny. Competition from the United States and Germany, and Britain's relative economic decline, were raising anxieties about the future of the empire and threatening the prosperity of the middle classes. Seeley offered a strategy for national renewal. The security of England as a world power could only be protected through overseas expansion and a form of federation with her Anglo-Saxon dominions. These colonies, he argued, would become part of a moral, racial, organic unity: a 'Greater Britain'. Seeley's imperialism was more an idealistic call to arms than an economic strategy, but *The Expansion of England* was a major factor in converting the middle classes to the New Imperialism. One of the most influential propagandists of Seeley's imperial unity was Lord Milner, the High Commissioner in South Africa between 1897 and 1905. 'Imperialism,' he wrote, ' has all the depth and comprehensiveness of a religious faith:'

> Its significance is moral even more than material... It is a question of preserving the unity of a great race, of enabling it, by maintaining that unity, to develop freely on its own lines, and to continue to fulfil its distinctive mission in the world.'[17]

Providence had given the Englishman his mission of civilising the world. For men like Seeley and Milner, this imperial mission would reinvigorate the English race and reforge the links between individual duty and national destiny. Empire must become the motivating principle of English character.

Henry Newbolt, in his poem, *Vitai Lampada* identified games as the link between manliness and the religious calling of imperialism:

> There's a breathless hush in the Close tonight –
>   Ten to make and the match to win –
> A bumping pitch and a blinding light,
>   An hour to play and the last man in.
> And it's not for the sake of a ribboned coat,
>   Or the selfish hope of a season's fame,
> But his Captain's hand on his shoulder smote –
> 'Play up! play up! and play the game!'
>
> The sand of the desert is sodden red, –
>   Red with the wreck of a square that broke; –
> The Gatling's jammed and the Colonel dead,
>   And the regiment blind with dust and smoke.
> The river of death has brimmed his banks,
>   And England's far, and Honour a name,
> But the voice of a schoolboy rallies the ranks:
> 'Play up! Play up! and play the game!'[18]

In the final verse, Newbolt urges all the sons of the School to carry this creed like a torch in flame untill their death: 'And falling fling to the host behind.' The language of games – its asceticism, its binding of the individual into the group and its obeisance to a force greater than the sum of its players was turned into a secularised version of Calvinist theology, the puritan's predestinarian religion. 'Playing the Great Game' became a 'calling' for the imperial mission, and its promise of transcendence drew individual men into its epoch-making, historical forces. 'Playing the Great Game,' wrote Hannah Arendt, 'a man may feel as though he lives the only life worth while because he has been stripped of everything... Life itself seems to be left in a fantastically intensified purity, when man has cut himself off from all ordinary social ties'.[19]

'the brave bright days of his boyhood'

The stiff upper lip and disciplined body of the games ethic were a far remove from the more androgynous and emotional manliness of the early Victorians. It was a masculinity for an imperial nation whose priority was the creation of an elite of soldiers and administrators. But the historical shift in meanings of masculinity was not solely determined by imperial demand. In his essay, 'Manliness and Domesticity', John Tosh suggests that the shift began in the 1850s-70s, before imperialism had become a significant ideology amongst the middle classes. The generation which grew up after 1860 displayed an insecurity in their masculine identities which manifested itself in a flight from domesticity, a growing disparagement of the 'feminine', a readiness to go abroad and an increasing refusal amongst late Victorian men to marry. It was a phenomenon 'rooted in the first instance in the reaction of young middle-class men against domestic emotions and domestic constraints.'[20] The cause of this reaction lay in the separation of manliness from domesticity and the 'sharp division of gender attributes within the mid-Victorian family'. Claudia Nelson has also noted that during the last half of the century there was a sharpening divide between men and women's gender identities: 'in boy's fiction and sexology alike [there was] a gradual reclassification of the attitudes and behavioural patterns considered appropriate to men, often combined with a rejection of qualities associated with femininity.'[21] The historian Lawrence Stone defined this polarisation of gender as the 'Victorian revival of patriarchy.'[22]

By the middle of the century, the growing separation of work from the home had distanced men from family life and contributed to the feminising of domesticity. In the home the mother/child culture became central, and mothering was the emotional hub of family life.

The influence of manly codes of hard work and delayed gratification gave rise to a more formal and distant father figure whose principle duties were to provide, to instruct his children and to discipline them. Consequently the language of emotions – expressions of need, pleasure, pain and vulnerability – were feminised in a domestic world clearly delimited from the public world of men and masculinity. The mother became the ideological centre of the Victorian bourgeois ideal, endowed with a sacred mission to raise her children and provide a haven for her husband away from the corrupting world of money and business. She was portrayed as an ethereal presence, but in reality she commanded domestic power and her control in the home was seen as a potential threat to male dominance. Motherhood came under intense scrutiny. In her book, *The Mothers of England, Their Influence and Responsibility* (1843), Sarah Ellis castigated mothers who had 'ungoverned springs of tenderness and love' toward their offspring. She warned that an overabundance of maternal affection would damage her children and lead to the neglect of her wifely duties. A mother's love must never 'be concentrated into one force, so as to burn with dangerous and destructive intensity'.[23] At once idealised and demonised, the Victorian middle class mother was charged with the future health of the race and the proper manliness of her sons. Her body and emotions were subjected to a variety of taboos and regulatory practices which sought to protect the conjugal rights of her husband and safeguard her sons from the thraldom of her femininity.

The drama of this historically specific family – the domestic division of labour, the polarisation of masculinity and femininity, the male anxieties and fantasies about the power and influence of mothers – was central to the evolution of Freud's psychoanalytic writings. In his 1909 essay, 'Family Romances' Freud presents the reader with an archetype of the mid- and late-Victorian family and the struggle of its children to become independent from parental authority. He argued that the sexual rivalries initiated by the oedipus complex ensured that the boy had a far more intense desire to get free from the father than from the mother.[24] Freud claimed that his oedipus complex was universal, but it is principally a male-centred story about the boy's acquisition of gender identity and sexuality. The father is presented as the key psychological figure who intrudes upon the infant-mother relationship, initiating the oedipus complex and sexual differentiation. He brings language, individuation and access to culture; a process which ensures the dissolution of the infant's bond with the mother and consigns their bond to the unconscious. At the same time his rivalry with his son for the mother threatens the boy with castration and heralds his wish to become like his father. This sexual rivalry produces a desire in the boy to escape his father's dominating presence and establish a heterosexual masculine position of his own. In Freud's oedipus complex, the drama resides with the father and son in their conflict over the mother. In contrast to the male actors, Freud can only eulogise the mother-son relationship as 'the most perfect, the most free from ambivalence of all human relationships.'[25]

Freud's emphasis on the father is a product of the patriarchal demonisation and idealisation of mothers. When Freud wrote 'I cannot think of any need in childhood as strong as the need for a father's protection' he echoed the Victorian anxiety that the male child needed to be protected from maternal love.[26] Freud reiterated the special bond between mother and son in several of his essays, but his glowing remarks do not disguise the 'terrifying impression of helplessness' he perceived in the infant's dependency upon its mother.[27] In Freudian psychoanalysis the mother is incapable of nurturing her young son into independence. She becomes the potential gorgon who will deny men their potency and autonomy and turn them to blocks of stone: 'even marriage is not made secure until the wife has succeeded in making her husband her child as well as acting as mother to him.'[28] Freud's preoccupation with the father's role in rescuing the boy from his mother, left his analysis of the mother–son relationship undeveloped. 'Everything in the sphere of this first attachment to the mother,' he wrote, 'seemed to me so difficult to grasp in analysis – so grey with age and shadowy and almost impossible to revivify.'[29] It was the psychoanalyst Melanie Klein who challenged Freud's neglect of this relationship. She argued that a boy's sense of self is defined in the processes of separating, distancing and differing from his mother.[30] The mother-son relationship is central to the making of masculinity.

The patriarchal demand on a small boy to break his maternal attachment derives from a cultural pathology, born of an anxiety to wean sons away from the influence of their mothers. Consequently, a small boy's bond with his mother is frequently broken before he is ready to cope with its loss. What feels lost in this premature separation is not his actual mother but the feeling of her aliveness inside him (what is termed the maternal object), and with it an inner sense of his ontological security. In 'Mourning and Melancholia' Freud described such an inner loss: 'The object has not perhaps actually died, but has been lost

as an object of love.'³¹ Mourning becomes a central preoccupation of
the boy's developing psyche. The compensation of his father's love is
denied by the taboo on feelings between males, and compounded by
his absence from the home. In a patriarchal culture which denigrates
'weakness' in boys and men, it is impossible for the boy to grieve, and
there can be no end to his mother's dying. Loss holds him prisoner and
he is arrested in his capacity to love another. Misogynistic rejection and
emotional need alternate in the boy's attempt to establish his independence from his mother. Locked away in boarding schools, the loss was
made inexorable, a boy's mother became an impossibly idealised object
encased in a fantasy home steeped in tender love and care.

The gendered order of the Victorian middle-class family produced an
intense ambivalence in the masculinity of its sons. A boy's unresolved
need for his mother continually threatened to undermine his tenuous
identifications with his emotionally distant, often absent, father.
Through the vestiges of his continuing attachment to his mother, he
retains an identification with her, adopting a 'feminine attitude' toward
his father and taking the place of his mother as the love object of his
father. Thus a cultural construction of manliness which had been intent
on ironing out all traces of 'feminine feelings' had the converse effect;
inscribing homoerotic desire into the psychic structure of masculinity.
The ambivalence of gender identity in these mother's boys found a
cultural expression in the cult of Little Lord Fauntleroy. Written by
Frances Hodgson Burnett and published in 1886, the novel is the story
of a little boy, Cedric Errol, who must live with his estranged and a
cold-hearted grandfather in order to gain his inheritance and earldom.
The grandfather refuses to allow the boy's mother to live with them and
so the young hero rejects his patriarchal heritage. Burnett was no radical feminist, and the boy eventually adopts his new status, thus restor-
ing the gender order. But the popularity of the story amongst women of
the time suggest that the effeminacy of this mother's boy was an antidote to the crude and pugnacious manliness of the era.

Perhaps more significantly, it was a recognition of the pressures
placed on the relationship of mothers and sons by a male dominated
society. The Hungarian anglophile Emil Reich reported: 'From the
very earliest childhood the English boy is subjected to methodical will-
culture; he is soon trained to suppress to the uttermost all external signs
of emotion.'³² The first step in achieving this condition was to remove
boys from their homes. The punitive regime of the boarding school
was the cultural enforcement of the castration complex which would

'smash to pieces' the boy's attachment to his mother.[33] Bereft of their mothers, patriarchal bourgeois culture could only instil in its sons an illusion of their complete autonomy. Boys were forced to develop their own autarchic emotional economy. In childhood, solitude created anxiety, in adulthood it became a virtue. In his aloneness the man imagines himself freed of social relations and untied from all emotional dependency on women. But, in spite of adopting the defensive ego boundaries and manly postures prescribed him, he could never fully repress the trauma of maternal loss, nor succeed in establishing an unambiguous adult heterosexuality.

The Englishman as a Perpetual Adolescent

John Tosh's work is based on the marriage and family of Edward White Benson (1829-1896), headmaster of Wellington school and later Archbishop of Canterbury. He highlights the impact of family life on the three Benson sons, Fred, Arthur and Hugh. In adulthood they avoided sexual relationships and lived exclusively amongst men. All three hovered on the edge of the Uranian group of writers who eulogised the spiritual and aesthetic appeal of adolescent boys. This distancing from women and heterosexuality was not confined to a small group of aesthetes. The cultivation of male emotional friendships or 'manly love' was widely shared amongst men of their class. David Newsome in his book on the public schools, *Godliness and Good Learning*, has noted the 'tendency to emotionalism and passionate friendship' of the early and mid-Victorian period. 'The association between master and pupil seems to have often been very intimate, admitting of expressions of emotion on both sides.'[34] The muscular Christianity of Thomas Hughes and Charles Kingsley and the anglo-catholicism of the Oxford movement, in their different ways, encouraged male passionate friendship and contributed to the first wave of homosexual sentiment in mid-Victorian society. In secular culture, the Victorian fascination with mediaeval chivalry made close male friendship a knightly virtue. The biblical words of David, as he mourns the loss of his friend, Jonathan, were a recurrent text in these discourses of male companionship: 'I am distressed for thee, my brother Jonathan: very pleasant hast thou been unto me; thy love for me was wonderful, passing the love of women' (2 Samuel ch.1. v.26). The growing significance of games and the centrality of Greek classics in public school education fostered this culture of

23

close male friendships and encouraged the worship of the young male body. As Martin Green has noted, one striking feature of late Victorian culture was its emotional focus on boys.[35]

Cyril Connolly, in *The Enemies of Promise* written in 1938, offers his 'theory of permanent adolescence' to explain the late Victorian preoccupation with boys:

> the experience undergone by boys at the great public schools, their glories and disappointments, are so intense as to dominate their lives and arrest their development. From these it results that the greater part of the ruling class remains adolescent, school-minded, self-conscious.[36]

The ex-public school archetype inhabited the crammers, regiments, City firms and all-male clubs as though they were surrogate schools: 'they behave like a lot of adolescents – oh, very well brought up adolescents – with the run of the tuck shop.'[37] The experience of adolescence touches on the central predicament of upper-middle-class Victorian masculinity. Adolescence is a period when intense sexual feelings coexist with the revived emotional ties of infancy. For Victorian, adolescent, public school boys, an unresolved need for their mothers and an exclusive male culture heightened their sexual uncertainty and frequently ensured that the troubling dilemma of their relationship to women continued into adulthood. 'Every human being', wrote Freud 'has originally two sexual objects – himself and the woman who nurses him . . . we are postulating a primary narcissism in everyone.'[38] Adolescence involves a search for new love objects, but a boy's fear of adult female sexuality can deflect desire back onto the two original sexual objects, his mother and himself. He worships his mother as his lost moment of plenitude; but his idealisation is a corollary to his fear of her engulfment of him.[39] Such a narcissist can only love the boy he longed to be. 'What he projects before him as his ideal,' wrote Freud, 'is the substitute for the lost narcissism of his childhood in which he was his own ideal.'[40] Unlike Little Lord Fauntleroy, for such a narcissist, the liberation from the shadow of his mother is continuously postponed and he remains something of a perpetual adolescent. Trapped, he nourishes a secret craving for the body of the boy. In its innocence, he imagines he can recapture his own future, and in his repressed homoerotic desire for it he strives to discover his sense of destiny.

This predicament of late Victorian masculinity was epitomised by J.M. Barrie's *Peter Pan*. In 1901, aged 40, Barrie spent the summer at

Black Lake Cottage in Surrey, playing adventure games and cultivating his relationship with the young Llewelyn Davies boys. Denis Mackail, in his official biography wrote, 'if Barrie is besotted with these boys and his games, if sometimes his single-minded concentration on them is really a little excessive and alarming, no-one can stop him, and he is obviously so gloriously happy, too.' Barrie's obsession with these children inspired his creation of *Peter Pan*. First performed in 1904, Peter Pan was a sentimental, whimsical celebration of childhood. It was also the culminating adventure story of the Victorian era and revealed what had been repressed and denied in the imperial fantasy of manly racial supremacy – the domestic world of mothers, sexuality and emotional need. It was an act of acute, if unconscious, reflexivity.

Instead of adventuring overseas, Barrie turned inward, into his unconscious, to create the Neverland, an island which Michael Egan describes as 'a vast, symbolic metaphor', 'a poetic version of the Freudian id . . . the child's mind during sleep.'[41] But the topography of Neverland does not belong to a child. It is symbolic of the psyche of late Victorian masculinity. As Jacqueline Rose points out; 'Behind Peter Pan lies the desire of a man for a little boy (or boys)'.[42] This was not just his confused longing for the Llewelyn Davies boys, but for his own lost boyishness. In his popular novel *Tommy and Grizel* (1900) Barrie anticipated the themes of Peter Pan: 'He was a boy only . . . And boys cannot love. Oh is it not cruel to ask a boy to love? . . . He was a boy who could not grow up.' This is the story of a mother's boy, faced with the troubling dilemma of his adult heterosexuality. When Peter Pan is confronted with the desires of Wendy, Tinkerbell and Tiger-Lily, he denies their sexuality and reframes their demands as their longing to meet his own infantile need.

> *Peter.* Now what is it you want?
> *Tiger-Lily.* Want to be your Squaw.
> *Peter.* Is that what you want, Wendy?
> *Wendy.* I suppose it is Peter.
> *Peter.* Is that what you want Tink?
> Bells answer.
> *Peter.* You all three want that. Very well – that's
> really wishing to be my mother.[43]

Peter Pan is neither child nor adult, he is narcissistic, asexual and appalled by the body and carnality. He longs for a mother, yet is unable

25

to endure any form of emotional dependency. When Peter Pan says 'to die will be an awfully big adventure' he expresses the fatalism of the interminable Old Boy, locked into the maudlin glow of an idealised boyhood when life before the demands of women and adult sexuality was simple and pure. Imperial manliness, in its production of emotionally repressed, sexually confused, mother fixated, women fearing men, fostered in them a morbid nostalgia for 'the brave bright days of his boyhood.'⁴⁴ In the body of the boy, the narcissist had hoped to discover his sense of aliveness and destiny. Instead he finds only romanticism and a death wish.

The story of the Empire is full of mother's boys – repressed, sentimental, loving boys in general because it was a way of loving the boyishness in themselves. Lytton Strachey, writing on General Gordon, the martyred hero and maverick of Khartoum, remarks how he was 'particularly fond of boys'. Gordon was engaged as a military engineer in Gravesend before his assignment to the Sudan: 'Ragged street Arabs and rough sailor lads crowded about him. They were made free of his house and garden.'⁴⁵ Gordon's narcissism led him to eulogise boys and to replace his idealised mother with a fatalistic, Old Testament religion, asceticism and a megalomaniac belief in his own divine fate. When Lord Milner was appointed High Commissioner in South Africa, he recruited to South Africa university graduates, mainly from All Souls and New College, Oxford. A Johannesburg lawyer, Sir William Marriot, nicknamed them the 'Kindergarten' and the name stuck. Robert Baden-Powell, founder of the Boy Scout Movement, developed a close, life-long and chaste relationship to Kenneth McLaren, nicknamed 'The Boy' on account of his youthful looks. During the Matebele campaign of 1896, Baden-Powell, aged thirty-nine, kept a daily diary for his mother. Celibate and an ardent voice against the vices of boyhood masturbation, he finally married at the age of fifty-five. Like Robert Scott, he named his first born Peter, after Peter Pan. Lord Kitchener, born in 1850 to an adored mother who died when he was fourteen, surrounded himself with young unmarried officers. Known as his 'cubs', he called them 'my happy family of boys'. From 1907 until his death in 1916 his constant and inseparable companion was Captain O.A. Fitzgerald. Rudyard Kipling was torn from his mother when he was six years old to attend school in England. He called his foster home 'the House of Desolation'. His 'terrors' in this 'Hell' left him with a nervous breakdown and a deep sense of maternal betrayal. His emotional life atrophied at the level of the adolescent and ensured that his youthful heroes never reached beyond puberty. The figure of the boy in all the great adventure stories of the era represented the repressed longing of these men for all they had been forced to renounce – maternal love, their own bodies, sexual desire.

The Troubling Dilemma of Homosexuality

The infatuation with boys and boyishness goes to the heart of late Victorian manliness, and with it travels the more awkward desires of homosexuality. In his 'theory of permanent adolescence', Connolly adds that, in the last analysis, his archetypal English, upper-middle-class masculinity was homosexual. But this attaches a too rigid category to what is a wider, more complex phenomenon, and it fails to address the historical differences in relations between men. Eve Kosofsky Sedgwick uses the phrase homosocial desire to describe male-to-male attitudes and practices. She argues that there is a continuum of relations between men which includes emotional friendship, mentorship between older and younger boys, homoeroticism, pederasty and homosexuality. This continuum is, however, disrupted by homosexuality.[46] Sedgwick argues that homophobia creates a boundary in the continuum between sexual and nonsexual male bonds. She also emphasises that homosociality is not just an affair between men. It is homophobic in its outlawing of homosexuality but it is also misogynistic in its repression and denigration of female power and authority. The trial of Oscar Wilde in 1895, and the frequent public attacks on decadence, signalled the reassertion of a sound manly character in public life. A homosexual identity, as distinct from the Victorian tradition of male friendship, became a new object of regulation, its deviant nature signified by feminine traits and characteristics. The exclusion of women and the feminine now became a defining factor of manliness, a discourse which extended to parts of the early homosexual rights movement. John Addington Symonds, one of its founding figures, believed that the absence of women from his private life enhanced his masculinity: 'I am more masculine than many men I know who adore women. I have no feminine feelings for the males who rouse my desire'.[47]

By the end of the century the schism between sexual and non-sexual relations between men had been widened. Nonetheless, countless public school stories depicted romances between boys, drawing an ambiguous line between carnal desire and chaste romance. The enduring popularity of male romantic adolescent love is evident in Ernest Raymond's first and highly successful novel, *Tell England*, which was published in 1922. The story follows the Edwardian, schoolboy friendship of Rupert Ray and Edgar Doe to their eventual deaths in the First World War. In an early part of the book, the two boys are lying in their beds in the dormitory. They have just been beaten by their housemaster Radley. 'I feel I can tell you things I wouldn't tell anybody else,' says Doe. He admits to liking their manly housemaster, Radley, more than anyone else in the world – 'I simply loved being whacked by him'. Doe is embarrassed by his confession and Ray tries to make light of it. When Doe falls asleep. Ray is left alone with his thoughts.

> Doe's remark, I reflected, was like that of a schoolgirl who adored her mistress. Perhaps Doe was a girl. After all, I had no certain knowledge that he wasn't a girl with his hair cut short. I pictured him, then, with his hair, paler than straw, reaching down beneath his shoulders, and with his brown eyes and parted lips wearing a feminine appearance. As I produced this strange figure, I began to feel, somewhere in the region of my waist, motions of calf-love for the girl Doe that I had created. But, as Doe's prowess at cricket asserted itself upon my mind, his gender became conclusively established, and – ah, well I was half asleep (p41).

Doe's sexual ambiguity confronts Ray with the question, 'Is he a boy or a girl?'; and with the advent of his own sexual desire for Doe, a further question 'Am I a boy or a girl?'. It is the oedipal dilemma of the hysteric, the moment when the subject, in full recognition of sexual difference, must renounce the mother and identify with the father. There can be no resolution to this dilemma, only an oscillation between the choices of sexual object. Rupert Ray must call upon the games ethic, the homophobic emblem of manliness, to rescue himself from his sexual ambivalence. The cricket bat confirms Doe's maleness; no girl could ever wield it as he does. Ray represses his homosexuality but it remains the instinctual basis for his love of Doe – 'this feeling of love at first sight for the girl Doe, who never existed, I count as one of the strongest forces that helped to create my later affection for the real Edgar Gray Doe'(p42).

Doe falls under the influence of an older schoolboy called Reedham, a Wildean character who introduces him to drugs and drink and other unnamed vices. Doe later confesses to Ray that he and Freedham 'tried everything'. Doe eventually breaks with Reedham when he realises that his love for Ray is superior to Reedham's more carnal pleasures: 'Life is what feeling you get out of it and the highest types of feeling are mystical and intellectual.' The love between Doe and Ray is confirmed, but it has been disconnected from the body and sex and it must find its expression in some object which transcends them both. *Tell England* ends on the Western Front. Doe has been killed in Gallipoli. It is the eve of battle and Ray is reading a letter from his mother. War and death, she reminds him, have transferred ordinary young men from undistinguished valleys to the mountain tops; 'remember how I used to call you 'my mountain boy'? The name has a new meaning now. Even if you are in danger at this time, I try to be proud. I think of you as on white heights.' This is the apotheosis of the 'Great Game' and Ray reflects on the purity to be found in death and suffering. 'I try to recapture that moment of ideal patriotism . . . I see a death in No Man's Land tomorrow as a wonderful thing . . . Perhaps it is not ill to die standing like that in front of your nation' (p319). He reflects on his mother's love for him and on the selfless death of Doe. In his willingness to die for his mother country, he has discovered the Holy Grail. 'I have the strange idea that very likely I, too shall find beauty in the morning.' To give himself to the 'white heights' of national destiny is to transcend the body and sex. It is the 'Great Game', Ray's romanticised expression of the death wish – the desire to erase his sexual identity and return to the plenitude of his mother: 'I shall only return her what is her own'. Only in the 'cleanness' of a noble death can he resolve the troubling contradictions of his sexual identity and embrace what has been lost and denied; mother love and homosexual desire.

Imperialism and the denial of homosexual desire

In his case study of the Judge, Daniel Paul Schreber, Freud argued that the repression of homosexuality creates the conditions for paranoia. According to Freud, the proposition 'I(a man) love him (a man)' is transformed in the psyche to become 'I do not love him – I hate him, because HE PERSECUTES ME.'[48] This denial and splitting off of unacceptable feelings aligns with the race-thinking and cultural monologism of imperialism. Like war, the imperial mission offered men the opportunity to displace their homosexual desire. The empire provided an ideal screen for its projection onto black and brown young men. This is what Edward Said is pointing towards, when he describes the psychological character of Orientalism as 'a form of paranoia'.[49] One of the central imperatives of colonialist culture was the white man's fear of the sexually voracious native. While women were constructed as the primary victims of this black and brown peril, its impetus lay in the projective fantasies of the white man who was enmeshed in anxieties of homosexual rape. This homoerotic tension found a representation in many of the adventure stories of the period, particularly when Englishmen donned a disguise to pass themselves off as a native.

The imperial adventure story was exemplified in the work of G.A Henty, (1832–1902), who during the late 1890's sold around 150,000 books a year. His work is infused with the language of 'manliness, steadfastness and courage'. According to his biographer, 'there was nothing namby-pamby in Henty's writings ... he never made his works sickly by the introduction of what an effeminate writer would term the tender passion.'[50] But a closer examination of some of Henty's work reveals the translation of repressed homosexual desire into the colonial world of racial difference. *With Kitchener in the Soudan*, is the story of a boy's adventure as a young army officer in the Sudan. Gregory Hilliard's father, an interpreter, has disappeared in the disastrous attempt to relieve General Gordon, besieged in Khartoum. His father could speak the Arabic dialects, and because he dressed up as a native, Gregory believes he may have escaped the massacre of the relief column. When he is fifteen his mother dies of consumption and he determines to discover his father's fate. He too can speak half a dozen Arabic dialects and he joins General Kitchener's expeditionary force as an interpreter.

As befitting a white officer, Gregory acquires a servant, Zaki, a youth of his own age. The racialised hierarchy of master and servant, white over black, is firmly established from the beginning. Zaki calls Gregory 'my lord' and 'master', and Gregory refers to Zaki as his 'man' or his 'boy' – 'Zaki's only regret was that he could not do more for his master.' Within this Manichean universe, Gregory volunteers to disguise himself as a Dervish to spy on the enemy forces. His act of cultural cross-dressing involves an elaborate ritual. Zaki shaves Gregory's head, boils herbs to make a dye and paints his skin from head to toe. Finally he dresses him in the clothes of a Dervish.

Like a man dressing as a woman, Gregory's disguise is fetishistic. Freud explains the fetish as an object which is a 'substitute for the woman's (mother's) penis that the little boy once believed in . . .'[51] The castration complex inaugurates sexual difference and disillusions the boy's belief in her sameness. But if his mother has lost her penis, it is possible that he may lose his own. The fetish is 'a token of triumph over the threat of castration and a protection against it. It also saves the fetishist from becoming a homosexual.'[52] By adopting a fetish a boy can evade the oedipal injunction to give up his mother. He can embrace a 'feminine attitude' and at the same time avoid a homosexual object choice. By defining it as a phallic icon, Freud constructs fetishism as a perversity which secures heterosexual masculinity against its own inherent instability. A less reductionist analysis of the fetish would define it as a cultural object which symbolises a conflict of differences. It embodies two imaginary positions, the masculine and the feminine, heterosexuality and homosexuality. By dressing as a woman, a man negotiates the ambivalence of his own sexual identity. In this temporary upsetting of sexual difference, he parodies the original sexual object of his mother. This is not so much a transgression of his gender identity as an imposition of his power over his mother. At the same time he can transgress the taboos of homophobia and relate to men as a woman, adopting an imaginary homosexual object choice.

Gregory is both an exhibitionist and a voyeur. The masochistic thrill of discovery lies in his own repressed desire for these men. But at the same time his cross-dressing is an expression of his triumphal omnipotence and surveillance over them. He has been able to cross the border of difference, to get inside their skin. The homophobic boyhoods of Englishmen exacerbated the autoerotic desire to spy on the bodies of others. The object of the Englishman's desire is his own body which has been denied him. Gregory's cross-dressing represents a central feature of colonial power – the imperialist's attempt to see and to know his own repressed homoerotic desire in the lives of another 'primitive' race. Gregory is but one more fictitious secret agent of the 'Great Game'. He no longer plays the game for nation and empire, but for the unimaginable and eroticised power it offers him.

As Gregory makes his escape from the Dervish camp, one of the sheiks discovers him: 'without hesitation [he] snatched his own knife from the sash and drove it deep into his assailant's body' (p126). By stabbing a high born Arab, Gregory reestablishes his mastery and the homophobic Manichean universe. Escaping the scene of racial ambivalence, Gregory knows which side he belongs to; as a white man he clings to the racial totem of his skin colour. It signifies his separateness from and supremacy over black and brown men and it is his defence against his own transgressive, homosexual desires. At the end of the book, back in England with his rightful inheritance restored, Gregory offers Zaki his freedom: 'Zaki shook his head. 'I should be a fool to wish to be my own master,' he said, 'after having such a good one at present.' It is one of the functions of racial mastery to contain the scene of male hysteria behind the tight ropes of its ethnic absolutism.

The Narcissism of Englishmen

In *Tell England*, death is the symbol of transcendence; in Henty's story it is race. Both represent metaphorical attempts to displace confused emotions and taboo sexualities from the bodies of Englishmen. Narcissism was central to the psychopathology of imperialism. It was characterised by an asceticism, an affective immaturity and a tendency towards the denial of desire and instinctual life. Strachey's description of Gordon's fanatical evangelicism and contempt for the body revealed a man torn between the flesh and spirit, between his ego and its renunciation. Gordon, like other imperialists, transfigured desires of the flesh into a metaphysical imperial quest 'for fame and influence, for the swaying of multitudes, and for that kind of enlarged and intensified existence where breath breathes most – even in the mouths of men'.[53]

The 'white heights' of the imperial mission offered a reason for the extinguishing of instinctual life. This relates to Andre Green's analysis of narcissism. According to Green,

> The body as an appearance and source of pleasure, of seduction and conquest of others is banished. In the case of the moral narcissist, hell is not other people – narcissism has eliminated them, but rather, the body. The body is the Other, resurrected in spite of attempts to wipe out its traces. The body is a limitation, a servitude, a termination.[54]

The body and its sexualities were indeed the source of the imperial Englishman's shame. And for Green these vicissitudes of the body are rooted in the relationship with the mother. The suppression of feelings and 'the feminine' has the effect of turning the son's sexual desire into an expression of need. In his mind, his mother assumes an omnipotence because only she can satisfy his need. He idealises her, but he experiences her as a persecutor, an ailing woman who constantly demands his love and attention. He must constantly acquiesce in her demands, for only when she is alive can he also live. This fantasy of the persecuting mother reduces men to a state of helplessness. A state which so troubled Freud; 'we already know ... that this helplessness lasts throughout life [and makes it] necessary to cling to the existence of a father.'[55] What frightened Freud was the failure of the father to act as a protector against the mother. In the face of the father's unreliability, religion and the esoteric become the illusory substitutes – 'the benevolent rule of a divine Providence allays our fears of the dangers of life.'[56] To attain liberation from his servitude to his mother, the son must find a reason to extinguish his instinctual life and transpose it onto a metaphysical plane; to submerge himself in intellectual life, to follow a cause or to become part of some bigger and greater scheme of things.

Lionel Johnson, in 'Winchester College' (1893), a poem celebrating the college's five hundredth anniversary, likened his old school to maternal love:

> Witness and interpreter
> Mother mine: loved Winchester.

In another poem, 'Winchester Close', school becomes his maternal home:

> first-born thou,
> Who stateliest now
> The crown of ages weariest
>
> To know me Thine,
> And know thee mine
> Could comfort many a sorrow.

Maternal loss is displaced into a nostalgic sense of union with his old school and projected back in time to signify a homosocial, racial continuum.

> Before us, years that charmed full well.
> Five centuries behind us.
>
> . . .
>
> Heirs of old race
> In that fair place:
> One fellowship unbroken.[57]

This is the archaic motherland to which men offer up their lives. But in truth they have already given up their lives to a single woman. Fashioned in the narcissist's projection of his dependency on his mother and struggle to be free of her, imperialism offered an outlet for an infantile unbounded desire. The son's sacrifice of his own life for his mother would not be wasted if history afforded him the omnipotence he longed for. The imperial mission, the 'white heights' of English manliness, gave him the opportunity to escape from his servitude by transferring his identification to the creed of a brotherhood in service to a higher cause. Imperialism became a divinity, an autoerotic pleasure offering itself as an object of love.

This transfer of ego-subordination from the mother to an imperial mission cultivated a demand for individual sacrifice and a tantalising culture of the will to power. In Henry Newbolt's poem, 'Clifton Chapel', a father offers his son the symbol of imperial transcendence and patriarchal continuity in the brotherhood of his new school.

> This is the Chapel: here my son,
>   Your father thought the thoughts of youth,
> And heard the words that one by one
>   The touch of Life has turned to truth.
> Here in a day that is not far,
>   You too may speak with noble Ghosts
> Of manhood and the vows of war
>   You made before the Lord of Hosts.
>
> To set the cause above renown,
>   To love the game beyond the prize,
> To honour, while you strike him down,
>   The foe that comes with fearless eyes;
> To count the life of battle good,
>   And dear the land that gave you birth,
> And dearer yet the brotherhood
>   That binds the brave of all the earth –
>
> My son, the oath is yours: the end
>   Is His, Who built the world of strife,
> Who gave His children Pain for friend,
>   And Death for surest hope of life.
> Today and here the fight's begun,

Of the great fellowship you're free;
henceforth the school and you are one
And what You are, the race shall be.[58]

The poem idealises the obliteration of the self and its mergence with a racial imperial destiny. The mother has been banished. In her place the father offers the fellowship of other men, but the price is submission to the immortality of *Pro Patria Mori*. Her suppression promised men a resolution to the predicaments of sexual difference. But in truth the ascetic, desexualised, narcissistic culture of imperial manliness reduced the subject to the zero of himself. It paved the way to a culture of death.

Imperialism, with its male fraternity, its hard work, and opportunities for escape and ultimately war, offered both death and immortality. As Benedict Anderson has pointed out, there is no more arresting emblem of nationalism than the cenotaph to the Unknown Soldier. To give one's life for one's country is to transform violent, meaningless, catastrophic death into an eternal heroism, a surrender to the transcendent symbols of race and Empire. 'It is the magic of nationalism to turn chance into destiny.'[59] Fatality is transformed into continuity. The imperial race glides out of an immemorial past and sails majestically into a limitless future carrying her sons forward with the promise of her eternal gratitude for their sacrifice.

The last word should go to J.M Barrie, because he brought these myths home. In *Peter Pan* time future is suspended and with it time past. The Neverland is a place where Hook and Pan are fated by the absent mother they both dread and long for – they are both interred in an unchanging present. Into this breach steps Wendy, the adolescent fantasy of the asexual, perfect mother. Only she is destined for a real, temporal life of maturity and old age. In his whimsical, sentimental way Barrie positioned the figure of the mother in the imperialist rhetoric of sacrifice and immortality. Hook has captured the Lost Boys and is about to make them walk the plank: 'At this moment Wendy was grand. 'These are my last words, dear boys,' she said firmly. 'I feel that I have a message to you from your real mothers, and it is this: "We hope our sons will die like Englishmen."'[60] For men to reject life demands a point of departure and that lies with the mother. The vestiges of her body, the inextinguishable hope for her love, remains with the narcissist and it is she – 'woman'- who will be blamed for the private catastrophe of his death. Behind every myth of the imperial hero lies the fantasy of the mother who refused him his life.

Notes

1. For discussion of Victorian boy's fiction and adventure stories see; Avery 1975, Boyd 1991, Bratton 1986, Carpenter 1985, Dunae 1980, Kiely 1971, Low 1990, MacKenzie 1984, Plotz 1992, Richardson 1993, Scott 1992, Turnbaugh 1975, Turner 1975.
2. Robert Falcon Scott (1975), *Scott's Journals*, ed. Peter Scott, Methuen, p.440.
3. Robert Cust (1899), *Life-Memoir*, Robert Needham, p.30.
4. *Ibid., p.88.*
5. *Cited in Dean Stanley (1844)*, Life of Dr Arnold, Ward, Lock and Co., p.69.
6. Achmed Abdullah and T. Compton Pakenham (1930), *Dreamers of Empire*, Harrup and Co., p.9.
7. Quote taken from, Ronald Hyams (1992), *Empire and Sexuality: The British Experience*, Manchester University Press, p.71-72.
8. Rev. J.E.C. Welldon (1895), Minutes of the Seventh Ordinary General Meeting of the Royal Colonial Institute, p.327-28.
9. *Ibid.*, pp.329, 331, 330.
10. See James Morris (1979), *Pax Britannica: The Climax of an Empire*, Penguin.
11. Thomas Hughes (1993), *Tom Brown's Schooldays*, Wordsworth Children's Classics, p.313.
12. Cited in Edward C. Mack (1971), *Public Schools and British Opinion since 1860*, Greenwood Press, Connecticut, p.123.
13. Henry Newbolt, (1918), *The Book of the Happy Warrior*, London. Quote from Jeffrey Richards (1987), 'Passing the Love of Women': manly love in Victorian Society', in *Manliness and Morality Middle Class Masculinity in Britain and America, 1800-1940*, eds. J.A. Mangan and James Walvin, Manchester University Press.
14. Rev. J.E.C. Welldon, *op.cit.*, p.329.
15. Philip Mason (1993), *The English Gentleman: The Rise and Fall of an Ideal*, Pimlico, p.161.
16. John Robert Seeley (1883), *The Expansion of England*, Boston, p.174-75.
17. Lord Milner (1913), 'Introduction' to *The Nation and the Empire*, Constable, p.xxxii.

18. Henry Newbolt, *Collected Poems of Henry Newbolt 1897-1907*, Thomas Nelson, London.
19. Hannah Arendt (1986), *The Origins of Totalitarianism*, Andre Deutsch, p.217.
20. John Tosh (1991), 'Domesticity and Manliness' in *Manful Assertions Masculinities in Britain since 1800*, eds Michael Roper and John Tosh, Routledge, p.68.
21. Claudia Nelson (1989), 'Sex and the Single Boy: Ideals of Manliness and Sexuality in Victorian Literature for Boys' in *Victorian Studies*, No. 4, Vol.2, p.545.
22. Lawrence Stone (1976), *The Family, Sex and Marriage in England, 1500-1800*, Weidenfield and Nicolson, p.665.
23. Cited in Sally Shuttleworth (1992), 'Demonic Mothers: Ideologies of bourgeois motherhood in the mid-Victorian era', in *Rewriting the Victorians: Theory History and the Politics of Gender*, ed. Linda M. Shires, Routledge, p.43-44.
24. S. Freud (1909) 'Family Romances', *PFL*, Vol. 7, p.222.
25. S. Freud (1933[32]), 'Femininity', *PFL*, Vol. 2, p.168.
26. S. Freud (1930[1929]), 'Civilisation and its Discontents', *PFL*, Vol. 12, p.260.
27. See for example S.Freud (1916[1915-1916]),'The Archaic and Infantile Features of Dreams' in *PFL*, 1, p.24. And S. Freud (1914), 'On Narcissism: An Introduction', *PFL*, 11, p.82.
28. S. Freud (1933[1932]) 'Femininity', *PFL*, Vol. 2, p.168.
29. S. Freud (1931), 'Female Sexuality', *PFL*, Vol. 7, p.373.
30. M. Klein (1928), 'Early Stages of the Oedipus Complex' in *The Selected Melanie Klein*, ed. Juliet Mitchell, Penguin.
31. S. Freud (1917[1915]), 'Mourning and Melancholia', *PFL*, 11, p. 253.
32. Cited in H. John Field (1982), *Toward a Programme of Imperial Life: The British Empire at the Turn of the Century*, Clio Press, Oxford, p.39.
33. S. Freud (1925j), 'Some Psychical Consequences of the Anatomical Distinction Between the Sexes' in *PFL*, Vol. 7, p.341.
34. David Newsome (1961), *Godliness and Good Learning: Four Studies on a Victorian Ideal*, London, p.83.
35. Martin Green (1980), *Dreams of Adventure, Deeds of Empire*, Routledge & Kegan Paul.
36. Cyril Connolly (1988), *The Enemies of Promise*, Andre Deutsch, p.271.
37. Richard Gordon (1988), *A Gentleman's Club*, Arrow, p.95. Quote taken from P.J. Rich (1991), *Chains of Empire: English Public Schools, Masonic Cabalism, Historical Causality, and Imperial Clubdom*, Regency Press.

38. S. Freud (1914), 'On Narcissism: An Introduction' in *PFL*, Vol.11, p.81-82.
39. M. Klein (1946), 'Notes on Some Schizoid Mechanisms' in Juliet Mitchell, *op.cit.*
40. S. Freud, 'On Narcissism', *op.cit.* p.88.
41. Michael Egan (1982), 'The Neverland of Id: Barrie, Peter Pan and Freud' in *Children's Literature*, Vol. 10, p.37.
42. Jacqueline Rose (1984), *The Case of Peter Pan or The Impossibility of Children's Fiction*, Macmillan, p.3.
43. J.M. Barrie (1904-5B), *Peter Pan*, The Walter Beinecke collection, Act ii, Scene iii, p.26.
44. 'It's a toast which I hope everyone of us, wherever he may go hereafter, will never fail to drink when he thinks of the brave bright days of his boyhood. It's a toast which should bind us all together, and to those who've gone before and who'll come after us here. It is the dear old School-house – the best house of the best school in England.' 'Old Brooke' in *Tom Brown's School Days*.
45. Lytton Strachey (1979), *Eminent Victorians*, Chatto and Windus, p.21.
46. Eve Kosofsky Sedgwick (1985), *Between Men: English Literature and Male Homosocial Desire*, Columbia University Press.
47. John Addington Symonds (1984), *op.cit.* p.64.
48. S. Freud (1911[1910]), 'Psychoanalytical Notes On An Autobiographical Account of a Case of Paranoia (Dementia Paranoids), in *PFL*, Vol. 9, p.201.
49. Edward Said (1991), *Orientalism*, Penguin, p.72.
50. Cited in Michael C.C. Adams (1990), *The Great Adventure: Male Desire and the Coming of World War 1*, Indiana University Press, p.30.
51. S. Freud (1927), 'Fetishism' in *PFL*, Vol. 7, p.352.
52. *Ibid.*, p.353-54.
53. Lytton Strachey (1979), *op.cit.*, p.215.
54. Andre Green (1986), 'Moral Narcissism' in *On Private Madness*, Hogarth Press, p.127.
55. S. Freud (1927) 'The Future of an Illusion', *PFL*, Vol. 12, p.212.
56. *Ibid.*
57. Poems taken from E.C. Mack (1971), *op.cit.* pp 145-46.
58. Henry Newbolt, 'Clifton Chapel' in *Collected Poems of Henry Newbolt*, *op.cit.*
59. Benedict Anderson (1983), *Imagined Communities*, Verso, p.19.
60. J.M. Barrie, (1991), *Peter Pan*, Puffin Books, p.173.

3

'UNDER AN ENGLISH HEAVEN.' RUPERT BROOKE AND THE SEARCH FOR AN ENGLISH ARCADY

In January 1915, the poet Rupert Brooke sent the actor John Drinkwater an invitation: 'Come and die. It will be great fun.'[1] He had just returned from the ill-fated expedition to save Antwerp from the German advance. He urged Drinkwater not to get left out, but to mix in with the French: 'I want to mix a few sacred and Apollonian English ashes with theirs. Lest England be shamed.' After a couple of weeks kicking his heels in an army camp at Blandford, Dorset, Brooke embarked for the Dardanelles. 'It's too wonderful', he wrote to his friend, Dudley Ward. 'We're going in four days. And the best expedition of the war.'[2] He informed his mother the fighting would last between two and six weeks: he would be home in May. On 23 April, aboard the French hospital ship *Duguay-Trouin*, Brooke died of blood poisoning from an infected mosquito bite. He was twenty-seven years old.

Three weeks before his death, the Dean of St Paul's had praised Brooke's 'pure and elevated patriotism', to an Easter Sunday congregation of widows, parents and orphans. He went on to recite Brooke's 1914 Sonnet, 'The Soldier':

> If I should die, think only this of me:
>   That there's some corner of a foreign field
> That is forever England. There shall be
>   In that rich earth a richer dust concealed:
> A dust whom England bore, shaped, made aware,
>   Gave, once, her flowers to love, her ways to roam,

A body of England's, breathing English air,
Washed by the rivers, blest by suns of home.[3]

The Times carried a report of the sermon, and the sonnet's pastoral evocation of patriotism and loss transformed a mediocre poet into an icon of Englishness.

The irony of Rupert Brooke's death by a mosquito bite was lost in the clamorous appeal to England's sons to follow his example and do their duty. On 26 April, Winston Churchill, First Lord of the Admiralty wrote his obituary in *The Times*.

> Rupert Brooke is dead ... A voice had become audible, a note had been struck, more true, more thrilling, more able to do justice to the nobility of our youth in arms engaged in this present war, than any other-more able to express their thoughts of self-surrender ... He expected to die. He was willing to die for the dear England whose beauty and majesty he knew; and he advanced toward the brink in perfect serenity, with absolute conviction of the rightness of his country's cause, and a heart devoid of hate for fellow-men.[4]

Churchill had met Brooke through his private secretary Edward Marsh, and had secured him a commission in the Royal Naval, 'Hood Battalion'. With an eye on the opponents of his Gallipoli campaign and a predilection for Greek beauty and tragedy, he turned his young protégé into public property. The image of Brooke as a warrior poet became the rallying-cry for a volunteer army. Between the annihilation of the regular army in 1914 and the introduction of conscription in 1917, two and a half million young men joined the colours. Rupert Brooke became 'the incarnate symbol of the spirit of 1914'; the embodiment of patriotic, youthful sacrifice.

On 3 May, *The Sphere* established an historical dimension to the burgeoning myth, declaring him 'the only English poet of any consideration who has given his life in his country's wars since Philip Sydney received his death wound under the walls of Zutphen in 1586'. Tributes and elegies poured into newspapers. The editor of the *Nation* bewailed the execrable verse which flooded his office; 'I should be afraid to say,' he wrote in his editorial, 'how many poems commemorative of R.B. I have received since his untimely death.' One month after he died, a collection of his poems, *1914 and Other Poems* was published. Eighteen months later it had been through fourteen impressions. By August

1916, Brooke's first volume, *Poems* (1911), had been reprinted ten times and by 1932 had sold 100,000 copies. In 1919, the Commander-in-Chief of the Dardanelles, Sir Ian Hamilton, gave an address at the unveiling of a commemorative plaque in the Chapel of Brooke's old school, Rugby. 'I have seen famous men and brilliant figures in my day, but never one so thrilling, so vital as that of our hero. Like a prince he would enter a room, like a prince quite unconscious of his own royalty, and by that mere act put a spell upon everyone around him.'[5] By 1954, some 600,000 copies of the various editions had been sold. There were one hundred poets of Brooke's generation publishing in London; only Yeats, Eliot and Pound are as well known and as widely read. When Sir Edward Grey had declared in 1914 that the 'lights are going out all over Europe', it was the image of Rupert Brooke, the golden haired Adonis, who lit the way. 'No-one ever looked so much like a poet as he did . . . an ideal English poet, a Rugby and Cambridge poet, a healthy, pink-cheeked, blond, games playing poet.'[6]

Rupert Brooke

Rupert Brooke was born on 3 August, 1887, the second of three sons, to a dominant and puritanical mother. Mrs Brooke had desperately wanted a daughter to replace her second child who had died in infancy. Rupert became his mother's special son; cosseted by her during his frequent bouts of ill-health and subject to her stern injunctions when he erred from her wishes. In contrast, his father, a housemaster at Rugby School, was an ineffectual, diffident man. According to Brooke's biographer, Christopher Hassall, 'The nearest he ever got to intimacy with his father was over a Latin or Greek grammar.'[7] Throughout his life, Brooke remained emotionally subservient to his mother, nick-naming her 'The Ranee' in reference to the Brookes' of Sarawak, and as a sideswipe at her domineering manner. He fought and argued with her. But each attempt to assert his autonomy precipitated his emotional need and ended in a bout of illness and a retreat back into her care. This never-ending cycle of flight and collapse bred a romantic escapism and a deep-seated fatalism in his personality, leaving him prone to periods of manic enthusiasm and fits of depression.

Brooke went to King's College Cambridge in 1906, aged twenty. His friend, the future Labour politician Hugh Dalton, persuaded him to join the Fabian Society, enticing him with romantic tales of class struggle. But Brooke remained an aesthete at heart and sceptical of the Fabians' industrial and bureaucratic ethos. His commitment was to the pastoralism of the New Life: 'I'm not your sort of Socialist,' he told Dalton, ' I'm a William Morris sort of Socialist.' It was an anti-industrial and agrarian socialism. In 1887, Morris had told the Hammersmith Branch of the Socialist League, 'I must tell you that my special leading motive as a Socialist is hatred of civilisation.'[8]

> It has covered the merry green fields with the hovels of slaves and blighted the flowers and trees with poisonous gases, and turned rivers into sewers; till over many parts of Britain the common people have forgotten what a field or flower is like, and their idea of beauty is a gas-poisoned gin-palace or a tawdry theatre.'[9]

The best known advocate of the New Life was Edward Carpenter (1844-1929) who set up his Millthorpe Colony, near Sheffield, in 1880.[10] Alongside a band of followers, he practised rural self-sufficiency and a lifestyle of nudity, vegetarianism, sunbathing and sandals. He denounced the evils of industrialism in political activism and verse:

> Forget six counties overhung with smoke,
> Forget the snorting steam and the piston stroke,
> Forget the spreading of the hideous town;
> Think rather of the pack-horse on the down
> And dream of London, small, and white, and clean.
>
> 'The Earthly Paradise' (1870)

It was this utopian aesthetic which appealed to Brooke. His rebellion was less against capitalism than against adult society, particularly his own parents. 'I'm terribly Fabian,' he told a friend, 'which in our family is synonymous with "atheistical", "Roman Catholic", "vulgar", "conceited" and "unpractical".'[11] His ambition to be a poet was matched by his romantic yearning to live like a poet and follow the New Life. To be one of nature's children, he imagined, offered a prolonged adolescence and the evasion of adulthood.

Brooke quickly became a prominent figure in Cambridge undergraduate life. His homoerotic appeal and intellectual flamboyance ensured his election to the elite and secretive male cabal of the Apostles. He now had one foot in Bloomsbury and one in the Fabians, but the focus of his life became a small group of men and women whom Virginia Woolf later dubbed the 'Neo-pagans'. The central group of Neo-pagans consisted of Brooke, Justin Brooke, (whose father built up the tea company Brooke Bond) Jacques Raverat, Gwen and Frances Darwin, Ka Cox (the treasurer of the Cambridge Fabian Society) and the Olivier Sisters – Bryn, Daphne, Margery and Noel. Their father, Sydney Olivier, was the Governor of Jamaica and a founding member of the Fabians. The sisters had been raised liberally; Noel attended Bedales, a progressive public school whose headmaster and founder, J.H. Badley, was a follower of Edward Carpenter. Justin Brooke and Jacques Raverat were both ex-pupils and had introduced Brooke to its spartan, back-to-nature philosophy. In 1909, he wrote to his cousin Erica Cotterill, 'I am leading the healthy life. I rise early, . . . eat no meat, wear very little, do not part my hair, take frequent cold baths . . . it is all part of my scheme of returning to nature.'[12] It was the lifestyle of country walks, bare feet and camping which drew the circle together around the central figure of Brooke. What inspired them were not ideologies of socialism or the aesthetics of art, but the fact of being young in a new century. They first came together as a group to rehearse a production of Milton's masque, *Comus*. Brooke cajoled them into an oath which forbade them to marry or become engaged within six months of its performance. Friendship and youth sustained their circle; what eventually pulled it apart was sexuality. The pact was soon broken by the marriage of Frances Darwin to a young Don, Francis Cornford. Gwen Darwin and Jacques Raverat followed their example; but by this time Brooke too was embroiled in his own tortuous courtships.

Brooke had first met Noel Olivier on 10 May, 1908, during a Fabian Society dinner. She was fifteen years old and, like her sisters, she had been encouraged to discard the oppressive Victorian codes of femininity. Despite her age, Brooke was immediately infatuated with her and began a correspondence. Before long, Margery was warning him off her younger sister, for his 'wild writing'. Love, she insisted, only ruined young women. But Brooke's infatuation with Noel had grown into an obsession.

26th Oct. 1910. The Orchard, Grantchester

Most holy,

Just to get in touch with you, to get the right attitude, I've been up to look at you. You sit on my garish bedroom mantel-piece now (you wrin-

kled a vast nose of disapproval, you remember, at your continual, trai-
torous presence in *this* room). Occasionally I go and stare. You never say
anything. You are brown and discreet.[13]

Which was the problem. Noel would not respond to Brooke's impas-
sioned declarations of love. Brooke's social non-conformity did not
encompass sexuality; the Neo-pagans circle had dispensed with the
prudery of the Victorian age, but had not been able to renounce its
censorious attitude toward sexual relations. The Neo-pagans had
broken the taboo against mixed company, but sex was still inconceiv-
able outside the strict marital codes of bourgeois life. Brooke's growing sexual confusion and frustration were compounded by his
emotional dependence on his mother who repeatedly complained
about his friendship with the 'fast' Olivier girls. In January 1910 his
father had died and, despite his peripheral role in Brooke's life, it trig-
gered the beginning of a personal crisis. His virginity had become a
cruel and humiliating symbol of his unmanliness.

Brooke conspired to end the 'shame of being a virgin'. He invited
the younger brother of an old school friend to stay with him. Sexual
attraction was mutual and it required little persuasion by Brooke to
seduce the boy. Brooke later confessed the incident to his friend, James
Strachey: 'I thought of him entirely in the third person. At length the
waves grew more terrific: my control of the situation was over; I
treated him with the utmost violence, to which he more quietly, but
incessantly, responded.'[14] The day after his initiation into sexual intercourse, Brooke accompanied the boy to the railway station. Neither
mentioned the incident again. The secret and manipulative nature of his
homosexual passion had only reinforced the impasse of his heterosexuality, and revealed a self-disgust, and a loathing of carnality.
Disenchanted by Noel Olivier's reticence, Brooke started to foster a
deeper intimacy with Ka Cox. She was older than Noel and a woman
of independent means. While Noel was aloof and withdrawn, Cox was
more expansive and giving. By June Brooke was wooing two women.
Ka Cox he idealised as a surrogate mother, Noel Olivier as pure and
virginal; both were unobtainable. In 1911, on a visit to Munich to learn
German for his thesis on Elizabethan drama, Brooke met Elizabeth van
Rysselberghe, the daughter of the Belgian, neo-Impressionist painter.
She fell in love with him. Brooke was presented with the opportunity
for a passionate affair in a foreign city, away from censorious, prying
eyes. In his sonnet 'Lust' he described how he 'starved' for her. But as

soon as she responded to him, his desire collapsed – 'Quieter than a dead man on a bed.' His desperation for heterosexual experience was equally matched by his fear and disgust of female sexuality.

Noel Olivier continued to remain aloof. Brooke decided to stake everything on Ka Cox and announce his desire to marry her. But, on a reading party in Lulworth Cove in January 1912, she declared her love for the painter Henry Lamb. Brooke felt betrayed and humiliated. He imagined the more experienced Lamb had already slept with her. The following month he accused her of naivete - 'The creature slimed down to Lulworth; knowing about women, knowing he could possibly get you.'[15] He disintegrated into a state of paranoia. His principal persecutor was Lytton Strachey who had arranged for Lamb to come to Lulworth in order to foster his relationship with Cox: 'Lytton "hovering" with a fond paternal anxiousness in the background, eying the two young loves at their sport:- it was the filthiest filthiest part of the most unbearably sickening disgusting blinding nightmare.'[16] Strachey had not deserved to be singled out for this vituperative hatred, but his homosexuality and casual attitude toward sex flaunted what Brooke was desperately attempting to control within himself.

He escaped the reading party at the earliest opportunity and made his way to Jacques and Gwen Raverat, who were staying in Studland. Realising the serious state he was in, they took him to Dr. Craig in Harley Street, who pronounced that Brooke was 'in a state of severe breakdown'. The cure was rest and 'stuffing'. Within weeks, his mother had taken charge and Brooke was in a Cannes hotel, under her care. Forced into a state of isolation and idleness he had little to distract him from his mental anguish. 'I couldn't eat or sleep or do anything but torture myself. It was the most ghastly pain imaginable, worse than any physical pain, dragging on, unending. It was madness - I can't describe it.'[17] Filled with self-recrimination, he bombarded Cox with frantic, manic declarations of love and need; 'By God! *you're* sane, with your splendid strength and beauty. But I've been half-mad, alone. Oh, it's all mixed up with this chastity.'[18] At the same time he was overwhelmed and frightened by her. He felt invaded;

> Loving you implies a geometrical progression. One gets worse and worse. You grow on one, so. It's a pervading, irresistible thing, 'Ka'. It's like having black- beetles in the house. 'I've got Ka in the body . . . My dear, I've tried *everything* . . . Put down carbolic? My dear, Yes! . . .' So, I tell you, I get frightened.[19]

He wheedled and cajoled her into meeting him in Munich. She agreed. At the end of January, Brooke escaped the control of his mother by concocting a story about visiting an old school friend. He met Cox in Verona and they spent three weeks together. Brooke wrote to James Strachey, 'I really rather believe she's pulled me through.'[20] Four days before their homecoming, they finally achieved the consummation Brooke believed would rescue him from mental anguish. He had heeded the advice of his friend, James Strachey and equipped himself with contraceptive devices. Most likely it was a clumsy and self-conscious event, but in March Brooke was writing to Cox: 'Dearest: I'm getting ravenous with passion. Oh, I love you . . . Love, love, love: It takes me like a tide.'[21]

And like the sea, she flooded his life; 'You, oh you. You fill one's horizon - one's narrow horizon- and one's life. Ka, and her dresses, and her walk - it comes round and over one.'[22] In May, for the second time in four months, Brooke and Cox found themselves alone and abroad, this time staying in Berlin. Brooke wrote to Jacques Raverat, 'I was in a mere stupor those weeks in Berlin; dead, dead, dead. I hadn't a flicker of emotion left for any living person.'[23] He felt nothing toward Cox; 'I felt utterly without 'love' for her: and extremely dead.'[24] Cox, the surrogate mother, became subject to his peevish demands: 'you mayn't foolishly and unthinkingly get tired and ill and miserable: because you make me tired and ill and miserable.'[25] Sex had released a stream of misogynistic loathing for her body. He wrote to Jacques Raverat: 'it's hard to get up love for anyone whom one associates only with the evil things of one's life: and whom one always catches oneself thinking degraded, slightly noisome or at least contemptible'.[26] But he is afraid to leave her - 'I'm terrified of leaving her'.[27] Brooke was riven with the fear that Henry Lamb might take Cox away from him. His dependency and jealousy transformed her from a luxuriant sea into something monstrous. 'There is a feeling of staleness, ugliness, trustlessness about her . . . Dirt.'[28] He told Noel Olivier, 'Ka is unclean'.[29] It was the unobtainable Noel, the virginal schoolgirl, who retained his fascination and desire. While Ka had descended to the status of a whore, Noel was elevated into a madonna. To Dudley Ward he proclaimed, 'Noel is the finest thing I've ever seen in the world, and Ka - isn't.'[30]

In 1913, Brooke escaped his claustrophobic and emotionally unstable life in England and travelled to America and the South Seas. He turned his back on the anti-Victorian influences of Aestheticism, the

New Life, Fabianism and Bloomsbury, which had been so important in shaping his life. On his return the following year, he gravitated towards Edward Marsh and his elite social circle in London. Brooke had first met Marsh at Cambridge, in 1906, when the older man had watched him play the part of the herald in a production of *Eumenides*. He had been Brooke's literary mentor and father figure and undoubtedly loved Brooke in that sublimated asexual Victorian way. But he was a man with little understanding of Brooke's emotional traumas, and out of kilter with the sensual pleasures of Neo-paganism. Amidst the emotional wreckage of his life Brooke sought security in conformity and became an increasingly outspoken misogynist, homophobe and anti-Semite. As his Cambridge friend and confidante, Frances Cornford had pointed out, nobody could miss Brooke's streak of puritanism, if they cared to look – 'the scorn and sternness in his face when he spoke of things that he hated, things corrupt and unclean'.[31] Brooke's madness brought to the surface the 'uncleanness' he hated most; women, Jews and his own ambiguous sexuality. 'I've a sort of hunger for cleanness,' he told Raverat.[32]

His poetry had been a means of expressing emotions which had been denied an outlet in his personal life. As Brooke exchanged his youthful idealism for a bourgeois and anodyne conservativism, his poetry became preoccupied with a sense of ending. In 'The Funeral of Youth: Threnody' (1913), he described the 'scatter'd friends' who arrive at the graveside to pay their last respects to dead *Youth*. Amongst many, there are '*Lust*, poor snivelling boy', '*Grief*', '*Romance*', '*Ignorance*', '*Generosity*', '*Friendship*', '*Imagination*.' They were 'met once more together': 'All, except only *Love*. *Love* had died long ago.' He wrote to Jacques Raverat, 'Friendship is always exciting and yet always safe. There is no lust in it and therefore no poison ... I will not love and I will not be loved.'[33] His Neo-pagan circle had failed to delay adulthood and hold back the inevitability of sexual desire. Brooke could no longer hide in the fantasies of an eternal, asexual youth. He cultivated an air of urbane sophistication and found a ready and admiring audience amongst Marsh's social circle of Asquiths and Churchills. Their formality and restrained company helped to contain the contradictions of his emotional and sexual life, which began to find an outlet in his rising ambition for fame and success. It was this political and social milieu, oblivious of or uninterested in his past life, which established the birth of his legend as a national hero.

The Making of a Legend

However cynically his image was exploited, its poignancy and endurance went far beyond crude Churchillian war propaganda. His mythical appeal amongst large swathes of middle-class England lay in a nostalgia for something past and lost. The stage for this image had already been well-established before the outbreak of war. During his life, Brooke succeeded in weaving an astonishing web of homoerotic fascination and desire around himself. James Strachey, his most loyal and longest friend, had been passionately in love with Brooke at Cambridge. Brooke's repeated rebuffs had only intensified his desire.

> This afternoon for the first time in my life, I saw Rupert naked. Can't we imagine what *you*'ld say on such an occasion? . . . But I'm simply inadequate of course. So I say nothing, except that I didn't have an erection – which was .. fortunate?, as I was naked too. I thought him - if you'ld like to have a pendant - 'absolutely beautiful.'[34]

The poet Edward Thomas, visiting him at his lodgings in the village of Grantchester, thought his 'steady blue eyes' and 'clear rosy skin' gave him the look of a 'great girl'. W.B. Yeats described him as 'the handsomest man in England', which later became transcribed in *The Little Review* as 'The most beautiful man in England'.[35] To men like Hugh Dalton he became a nostalgic figure of a 'golden time' of prewar, youthful freedom and happiness.[36] Robert Graves, who had never met Brooke, wrote to Edward Marsh in 1916: 'This afternoon I had a . . . waking dream about meeting and making friends with Rupert; it was absolutely vivid and I feel I now know him ten times better than before.'[37] In July 1918, the war almost over, Graves wrote again: 'I regret the meeting you promised me in 1914 with Rupert never came off . . . I'm much more of an optimist than any of my friends . . . but my capacity for such prehistoric happiness as Rupert had is nothing.'[38] Four decades after Brooke's death, Dalton wrote; 'No Cambridge friendship of mine meant more to me than this, and the radiance of his memory still lights my path . . . He was to all of us who loved him, a child of the Tir Nan' Og, the Land of the Forever Young.'[39]

In Rupert Brooke, English patriotism found an object to covet, a' man as beautiful as the English landscape - 'There was something dateless about his beauty which makes it easy to picture him in other centuries, yet always in England.'[40] Henry James, in old age, trying to recapture something of his own lost desire, associated Brooke with a pastoral scene. 'He reappears to me as with his felicities all most promptly divinable, in that splendid setting of the river at the "backs".'[41] Brooke was 'the social instincts of the race, poetically expressed'. He was 'the natural accommodation of the English spirit, this extraordinary beauty of the English aspect, this finest saturation of the English intelligence ... this ideal image of English youth.'[42] Others were no less effusive in linking the beautiful young man with the Anglo-Saxon race and the pastoral delights of the English landscape. In 1910, Dalton had written a review of Brooke for the University magazine, *Granta*. He described Brooke living in an idyllic pastoral world, in Grantchester.

> It is said that there he lives the rustic life, broken by occasional visits to Cambridge; that he keeps poetry and a cow, plays simple tunes on a pan pipe, bathes every evening at sunset, and takes all his meals in a rose garden.[43]

D.H. Lawrence was only too willing to perpetuate this Neo-pagan flavour. In April 1915, on hearing of Brooke's death, he wrote to the literary hostess Ottoline Morrell; 'I first heard of him as a Greek god under a Japanese sunshade, reading poetry in his pyjamas at Grantchester - at Grantchester upon the lawns where the river goes.'[44]

Behind these glowing tributes, Brooke's own life contained all the emotional contradictions and sexual tensions of the age. His masculinity was a legacy of Victorian, sexual prudery made increasingly fraught with self-doubt by the rise of feminism. He belonged to a middle-class generation torn between a new life of sexual emancipation and individual self-expression and the old patriarchal order of familial duty and Victorian formality. His attempt to reconcile these contradictions led him to embrace modernist art and poetry, but also too seek reassurance in a pastoralism invested with the unchanging traditional values and sexual hierarchies of Old England. His love of the revolutionary poetics of Diaghilev's ballet was continually tempered by his complaints of its cosmopolitan Jewish influences. In the end, Brooke chose romanticism and reaction over the modern. When Hugh Dalton showed him his *Granta* eulogy in 1909, Brooke told him, 'You might put in that my real life only began when I went to live at Grantchester.'[45] Here, living alone in the Old Vicarage, free of the compromising needs and demands of women, he was able to manufacture his own romantic identity as a *naif*, child poet. His lodgings were the inspiration for his best known poem, 'The Old Vicarage, Grantchester'. Written in Munich during his emotional crisis, it is a sentimental and nostalgic desire for home: 'Just now the lilac is in bloom/ All before my little room.'

> God! I will pack and take a train,
> And get me to England once again!
> For England's the one land, I know
> Where men with splendid Hearts may go:
> And Cambridgeshire, of all England,
> The shire for Men who Understand;
> And of *that* district I prefer
> The lovely hamlet Grantchester.

But belonging always evaded him and the Old Vicarage was never more than an idealised, imaginary home, just as it became for tens of thousands of readers. In spite of its significance in his own life, he spent remarkably little time living there. His adult life was a series of holidays and a constant moving around between friends; 'What I chiefly loathe and try and escape,' he explained to his friend Geoffrey Keynes, 'is not Cambridge nor Rugby nor London, but - Rupert Brooke. And I can only do this by rushing suddenly to places for a few days. He soon overtakes me.'[46] His frantic socialising was punctuated by frequent visits to his mother, to the home he was always trying to escape from.

Brooke's own life was an allegory of the Edwardian's anxious search for an English identity. He belonged to a bourgeois culture caught in the flux of modernity seeking an antidote for its social and sexual anxieties in an imaginary Arcady of rural England. Brooke's beauty, his romanticised and self-fabricated image of poet and child of nature, proved a receptive surface for personifying this idyll. His myth cultivated a homoerotic and nostalgic belief in a boyish innocence which deserted men when they entered heterosexual relationships. Its appeal was integral to the image of a prewar, Edwardian, pastoral age of innocence; an image of Southern landscapes and beautiful young men.

Pastoralism and English National Identity

By the end of the nineteenth century there was a vague but anxious desire amongst the middle classes to reinvent the English nation in an age of imperialism. A cultural movement began to emerge which claimed to reveal a 'true England'.[47] Foremost were the writers preoccupied with rural life; a diverse group of men from the cultural elite. Hillaire Belloc and G.K. Chesterton were radical English Nationalists, E.M. Forster was an antiimperialist liberal, A.E. Houseman was a liberal, D.H. Lawrence the one English writer who could be called a modernist. There was Thomas Hardy, W.H. Hudson, George Sturt and the nature poet Edward Thomas. And there were those, like Rupert Brooke, who found themselves temporarily or permanently housed under the title of 'Georgian poet': Lascelles Abercrombie, John Masefield, and Walter de la Mare. The nostalgia in their poetry and prose for a passing life of rural peace and solidity testified to a general disenchantment with everyday life. Despite their differing politics and aesthetic preoccupations, they shared an antipathy towards modernity and a belief in the regenerative power of nature. The symbolic geography they constructed of England as an Arcadian idyll gave a renewed political shape and meaning to Englishness.

The predominance of pastoral images in discourses of Englishness, derived from the peculiar social situation of England in the late nineteenth century. Since 1861, England had been an urban and industrial nation, its agriculture in decline. The aristocracy was powerful and wealthy enough and the historic unification of national life sufficiently strong, to allow a distinct rural society to disappear. As Paul Thompson wrote:

> Ruthless urbanisation had been one of the foundations of Britain's greater wealth. Left to the mercies of the market, unprotected by state subsidies, the Edwardian countryside was economically and socially moribund.[48]

William Morris recognised this landscape in decline, despoiled by exploitation, its people unable to appreciate its pleasures: 'all this country beauty so tragically incongruous in its richness with the country misery which cannot feel its existence.'[49] In spite of its economic ruin, the Edwardians 'rediscovered' rural England as a symbol of the country's unchanging essence. Their images and discourses of England and Englishness originated in the rural narratives of the 'South Country'; the cottages, meadows, woodlands and green rolling hills and hedgerows of Kent, Sussex and Surrey. Their literary and imaginative archaeology established England as an 'old country', its origins lost in the myths of time, its last recognisable moments the agrarian 'Merrie England' of Elizabeth 1.

They had a long tradition of pastoral representation to draw upon. The Romantic Poets of the late eighteenth century had used nature as a source of personal inspiration and a symbol of cultural and political aspirations. The Victorians reversed their meaning; what mattered was not cultivation and change but conservation and stasis. The upheavals of modernity - the mass exodus from the land and the rise of industrialism - established the village and the countryside as symbols of reassurance and continuity. The landscape painting of the early Victorians celebrated ownership of the land and hierarchies of gender, its ideological function to preserve the historical continuity of these relations within an emerging discourse of national identity. Landscape painting became the art genre of England, and established a dichotomy between the traditional harmony of the land and its people and the social upheavals of industrialisation. In an age of emigration and imperialism, exile from England encouraged these nostalgic and conservative images of a rural idyll. 'From about 1880', wrote Raymond Williams in *The Country and the City* (1973), 'there was ... a marked development of the idea of England as "home", in that special sense in which home is a memory and an ideal. Some of the images of "home" are of central London ... But many are of an ideal of rural England: its green peace contrasted with the tropical or arid places of actual work.'[50] J.S. Bratton shares his perspective and argues that the evocation of an English Arcady was the motive and reward for *the white man's burden*. The presentation of an idealised England as a motif and reward for the empire builder was the principle narrative structure of Victorian and Edwardian adventure stories. The idealisation of home was an 'adolescent boy's fantasy of motherhood ... a wonderland of crisp walks to church, holly berries, turkey and plum pudding, carol singers, mummers, presents, games and mince pies flaming with brandy.'[51] Like this idealisation of home, pastoralism regularly associated the countryside with maternal and feminine connotations of comfort, beauty and nurture.

The depiction of England as a mother to her sons became a powerful motif in imperialist ideology. In his short story, 'The Home-Coming of Vincent Brooke', the Imperial Proconsul and writer Sir Hugh Clifford describes a meeting with an old colonialist, Vincent Brooke, on board a home-bound ship.[52] He is seriously ill and desperate to see 'the England I have dreamed of so often' before he dies. 'I was

a boy, sir, when I quitted her, a boy with a boy's heart, a boy's understanding, a boy's callousness, a boy's love of adventure, I left her without a pang.' When Vincent Brooke felt the call of England and the
desire to return and was unable to, he experienced an intense longing
for his home. 'I who was born in her, I who love her, worship her, have
been banished from her shores for almost a lifetime . . . I know her sir
. . . My understanding of her has been bred of longing.' Clifford tries
to find consolation for this man's sacrifice in his commitment to the
imperial mission. Vincent Brooke is a man who dreamed of 'that vast,
free, unselfish Imperialism of which England - the England of our
dreams - is the centre, the inspiring spirit, the sustaining hope . . . "I am
going - Home!" he repeated softly in a kind of rapture, uttering with a
deep wonder and reverence. "Home! God grant that I may live to see
the white cliffs once more. Then I shall be content to die".' But this is
a classical oedipal drama and inevitably it ends in tragedy. The son
cannot return to his maternal origins and Vincent Brooke dies before
he sets eyes on England.

Feelings of loss and separation provided a textual quality to the
nostalgia for a motherland. But there were more material, social and
economic reasons for this turn to England and her countryside as a
source of security and identity. The English middle classes had grown
in power and confidence with the economic boom of the mid-nine-
teenth century. They had been spared the impact of Britain's subsequent decline in industrial output, because prices for food and basic
commodities had also fallen. But by the turn of the century, prices had
begun to climb faster than wages and the effect of the economic downturn was felt with a growing alarm. *The Times* edition of 6 January
1912, warned: 'the public must be prepared for a conflict between
Labour and Capital, or between employers and employed, upon a scale
as has never occurred before.' As Alan O'Day has argued; 'By the
beginning of the Edwardian age the economic foundations of the
liberal state were already insecure.'[53] Despite its continuing expansion,
British imperialism was becoming more defensive, turning inward to
its centre - an ailing England.

Slow but inexorable industrial decline shifted political and social
hegemony away from the North to financial capitalism in the South.
London became the heart of the Empire. But for the new Southern
middle classes in daily contact with the metropolis, it was rotten at the
core. Since the 1870s, commentators on the 'social question' had noted,
with growing apprehension, the failure of the labouring classes to

respond to legislative and charitable initiatives to raise their moral and social well-being. Unprecedented economic progress had not alleviated mass poverty nor the prospect of social unrest. One explanation put forward for the continuing ills of the urban poor was the concept of degeneration: social ills and moral depravity were not symptoms of too little civilisation, they were the consequences of too much. Poverty was the unfortunate consequence of progress, overabundance had enabled the lazy and feckless to flourish. The concept of degeneracy bore little relation to reality, but represented a moral panic in which the middle classes expressed their fear of the future, of the masses and of urban life in general. In the end it was war in South Africa which brought home the real extent of social deprivation and its dire consequence for nation and empire.

Increasing social insecurity and the rising industrial might of Germany and America gave the New Imperialism an added weight in national life. The empire signified Anglo-Saxon racial supremacy and Britain's prestige as a world power. The humiliating debacle of the Boer War (1899–1902) heralded a major social crisis and threatened to destroy the illusions of imperial greatness. Unemployment and the opportunity for adventure guaranteed a large number of volunteers at the outbreak of the war, but 330 out of every thousand volunteers were found to be unfit for service. They were too small, they suffered from weak lungs, bad hearts and rheumatic complaints, and had flat feet and bad teeth. By 1900, the figure had dropped to 280, but the standard of entry had been lowered. With initial rejections and subsequent losses of soldiers through ill-health, Major General Sir Frederick Maurice KCB, considered that only two out of every five volunteers had made effective soldiers.[54] The physical deterioration of 'the class which necessarily supplies the ranks of the army' was a potential national disaster. An interdepartmental Physical Deterioration Committee was set up by the government. In 1904 its report sparked off a widespread debate about 'the decline of the race'. The problem was located in childbearing, the upbringing of children and the supposed ignorance of working-class mothers in matters of healthcare and moral instruction. The argument for state intervention in the welfare of the national population grew. The Liberal MP, T.J. Macnamara, called for the introduction of school canteens, free transport and free baths for children. Writing in the *Contemporary Review* in 1905, he did not apologise for the fact that his proposals sounded like socialism: 'Because I know it also to be first rate Imperialism . . .

Empire cannot be built on rickety and flat-chested citizens.'[55]

By the end of the nineteenth century the theories of degeneracy had blended sin and crime into a medical discourse which proposed that the root of all social problems was a hereditary, personal pathology. Civilisation had enabled the 'unfit' to survive and unless they were checked the English race would be undermined and British imperialism would go the way of the Roman Empire and collapse from within. Sir Francis Galton took this social Darwinism to its logical conclusion in his theory and practice of Eugenics. The task of his Galton Laboratory at the University of London was to develop a practice of controlling 'the racial qualities of future generations'. The theory behind Eugenics was simple: if domestic violence, pauperism, alcoholism and criminality in working-class life could be attributed to heredity, it was possible, by controlling working class sexual reproduction, to breed these ills out of existence. Poverty would be ended and the racial stock revived. The task of the intellectual elite was to produce a nation 'healthy alike in mind and body'. In 1909, J.R. Inge, later to be Dean of St Paul's and the eulogiser of Rupert Brooke, called for 'any legislation' which would reduce the poor's desire to breed. Eugenics provided some of the central tenets for the foundation of the welfare state and the intellectual encouragement for a revived and racialised sense of Englishness and manhood. It also turned people's attention to the countryside as a bastion against degeneracy.

Robert Baden-Powell, the hero of Mafeking, and the subject of wild, jingoistic adulation during the Boer War, responded to the racial crisis with the formation of the Boy Scouts. He pronounced that only nature herself could revive the touchstones of English manliness - 'courage, endurance and self-reliance'. The solution to physical enfeeblement and racial degeneracy was imperial expansion and the opportunity for men to go overseas and test their manliness as pioneer farmers. 'Nature', he wrote, 'is being driven further and further out of the reach of the majority', with 'the artificial swamping out the natural in life.'[56] His *Scouting For Boys*, published in 1908, offered a peace-time solution to 'over-civilized' boys and young men whose only experience of life was the town or city. It was an imperialist's bible:

'scouts ... [are] real *men* in every sense of the word ... They are accustomed to take their lives in their hands, and to fling them down without hesitation if they can help their country by doing so.
They give up everything, their personal comforts and desires in order

to get their work done. They do not do all this for their own amusement, but because it is their duty to their King, fellow-countrymen, or employer.

Baden-Powell's vision of the outdoor life was resolutely anti-urban, masculine, anti-sensual and censorious of all expressions of sexuality. It drew upon the myth of the regenerative powers of rural England – a countryside inhabited by the squire and his *Country Life* country house, the bulwark against emasculating decadence and the degenerative influences of civilisation. Old England was the repository of the nation's moral character.

The imperialist sentiments of Baden-Powell appear far removed from the Socialist gospel of the New Life. But despite his separation from Baden-Powell in sensibility and politics, William Morris also viewed civilisation as emasculating: the City embodied decadent, wasteful luxury, breeding 'delicate invalid ladies' and the 'preposterous effeminacy' of the gentlemen's clubs, serviced by 'plush-breached flunkies'.[57] J.H. Badley, the founder of Bedales, welcomed the Boy Scout movement. The imperialist rural vision and the New Life were not mutually incompatible. A school like Bedales, with its rigid codes - 'we don't come to Camp to slack' - and its contempt for sensuality and decadence, could easily be absorbed into the more dominant discourses of imperial racial renewal. Both sought to defuse the sexual tensions and conflicts of late Victorian society in an anti-rationalist appeal to nature. Baden-Powell was an ardent proponent of the anti-masturbation campaigns, promoting the scouts as a form of sexual purity crusade for young men. For co-educational Bedales and its offspring the Neo-pagans, sexual relationships amongst the young were an explosive issue they attempted to defuse by separating sexuality from the body. While they advocated nude swimming and a cult of the body beautiful as prerequisites for physical and mental health, heterosexuality was subjected to a rigid code of chastity. Both imperialist and New Life versions of pastoralism were sustained by their belief in the corrupting influence of metropolitan life and the regenerative impulse of nature. The hegemonic concern was the revival of English ethnicity and its racial stock. Whether paganistic or conservative, the evocation of mother nature carried with it a strong hint of eugenics and an anti-cosmopolitan brand of nationalism.

English Nationalism and Anti-Semitism

Imperialists and New Lifers were not the only ones to make a political claim on English ruralism. Many Liberals and Radicals argued that imperialism, with its concern for territorial expansion, had neglected and betrayed the 'true' England. The Boer War presented the spectacle of a bullying, cosmopolitan society asserting itself over a rural, 'folk' culture. For these nationalists, the Boer were closer to the agrarian, organic community of Old England than the British government and its army. G.K. Chesterton exemplified their position: 'Is there anyone today who can reasonably doubt that what led us into error in our recent South African Politics was precisely our Imperialism, and not our Nationalism? Was precisely not our ancient interest in England, but our quite modern and frivolous interest in everywhere else?'[58] Pro-Boer, anti-imperialist sentiment frequently identified the greed of South African, Jewish financiers as the real cause of the war.[59] The figure of the Jew was endowed with the corrupting and destabilising influences of capitalism: the representative figure of a cosmopolitanism which was undermining the historical continuity of Old England and its homogeneous people.

The social transformations of modernity were breaking down community ties and vastly extending the prospects of individuality. A product of this destabilisation was the notion of the wanderer; the stranger who was everywhere out of place, 'a foreign body in our existence'.[60] The representative figure of the stranger in modernity was the Jew, who signified instability and embodied the gentile European fear of homelessness and cultural difference. It was a fear which preoccupied many of the Edwardian ruralists. The writer, Hillaire Belloc used the landscape and nature for metaphorical journeys in search of personal belonging and national identity. A close friend of Chesterton, Belloc was a Radical Liberal MP, an English Nationalist and an anti-Semite.[61] In *Hills and The Sea* (1906) he explored the feelings of dislocation and restlessness precipitated by modern society.

In an allegorical journey, two men embark upon 'a nobler kind of travel'. The purpose of their pilgrimage is an attempt to satisfy a 'divine thirst, for something that will not perish'. Belloc never clarifies this mystical goal, but towards the end of the book, in the vignette 'At the Sign of the Lion', he comes close to defining it in the form of a blood and soil nationalism. One of the travellers stays overnight in a country inn. He contemplates 'the corruption and the imminent danger of the time through which we must lead our lives . . . And, as I considered the ruin of the great cities and their slime, I felt as though I were in a fortress of virtue and of health' (p208). The inn offers a sense of home more familiar than the houses he has lived in. 'For nowadays we, who work in the State and are not idle, must be driven from one place to another' (p209). He strikes up a discussion with a man, a dispossessed aristocrat, about the purpose and meaning of the journey he has embarked upon. 'For my part, as I know of nothing else, I cannot but seek it in this visible good world. I seek it in Sussex, in the nature of my home, and in the tradition of my blood' (p210). The aristocrat argues that this journeying will lead nowhere. Life and the spirit are rooted in the present, in sensual feeling. Man is indissoluble with nature, a unity represented in the pagan figure of Pan: 'he revealed to them the life of trees and the spirits that haunt the cataracts, so that they heard voices calling where no one else had ever heard them, and they saw stones turned into animals and men' (p6). Belloc's allegory suggests that without out a sense of place, a national identity cannot take root. But the very nature of a future-oriented modern life mitigates against tradition and stability. Nationalism is the attempt to counter this threat of rootlessness. It is a search for an unambiguous identity, an 'us and them'. Its instinct is to search out the archaic and the prehistoric in which to embed its meaning and so place itself outside, raise itself above, the everyday life and language of modernity. The countryside functioned as a repository for the racial purity of 'us', its inert, mute landscape exorcising difference into one logical category of non-contradiction – nature. Here history ceases to exist in the mingling of blood and soil. In such a national conscience, the Jew represents everything that it seeks to eradicate.

In spite of the progressive leanings of the Neo-pagans, their belief in nature as a source of cultural identity left them exposed to this racial nationalism. Jacques Raverat, himself an anti-Semite, introduced Brooke to Belloc's work and Belloc became a powerful literary and political influence: ' I am thankful for such robust people, thinking of the swarms of decadent and immunised maggots that now swarm over the putrescent corpse of English Literature.'[62] In a letter to Lady Eileen Wellesley, written in August 1914, Brooke echoes Belloc's themes of alienation and homelessness.

> I find in myself two natures – not necessarily conflicting, but - different. There's half my heart which is normal & English – what's the word, not

quite 'good' or 'honourable' - *'straight'*, I think. But the other half is a wanderer and a solitary, selfish, unbound and doubtful. Half my heart is of England, the rest is looking for some home I haven't yet found.[63]

Brooke's anti-semitism was a projection of his own fractured identity, his own wandering aimless life: 'I seemed so remote and barren and stupid. I seemed to have missed everything.'[64] Its psychopathology is not simply racial, but a paranoia which grows out of the fear of cultural difference and sexual transgression. Anti-semitism represents the inordinate desire to be 'clean', to establish an external order which can ensure inner, psychological stability. Brooke learnt his anti-semitism from his friend Jacques Raverat and from Hillaire Belloc. But it was integrally a part of his own sexual prejudices and hatreds.

In 1914, on his sea-voyage back to England, Brooke wrote a letter to Helena, the six-month-old daughter of Frances Cornford. He looked forward to the theatres and supper parties, the 'arguments & hedges & roast beef & beer & misty half colours' of England.[65] But he dreaded London.

> London is full of 'Miles of shopping women, served by men,' and another Jew has bought a peerage, and I've a cold in my nose, and the ways are full of lean and vicious people, dirty, hermaphrodites and eunuchs, Stracheys, moral vagabonds, pitiable scum.

England, he wrote, had become a country 'ruled by women' who had feminised men. Back in England, Brooke wrote a review of the dramatist August Strindberg in the *Cambridge Magazine* (Oct. 1913): 'He is out to declare that men are men and women women'.[66] The enemy was feminism: 'The morbid symptom of lovelessness is that denial of sex called feminism, with it's resultant shallowness of woman and degradation of man.'[67] He contrasts Strindberg's work with Ibsen's adoption of 'feminism' and the way he crowded the theatre with 'petulant hermaphrodites'. In a letter to Noel Olivier, who was moving in the Bloomsbury circle, he echoed his paranoid jealousy of Henry Lamb, warning her: 'Lytton is filthy, & for God's sake don't touch him'.[68] He declaimed in another: 'the Stracheys are 'dangerous, spots of decay, menaces to all good. Even if one doesn't mind rats *qua* rats, one has to stamp out carriers of typhoid'.[69] With its associations of female emancipation and homosexuality, Bloomsbury became the 'pseudo-Jews'; the symbol of dirt, decay and transgression.

In his letter to Helena, Brooke offered an alternative, pastoral vision of home.

> Lately I have been having English thoughts - thoughts certainly of England – and even, faintly, yes, English thoughts - grey, quiet, misty, rather mad, slightly moral, shy & lovely thoughts. But very faintly so. England is too vague & hidden & fragmentary & forgotten a thing.[70]

His tentative attempt to imagine his national identity and belonging created an England of gossamer and ethereal femininity. A vision of 'misty half-colours', beautiful and quite harmless, just like Helena. Such an England represented the cleanness Brooke craved for, an ordered, patriarchal world, where female sexuality was impotent and women's bodies were boyish: a desexualised androgyny which banished the power of the maternal. In 1912, Brooke had written to Ka Cox giving her a precis of his sexual identity; 'I am here because ...Willie Brooke and Mary Cotterill got thrown together. And then they had a son and a daughter, and the daughter died, and while the mother was thinking of the daughter another child was born, and it was a son, but in consequence of all this very female in parts - . . . me.'[71] This short passage illuminates the source of Brooke's sexual ambiguity in his relationship with his mother. It is the oedipal scene of the hysteric; the boy who refuses an identification with his father and becomes his mother's daughter. It was the hermaphroditism he hated and for which he blamed women in general and his mother in particular. He projected his hatred into the imaginary bodies of Jews and intellectual young women who refused to accept their place and compounded his own insecurities. They were the cause of his sexual confusion and they became the carriers of his own 'uncleanness'. 'Manliness is the one hope of the world,' he told Virginia Woolf.[72] Manliness had been what most eluded him.

'Perilous paths and unlit darknesses': The Search for Male Desire

One of the most important dualisms in Western thought is the gendered polarity of culture and nature. Culture represents the world of the mind and the male subject. In the Freudian oedipus complex, it is initiated by the father and governed by activity, rationality, logic and objectivity. Nature is the world of the object, of non-identity, it

belongs to the body, to the feminine, the mother, it is governed by intu-
ition, emotions, passivity. The male, ruralist writers, those who
embraced paganism and called upon the god Pan, who sought an identification in the soft, rolling land of the South, appeared to transgress
this duality and abolish the distance between subject and object. W.H.
Hudson (1841–1922) the most influential prose writer of rural
England, believed in his indissoluble unity with nature:

> The blue sky, the brown soil beneath, the grass, the trees, the animals, the
> wind, the rain and the stars are never strange to me; for I am in, and of,
> and one, with them; and my flesh and the soil are one, and the winds and
> the tempests and the passions are one. I feel the strangeness only with
> regard to my fellow-men.[73]

In such an identification, the duality of subject and object, culture and
nature disappears. In 1938, the Marxist critic, Christopher Caudwell
wrote a stinging rebuke to D.H. Lawrence for his *participation
mystique* in the paganistic and nostalgic primitivism of Olde England.

> But it is Lawrence's final tragedy that his solution was ultimately Fascist
> . . . It was regressive. Lawrence wanted us to return to the past, to the
> 'Mother'. He sees human discontent as the yearning of the solar plexus
> for the umbilical connexion, and he demands the substitution for sharp
> sexual love of the unconscious fleshy identification of fetus with
> mother.[74]

Caudwell argued that nature, as symbolic of the transcendental lost
unity with the mother, swallows up the subject. Nature engulfs culture.
The language of the ruralists certainly did associate nature and the
countryside with feminine virtues and attributes. Vincent Brooke, the
exiled Imperialist, had a vision of England as his mother, but many of
the Edwardian writers inscribed in the countryside of their imagination
something more than a desire to immerse themselves in the 'promised
land' of a primal, undifferentiated union with the mother. They were
looking for something which was missing in their lives, which perhaps,
metaphorically speaking, was a part of the mother's body, but did not
belong to it.

During the Easter of 1909, Brooke spent several days with the
Olivier sisters at Bank in the New Forest. With the help of Dudley
Ward he had conspired to deceive his mother about his whereabouts:

For I was lost for four days - I went clean out of the knowledge of anyone in England but two or three - I turned, and turned, and covered my trail; and for three-four days, I was, for the first time in my life, a free man, and my own master! Oh! the joy of it! . . . I went dancing and leaping through the New Forest . . . and, in the end of the days, came to a Woman who was more glorious than the sun and stronger than the sea and kinder than the earth, who is a flower made out of fire, a star that laughs all day, whose brain is clean and clear like a man's and her heart is full of courage and kindness; and whom I love . . .[75]

In this pastoral theatre, Arcady is not a mother Brooke wants to fuse himself with in a search for ontological security, nor is it defined in connotations of his own repressed feminine attributes projected onto the landscape. It rings with a desire for his own masculine freedom from his mother and a recognition of his male heterosexual desire, a determination to establish a clear separation of subject and object. In a talk to the Carbonari, a discussion circle he started at Cambridge, Brooke identified the vagabond of the soul who rebels 'against the safeties and little confines of our ordinary life.'[76] But this wanderlust, 'Pan's flute in the distance', is an ominous threat. 'When industrialism has swamped the earth men will turn and look into their own souls and there may find many perilous paths and unlit darknesses.'[77] Brooke is afraid, because Pan symbolises both what he most wants and what he most fears. Pan is a metaphor for his turn to nature in search of sexual potency and identity. But he is also the figure of unrepressed sexuality who heralds the thoughtless abandonment of sexual ecstasy, the experience of *jouissance*, the dissolving of boundaries between self and other, subject and object. Brooke's 'deadness' is his defence against such a disintegration. He longs for sexual desire as a confirmation of his aliveness, but it is like having black-beetles in the house . . . 'I've got Ka in the body'.

Like Pan who is a part of nature, so the phallus is a part of the mother's body; the symbolic and idealised substitute for the unity of mother and child. Because it can never reoccur, it stands for something beyond the subject: desire. Desire is neither fully contained in the body nor entirely outside of it. It is what leads the subject away from undifferentiated union with the mother, it is the conveyor of the future. But because desire for the phallus originates in the body of the mother it is to her, metaphorically speaking, that men must return in order to seek it and to have it. In order to achieve a sense of their future, they must find it in the past. The narratives of pastoralism, the paganistic celebrations of communion with nature, were fuelled by the elusive quality of the phallus. The search for Arcady was not simply for Olde England. It was conducted in the hope she would yield up the phallocentric, heterosexual desire her sons believed she had dispossessed them of. Here men confronted the 'doubleness' or uncanniness of their pastoral quest. The maternal body which offers the key to the confirmation of their identity is also the site of its potential dissolution. Men like Brooke had rebelled against the world of the fathers only to discover in adulthood that their rebellion had been an affectation. They felt fated to remain the sexless sons of sexless men. Because female sexuality frightened them, because they felt unmanned, because a sexual language was denied them, their sexual ambivalence was metamorphosed into a search for Arcady, a desire to possess their own desire. For such men it was war and the promise of death which was to revive them. In the end, the world of the fathers came to their rescue and they made common cause in the name of England.

'Happy is England Now': August 1914[78]

War was a catharsis. Rupert Brooke informed John Drinkwater that the War offered a new beginning; 'I had hopes that England'ld get on her legs again, achieve youth and merriment, and slough the things I loathe - capitalism and feminism and hermaphroditism and the rest.'[79] It provided him with a renewed moral purpose. The army was the antidote to his loneliness, indecision and aimlessness. 'The central purpose of my life, the aim and end of it, now, the thing God wants of me, is to get good at beating Germans. That's sure. But that isn't what it was. What it was I never knew, and God knows I never found.'[80] Perhaps most important of all, war brought Brooke happiness. In a letter to Violet Asquith, he expressed his euphoria at the news of his imminent departure for the Dardanelles.

Monday

Oh Violet its too wonderful for belief . . . I've never been quite so happy in my life, I think. Not quite so *pervasively* happy; like a stream flowing entirely to one end. I suddenly realise that the ambition of my life has been – since I was two – to go on a military expedition against

Constantinople. And when I *thought* I was hungry, or sleepy, or falling in love, or aching to write a poem – *that* was what I really, blindly, wanted.[81]

August 1914 was an escape from modernity. The response to war in Britain was unequivocal. C.E. Playne wrote in 1928: 'The whole of youth rushed with blind nobility, but with utter heedlessness of causes, into the arena of war at the first possible moment.'[82] It was time to abandon Arcady, an opportunity to escape the restlessness and uncertainty of modernity and 'do the work of men'.[83] August 1914 symbolised a surrendering of the self to the compulsion of war, expressed in almost mystical terms as a stream of humanity, a form of release and freedom from the stifling confines of bourgeois, peace-time society. Where *The Times* had feared a revolution in 1912, there came a euphoric rallying to the nation in 1914. Young men escaped to a war conceived in a pastoral language of emancipation.

Brooke spent the early part of August writing a short story, 'An Unusual Young Man', for the *New Statesman*.[84] It is a thinly disguised portrait of his own preoccupations at the outbreak of war. The 'Young Man' is sitting on a beach in Cornwall when news of the war reaches him. He climbs a hill and contemplates the confusing images of 'Germany' and 'England'. He recalls his time in Berlin and Munich and the friends he knew. He cannot bring himself to hate them. Instead he feels a growing resentment at the imposition of military service: no more ballet, no more camping out, his friends would be killed. To escape these unpleasant thoughts he allows his mind to wonder off into fantasy. Two thoughts emerge – the death of his mother and his estrangement from the first woman he loved. He feels his mind divide into two halves. His upper, conscious mind runs about aimlessly – 'the light scurry of waves at full tide'(p219). But in his unconscious, the 'deeper waters are pausing and gathering and turning home' (p219). The word "England" seemed to flash like a line of foam' (p219) and he realised that she was in danger. It dawned on him that her earth had the same quality which he found in the body of his former lover. His astonishment grew as the full flood of 'England' swept him on from thought to thought: 'He felt the triumphant helplessness of a lover' (p220). He imagines the pastoral beauty of the Southern landscape and in it he sees 'the set of a mouth he knew for his mother's' and the face of his estranged lover; 'At the same time he was extraordinarily happy'. He knows if there is to be Armageddon, he must be there.

The significance of the story is not simply the maternal and feminine connotations of pastoralism: nature and the maternal/feminine have become one and he remains outside of them, a third term. The threat of external danger has enabled Brooke to achieve a separateness in the form of protector, a father figure defending 'his' women. War and the possibility of death delivered Brooke from his 'hermaphroditism' and his compromising dependence upon his mother and women. Together with hundreds of thousands of other men, he embarked upon the last great adventure and he embraced it with an almost transcendental sense of freedom.

'Peace'

Now, God be thanked Who has matched us with His hour
    And caught our youth, and wakened us from sleeping,
With hand made sure, clear eye, and sharpened power,
    To turn, as swimmers into cleanness leaping,
Glad from a world grown old and cold and weary,
    Leave the sick hearts that honour could not move,
And half-men, and their dirty songs and dreary,
    And all the little emptiness of love!

Oh! we, who have known shame, we have found release there,
    Where there's no ill, no grief, but sleep has mending,
    Naught broken save this body, lost but breath;
Nothing to shake the laughing heart's long peace there
    But only agony, and that has ending;
    And the worst friend and enemy is but death.[85]

It is not hard to guess who the half-men were – the Stracheys, the Jews and decadents and desexed hermaphrodites – Brooke's own lost half of himself. It is an indication of the levels of male frustration and sexual desperation in Edwardian society that his words became the 'incarnate symbol of 1914', that peace is equated with 'sleeping' and 'weariness'. It is a poem of Thanatos. The imagery of swimmers leaping into water is Brooke's death wish, the annihilation of the body and sexuality, the cleanness he craved, finally achieved in war and death.

'The Soldier' was Brooke's own epitaph, a lament for a life gladly handed over to the obedience and compulsion of war, a joyful aban-

donment of individuality. In the end what brought him peace of mind
was the knowledge of his own death. In a final, posthumous, regretful
letter to his former lover Ka Cox, he acknowledges her as 'the best
thing I found in life'. He hopes that she will be happy, marry and have
children. In his maudlin sentiments, perhaps the only line which rings
true is his concluding one: 'It's a good thing I die.'[86]

Notes

1 The Letters of Rupert Brooke (hereafter *LRB*) (1968), ed. Sir Geoffrey
 Keynes, Faber and Faber, p.655.
2 *LRB*, p.660.
3 Poems are taken from, *Poetical Works of Rupert Brooke*, (1977) Faber.
4 Cited in Christopher Hassall (1964), *Rupert Brooke a biography*, Faber,
 p.515.
5 Cited in John Lehmann (1980), *Rupert Brooke His Life and His Myth*,
 Weidenfeld and Nicolson, p.155.
6 Robert Brainard Pearsall (1974), *Rupert Brooke The Man and the Poet*,
 Rodopi N.V. Amsterdam, p.168.
7 Hassall, p.38.
8 William Morris (1979), 'The Society of the Future' in *Political Writings of
 William Morris*, ed. A.L. Morton, Lawrence and Wishart, p. 192.
9 *Ibid.* p.193.
10 See Sheila Rowbotham (1977), 'Edward Carpenter: Prophet of the New
 Life' in Socialism and the *New Life: The Personal and Sexual Politics of
 Edward Carpenter and Havelock Ellis*, Pluto Press.
11 *LRB*, p.79-80, Letter to St John Lucas, 1907.
12 *LRB*, p.159.
13 *Song of Love: The Letters of Rupert Brooke and Noel Olivier*, ed. Pippa
 Harris, Bloomsbury, p.53.
14 In Paul Delany (1987), *The Neo-Pagans: Friendship and Love in the Rupert
 Brooke Circle*, Macmillan, p.79.
15 *Song of Love*, p.153.
16 Delany, *op.cit.*, p.154.
17 Cited in *Song of Love*, p.157.
18 *LRB*, p.335.
19 *LRB*, p.337.
20 Cited in Hassall, p.321.
21 *LRB*, p.368.

22 *LRB*, p.369.
23 *LRB*, p.379.
24 *LRB*, p.381.
25 Delany, p.162.
26 *LRB*, p.382.
27 *LRB*, p.382.
28 *LRB*, p.379, Letter to Jacques Raverat, May 1912.
29 *Song of Love*, p.176.
30 *LRB*, p. 378.
31 Hassall, p. 278.
32 *LRB*, p.379.
33 *LRB*, p.539.
34 Delany, p.56.
35 Hassall, p.442.
36 In a letter to Edward Marsh, shortly after Brooke's death, Hugh Dalton wrote, 'we thought we had been too young to think, and soon we might be too busy, and ultimately we should be too old. The Golden time was now.' In Ben Pimlott (1985), *Hugh Dalton*, Jonathan Cape, p.38.
37 Robert Graves (1982), *In Broken Images. Selected Correspondence*, ed. Paul O'Prey, Mayer Bell Ltd, New York, p.56.
38 *Ibid*. p.100.
39 Ben Pimlott, *op.cit.*, p.66.
40 Frances Cornford, quoted in Hassall, p.277.
41 Henry James (1989), 'Preface' to *Rupert Brooke: Letters From America*, Sidgwick and Jackson, p.19.
42 *Ibid*. p.14.
43 *Granta*, 5 February, 1910.
44 Hassall, p.442.
45 Pimlott, *op.cit.*, p.62.
46 *LRB*, p.99.
47 See Alam Howkins, 'The Discovery of Rural England', in *Englishness, Politics and Culture 1880-1920*, Robert Colls and Phillip Dodd (eds), London 1986.
48 Paul Thompson (1992), *The Edwardians: The Remaking of British Society*, Routledge, p.24.
49 William Morris, 'Under an Elm-Tree: Or Thoughts in the Country-Side', *op.cit.*, p.217.
50 Raymond Williams (1973), *The Country and the City*, Paladin, p.281-82.
51 J.S. Bratton (1986), 'Of England Home and Duty: the image of England in Victorian and Edwardian juvenile fiction' in *Imperialism and Popular*

Culture, ed. J.M. MacKenzie, M.U.P, p.88.

52 Hugh Clifford (1929), 'The Home-Coming of Vincent Brooke' in *Bush-whacking and other Asiatic Tales and Memories*, William Heinemann, London.

53 Alan O'Day (1979), 'Introduction', *The Edwardian Age: Conflict and Stability 1900-1914*, ed. Alan O'Day, Macmillan, p.4.

54 Cited in Anna Davin (1978), 'Imperialism and Motherhood' in *The History Workshop Journal*, No. 5, Spring, p.15.

55 Cited in *ibid.*, p.17.

56 Cited in Tim Jeal (1989), *Baden-Powell*, Hutchinson, p.418.

57 William Morris (1979), 'The Society of the Future', *op.cit.*, p.193.

58 Cited in C.F.G. Masterman (1904), *England: A Nation The Papers of the Patriot Club*, p.38.

59 See Hannah Arendt (1973), *The Origins of Totalitarianism*, Andre Deutsch.

60 See Georg Simmel, (1908), 'The Stranger' in *Georg Simmel on Individuality and Social Forms*, ed. D. Levine, London, 1971.

61 Beloc was an Anglophile Frenchman who became a British citizen in 1902. He was elected to Parliament in 1906.

62 Hassall, p.171.

63 *LRB*, p.608.

64 *LRB*, p.623, Letter to Cathleen Nesbitt, October 1914.

65 *LRB*, p.573.

66 Hassall, p.378.

67 Robert Brainard Pearsall (1974), *Rupert Brooke: The Man and the Poet*, Rodopi N.V. Amsterdam, p.114.

68 *Song of Love*, p.177.

69 *Ibid.* p.213.

70 *LRB*, p.573.

71 *LRB*, p.375.

72 *The Question of Things Happening: The Letters of Virginia Woolf 1912-1922*, ed. Nigel Nicolson (1976), Hogarth Press, p.xvii.

73 Cited in H.E. Bates (1957), 'Introduction' to *Green Mansions*, W.H. Hudson, Collins, p.12.

74 Christopher Caudwell (1938), 'Studies in a Dying Culture', reprinted in *The Concept of Freedom* (1977), Lawrence and Wishart, p.19.

75 *LRB*, p.164.

76 Hassall, p.122-123.

77 *Ibid.* p.123.

78 'Happy is England Now' is the title of a poem by John Freeman (1914) 'happiest is England now/In those that fight, and watch with pride and

tears.' *Up the Line to Death: The War Poets 1914-1918*, (1976) Methuen.

79 *LRB*, p.654-655.

80 *LRB*, p.631.

81 *LRB*, p.62-663.

82 C.E. Playne (1928), *The Pre-War Mind in Britain*, London, p.163.

83 The line is from a poem by W.N. Hodgson, 'The Call'. It begins, 'Ah! we have dwelt in Arcady long time' and concludes, '[we] Went strongly forth to do the work of men.' *Up The Line to Death*, *op.cit.*, pp.9-10.

84 Rupert Brooke (1989), ' An Unusual Young Man' in, *Letters from America*, Sidgwick and Jackson, p.213-222.

85 From *The Poetical Works of Rupert Brooke*, *op.cit.*

86. *LRB*, p.669-670.

4

'WRECKED HOPES AND BROKEN DREAMS': T.E. SHAW AND THE DECLINE OF THE ENGLISH IMPERIAL MISSION[1]

Thomas Edward Shaw was a gifted writer, a literary critic, a political analyst and an aircraftman mechanic. In March 1935 he was discharged from the RAF. His papers included the comment: 'He is an exceptional airman in every respect and his character and general conduct have at all times been "very good"'. After thirteen years of life in a variety of barracks, he was frightened of being 'inutterably lost' in a future he imagined as 'an utterly blank wall'. Two months later, on 19 May after sustaining serious injuries in a motorcycle accident, he died. Thomas Edward Shaw had been T.E. Lawrence, the short, awkward looking man at the epicentre of the ubiquitous and golden legend of Lawrence of Arabia. He was seen by many of his generation as the greatest imperial hero in British history – in fact, the last great English hero. In the words of his friend Aubrey Herbert he was 'an odd gnome, half cad – with a touch of genius'.

Lawrence of Arabia

In 1917, the British newspaper magnate Lord Beaverbrook, eager to persuade the American public to join the war, arranged for American newspapermen to come to Europe. Lowell Thomas left his teaching job at Princeton University and arrived at the Western Front in the early months of 1917. The lack of heroic combat in the squalid slaughtering for a few hundred yards of mud offered nothing remotely optimistic for his reportage. He appealed to the writer and politician John Buchan, who was at the Ministry of Information, and closely involved in Beaverbrook's propaganda exercise. Buchan arranged for Thomas and his photographer Harry Chase to travel to General Allenby's head-quarters in the Middle East. Here Thomas found what he was looking for: 'My curiosity was excited by a single Bedouin who stood out in sharp relief from all his companions... His expression was serene, almost saintly, in it's selflessness and repose... "Who could he be?"'[2] Thomas was to spend the next decade answering his rhetorical question with an unabashed embellishment of the facts. In the process, he established his 'modern Arabian knight' as the world's first media star: 'This youth had virtually become the ruler of the Holy land of the Mohammedans, and commander-in-chief of many thousands of Bedouins mounted on racing camels and fleet Arabian horses. He was the terror of the Turks.'[3] With breathless vivacity, Thomas recon-structed the entire Allied Middle East campaign as a centrally organ-ised force emanating from this one mythical figure.

On 14 August, 1919, Thomas presented his travelogue, 'With Allenby in Palestine and the Conquest of Holy Arabia' to a packed Royal Opera House at Covent Garden. The two hour lecture was accompanied by lantern slides, film and a symphony orchestra. The star of the show was 'the mysterious blond Bedouin' in the white, silk robes of an Arabian Sharif. Thomas changed the title to 'With Allenby in Palestine and Lawrence in Arabia.' The popular myth of Lawrence of Arabia had been invented, its rumour mill fuelled by an enigmatic and reluctant hero. The show was a sell-out and was transferred to the Royal Albert Hall: 'my engagement was prolonged for months and months... Still the crowds came, including the Prime Minister and the Cabinet, MPs and their lordships from the House of Peers... More than a million people in London alone came to hear me tell about Lawrence.'[4] The Times of 7 November, 1919 declared: 'So great did his prestige become that the Arabs dowered him with supernatural powers, and King Hussein conferred upon him the unprecedented honour of creating him a Prince of Mecca.'[5] In 1920, the Strand Magazine serialised Thomas's story of Lawrence of Arabia. It pronounced him the 'The Uncrowned King of Arabia' and prefaced its first instalment with what had become accustomed exaggeration : 'One of our World Heroes. For many years he lived with the Arabs. To them he became a great white god.' Not to be outdone in hyperbole, Lloyd George pronounced: 'Everything that Mr Lowell Thomas says about

Colonel Lawrence is true.' With this endorsement, Thomas toured the English speaking dominions of the Empire. His lectures earned him a reputed one million dollars, making his venture one of the most successful of its kind in history.

The story of Lawrence of Arabia was a powerful and regenerative myth for a disenchanted age – a *Boy's Own*, mediaeval pageant of cavalry charges, guerrilla war and individual gallantry. The romantic Arcady of Rupert Brooke's August 1914 had been trampled into the mud of Flanders by modern, industrialised warfare. The noise, the claustrophobia of the labyrinthian trench system, the inability to vent aggression and anger on an enemy who remained invisible, the passive waiting and random, sudden death by high explosive had proved to be profoundly disempowering. The experience of disorientating, mean-ingless carnage precipitated an epidemic of male hysteria, and by 1916 cases of neurasthenia or shell shock accounted for as much as 40 per cent of the casualties on the Western Front. By the end of the war 80,000 cases had passed through army medical facilities.[6] Victorian imperial manliness, impervious to fear and contemptuous of any show of emotion, had thrived on tales of distant colonial skirmishes. It proved psychologically incapable of dealing with the new realities of warfare. Trapped in a narrow hole in the ground without the capacity to express their feelings of intolerable anxiety, men were forced to express their protest through their bodies. Shell shock was the soldiers' 'body language of masculine complaint': men collapsed into states of catatonia and uncontrollable crying, were struck dumb, blind and deaf, and incapacitated by horrific nightmares, paralysis and limb contrac-ture.[7] The war left many with permanent psychological trauma: 124,000 neurasthenic ex-servicemen applied for war disability pensions between 1919 and 1929.[8]

In contrast, the war mobilised women on an unprecedented scale, emancipating many from their Victorian entrapment: 'England was a world of women – women in uniforms' wrote Vera Brittain in *Testament of Youth*.[9] Women's enthusiasm for taking on men's jobs only reinforced the soldiers' belief that the war had undermined the rules which governed society and men's position in it. It had disabused them of their manly ideals and it had thrust British culture into the disorien-tating and transforming maelstrom of modernity. In the words of a contemporary song by Nina Macdonald: 'Girls are doing things / They've never done before... All the world is topsy turvy / Since the War began.'[10] It was women, rather than men, who were the first to break the cultural silence which surrounded shell shock. The young feminist Rebecca West, in her novel *The Return of the Soldier* (1918) portrayed shell shock as the destructive impact of manliness and militarism on men's lives. Her sensitivity was not reciprocated. Men's war poetry and prose, which began to appear in the 1920s, reviled the 'topsy turvy world' of women and 'the feminine'. In his poem 'In Parenthesis', David Jones equates female sexuality with death: 'But sweet sister death has gone debauched today / makes no coy veiling of her appetite but leers from you / to me with all her parts discovered.'[11] The veteran looked back on the war with horror, but also an intense, often homoerotic, nostalgia for a lost masculine community of soldiers. Henry Williamson captured this sense of loss when he wrote: 'I must return to my old comrades of the Great War – to the brown, the treeless, the flat and grave-set plain of Flanders – to the rolling, heat-miraged downlands of the Somme – for I am dead with them, and they live in me again.'[12]

Because Lawrence was young and had glamour, and most of all because he had had a 'good war', he remained untainted by any association with the older military caste of failed, walrus-moustached father figures who had caused so much needless death. He appealed to women, he appealed to ex-soldiers, he appealed to the Dandies and the young men who had rejected the manly stoicism of their father's generation. Like Prince Edward, Lawrence was symbolic of the 'new England', one of the *Sonnenkinder*, the 'Children of the Sun'.[13] Describing the wartime exploits of Lawrence and his brother officers, Thomas eulogised this romantic image of charismatic individualism and personal autonomy: 'Each man had his own task and went his own way. Each was a freelance and conducted himself with much the same freedom as did knights of old.'[14] The elements of mediaevalism and magic in the Lawrence of Arabia myth provided an escapist antidote to the routinized culture of modern peace-time capitalism and the insecurities of economic depression and labour unrest. His spectacle of male potency in a time of male impotence ensured that he lay in the interwar national imagination as 'one of the greatest Englishmen who has ever lived.'[15] Winston Churchill, with his penchant for dashing young men, described him as 'one of the greatest beings alive in our time... He looked what he was, one of nature's greatest princes... His pride and many of his virtues were superhuman.'[16] John Buchan, who met Lawrence in 1925, wrote in his memoir: 'I am not a very tractable person or much of a hero-worshipper, but I could have followed Lawrence over the edge of the world ... he was the only man of genius

I have ever known.'[17] If Rupert Brooke was the emblem of Old England, Lawrence of Arabia stood for its future.

Indirect Rule

The myth of Lawrence of Arabia grew directly out of the cult of indirect rule, which promoted strength of character as the primary requisite of imperial rule. Lowell Thomas had tried to enhance Lawrence's pedigree by claiming he was related to the originators of this ethos; the Lawrence brothers of the Punjab (see page 3). A fact which was untrue, but which did nothing to dissuade society from seeing in Lawrence the reincarnation of the 'Punjab creed'. In the early years of the twentieth century, its absolutist and charismatic form of colonial governance became official imperial policy and was given the name indirect rule (see page 4). The man credited with turning it into a ruling orthodoxy was Sir Frederick Lugard, the governor of Northern Nigeria. Instead of imposing a European dominated colonial bureaucracy, Lugard built up the native administrations into a structure through which he, a group of Residents (numbering 75 in 1906) and a small army, were able to control a population of seven million in a territory of 300,000 square miles. Charles Temple, whose father had ridden with John Lawrence, was one of Lugard's Residents. His book on indirect rule, *Native Races and Their Rulers* was published in 1910.

> By Indirect Rule I mean a system of administration which leaves in existence the administrative machinery which had been created by the natives themselves; which recognises the existence of Emirs, Chiefs and native Councils, native Courts of Justice, Mohammedan Courts, Pagan Courts, native Police controlled by a native executive, as real living forces, and not as curious and interesting pageantry; by which European influence is brought to bear on the native indirectly, through his chiefs ... and by which the European keeps himself a good deal in the background.[18]

Underlying this 'whisper behind the throne' was the racialised discourse of the imperial mission. 'The native is a human being like ourselves, but in a different stage of development. . . It is our great privilege and our great responsibility in this age . . . to control the development of literally hundreds of millions of human beings' (pp31-2).

T.E. Lawrence was to become the most famous advocate of this form of colonial governance. In 1910, aged 22, he left home for the British Museum's archeological dig at the ancient, Hittite city of Carchemish, in what is now South Central Turkey. His post had been secured by David Hogarth, the Keeper of the Ashmolean Museum and a well-known Orientalist, who had been his mentor at Oxford University. At Carchemish, Lawrence quickly learnt the art of wielding colonial authority, 'Punjab style'. He organised a vaccination programme amongst the local population, writing to his family doctor: 'I can get that done most easily, for the Arabs do what I want most charmingly.'[19] The site foreman, Hamoudi, portrayed him as an omniscient and charismatic figure: 'While we would twist and turn with our object far away, almost out of sight, he would smile and point out to us what we were after, and make us laugh, ashamed.'[20] Hamoudi claimed the source of Lawrence's authority lay in the Arabs' perception of his ability to 'outride, outwalk, outlast the best of them.'[21] Seven years later he was to put this authority into effect during the Arab revolt, providing the material for a definitive account of the practice of indirect rule.

At the outbreak of war in 1914 Lawrence joined the Geographical Section of the War Office and was posted to its Cairo Intelligence Department. Frustrated by the unimaginative regime of military life, he transferred to the newly created Arab Bureau, headed by Hogarth and staffed by an assortment of intellectuals and 'Arabophiles'. Under its auspices, Lawrence worked in the field as the confidante and adviser of Feisal, the commander of the Arab army under General Allenby, and the third son of Husayn Ibn Ali, the Sherif of Mecca. Husayn began the Arab Revolt against the Ottoman Empire in Mecca on 10 June, 1916.[22] For Lawrence and the Arab Bureau, the Revolt was, intended to establish the authority of Husayn's pro-British, traditionalist royal family over a burgeoning, pan Arab nationalism. Hashemite hegemony would comprehensively derail the German effort to orchestrate an Islamic Jihad against the allies. In this way it would contribute to an allied victory against the Turks. No less important, though not as immediate, it would serve to undermine France's claim to Syria. After Germany, the Arab Bureau's implacable enemy was France: 'So far as Syria is concerned it is France and not Turkey that is the enemy.'[23] For Lawrence, the French practice of Direct Rule and its imposition of European values would destroy the racial and cultural purity of the desert Arabs. The political ambition of the Arab Bureau, and Lawrence's own personal quest, was to gain a measure of independence for the Arabs under the tutelage of Britain: 'the Arabs should be our first brown dominion and not our last brown colony' he wrote to Lord Curzon.[24] Between October 1915 and March 1916 a correspondence between Husayn and Henry McMahon, the British High Commissioner in Cairo, appeared to endorse this ambition. In return for 'joint action' in the war, Britain would ensure Arab independence. But during the same period, the Government in London was engaged in secret negotiations with the French and Russians, haggling over a post-war carve-up of the Middle East with little concern for the wishes of the Arabs. The negotiations were ratified in the Sykes-Picot Agreement of 1916. It was a victory for the old-fashioned imperialists – represented by Cromer and Curzon – over the idealism of the Arab Bureau.

The Genealogy of Lawrence's Imperial Mission

The genealogy of Lawrence's imperialism went back to John Seeley, whose advocacy of a colonial nationalism and imperial federation underpinned the ethos of indirect rule. However, charismatic forms of political leadership were not the sole prerogative of imperialism. The threat of economic recession and the growing influence of socialistic doctrines of state intervention had encouraged ideas of strong, directive government. Joseph Chamberlain (1836-1914), a great admirer of Seeley, was the exemplary Bonapartist – or 'man of crisis' – who tried to achieve power through a populist, cross-class appeal. His brand of social imperialism was founded in protectionism, a closed empire market and a corporatism which would unite workers and factory owners beneath the common banner of a national and racial community. This fusion of nationalism and socialism constructed a new ideal of social authority and provided the political patronage and the ideological support for the development of indirect rule. Without Chamberlain's support, Lugard's administration in Northern Nigeria would have been impossible.[25]

If Chamberlain was the corporate manager of imperialism, Lord Milner was its visionary.[26] In 1897, Chamberlain, then Colonial Secretary, appointed Milner as High Commissioner in South Africa, encouraging him to build up a personal staff of young men to assist him in unifying the territories (see page 18). Milner's most significant recruits were Phillip Kerr (later Lord Lothian) and Lionel Curtis. Geoffrey Robinson (he later changed his name to Dawson) who had been Chamberlain's assistant private secretary also joined them. Leo Amery, a young correspondent on *The Times* was approached by Milner as a potential recruit but, unable to accept his invitation, recommended John Buchan in his place. In 1905, Milner returned to England, leaving his 'Kindergarten' of young men to complete the process of South African unification. In his farewell speech in Johannesburg, he declared his faith in Seeley's vision of a commonwealth of nations: the empire must become a common civilisation bound into a permanent organic union. In 1904, Milner became President of the Compatriots, a group formed by Leo Amery to promote imperial union. Amery described the group as 'a real brotherhood of those interested in Imperial unity all over the Empire.'[27] Milner had little sympathy with party politics and excelled in secretive ginger groups which avoided public scrutiny and flourished in a culture of ex-public school boy networks and oligarchies. He planned to establish similar groups in each dominion and build up an empire wide secret society dedicated to achieving political union.

His role as a trustee of the Rhodes Trust was crucial to his plans. Bequeathed by Cecil Rhodes, the aims of the Trust were to immortalise its founder and to create a secret society – 'between two and three thousand men in the prime of life, scattered all over the world' – which would carry out his dream of imperial union and Anglo-Saxon world domination.[28] In 1909, with South African Union assured, Lionel Curtis, Phillip Kerr and another member, R.H. Brand, returned home to initiate a joint venture with Milner and Amery. In September, the Round Table movement was formally inaugurated. Curtis, nicknamed 'the Prophet', was its driving force Milner acted as father figure, enhancing its credibility with his name and providing a source of finance via the Rhodes Trust. The goal of the Round Table movement was imperial federation; 'an organic union to be brought about by the establishment of an Imperial government constitutionally responsible to all electors of the Empire.'[29] Groups were established in the white dominions, and in 1910 the first issue of its journal, *Round Table* was published. In 1920, Lawrence made his own contribution to the journal. In 'The Changing East', he argued for a 'new Imperialism' which would balance British supremacy with the nationalistic aspirations of the Arabs.[30] The Round Table was to provide Lawrence with a lifelong connection to the political establishment, and with an ideological framework for his imperialist politics. Men like Buchan, Curtis, Kerr and Dawson became his friends, benefactors and political patrons.

In 1919 Lawrence wrote to a civil servant, G.J. Kidstone, explaining his motives for being involved in the Arab Revolt. 'You know how

Lionel Curtis has made his conception of the Empire – a Commonwealth of free peoples – generally accepted. I wanted to widen that idea beyond the Anglo-Saxon shape, and form a new nation of thinking people, all acclaiming our freedom, and demanding admittance into our Empire.'[31] The opportunity to realise his ambition had come on 2 October, 1918. After two years of guerrilla warfare, Lawrence entered Damascus, the spiritual centre of Syria, liberated from Turkish occupation. To preempt France's imperialist domination of the region, he contrived to enter the city in advance of Allied forces under General Sir Harry Chauvel, claiming Syria for the Sherif of Mecca. The plan misfired and he hurriedly presented a local pro-Hashemite nationalist, Shukri al Ayyubi, to Chauvel. This subterfuge contributed to the city's being plunged into a state of chaos, as Feisal's followers began looting and settling old enmities. The following day both Feisal and General Allenby arrived in the city, and a meeting was quickly arranged between them in the Victoria Hotel. Allenby informed Feisal of the Sykes-Picot Agreement, which gave Syria to the French and excluded an Arab administration from Palestine and the Lebanon. Feisal was bitter, and Allenby rounded on Lawrence, insisting he must have known about the 1916 agreement. Lawrence, who had known about this agreement – his subterfuge had been intended to spike French colonial ambition – denied all knowledge of it to Allenby. The meeting concluded in acrimony. Lawrence left the room and departed for England the following day. His war had ended abruptly in failure and disappointment. The goal of the liberation of Damascus from Ottoman rule had been achieved, but there would be no Arab dominion and no commonwealth. The triumph had been hopelessly soured by old-fashioned, imperialist geopolitics.

Home from Abroad

Lawrence had already had a premonition of the despair he was to feel. In July 1918, he had written to his university friend Vyvyan Richards: 'I have been so violently uprooted and plunged so deeply into a job too big for me, that everything feels unreal ... these years of detachment have cured me of any desire to do anything for myself. When they untie my bonds I will not find in me any spur to action.'[32] His knowledge of the Sykes-Picot Agreement had contributed to an increasing sense of guilt at his duplicity. He wrote bitterly about his betrayal of

Arab aspirations: 'The more we condemned and despised ourselves, the more we could cynically take pride in them, our creatures... They were our dupes, wholeheartedly fighting the enemy.'[33] In January 1919, Lawrence attended the Peace Conference in Versailles in a vain attempt to defend Arab independence from French colonialism, and to rectify his own and his country's duplicity in the Middle East. Lawrence wanted to make Feisal ruler of Syria and his brother Abdullah the ruler of Mesopotamia. But his plan met with increasing hostility from the Foreign Office, and the India Office, who had no interest in 'brown dominions' and no intention of offending their French ally. His efforts ended in ignominious failure.

In August, while Lowell Thomas was preparing for his opening night at Covent Garden, Lawrence returned to his family home in Oxford. During his absence, two of his younger brothers, Frank and Will, had been killed in France, and in April, while he was in Paris, his father had died from influenza. Like many another returning soldier, Lawrence was caught in the disorientating transition from war to peace, from abroad to home.

> In my case, the effort for these years to live in the dress of Arabs, and to imitate their mental foundation, quitted me of my English self, and let me look at the West and its conventions with new eyes: they destroyed it all for me... I had dropped one form and not taken on the other ... with a resultant feeling of intense loneliness in life, and a contempt, not for other men, but for all they do ... madness was very near, as I believe it would be near the man who could see things through the veils at once of two customs, two educations, two environments.[34]

Lawrence struggled to extricate himself from this fear of breakdown. In Paris he began writing *Seven Pillars of Wisdom*, an account of his two years in the desert. Back in England, Geoffrey Dawson secured a Fellowship for him at All Souls College, the spiritual home of the Kindergarten; but Lawrence was unable to settle in Oxford and he left for London. He adopted an assumed name and stayed in the sparsely furnished attic of the distinguished colonial architect Sir Herbert Baker. He wrote in a compulsive frenzy, claiming to write in sittings of 22-24 hours, averaging 1000-1500 words an hour. Sir Herbert Baker's testimony confirms that Lawrence was gripped by a manic form of asceticism. 'He refused all service and comfort, food, fire or hot water; he ate and bathed when he happened to go out... He worked timeless and sometimes around the sun; and once, he said, for two days without food or sleep, writing at his best until he became delirious.'[35] Lawrence finished the first draft of 250,000 words in five months, destroying his notes as he proceeded. He promptly lost the manuscript in the waiting room at Reading railway station. Cajoled by friends, he rewrote it in three months from memory. He then began recomposing the second draft, out of which a third version was extensively rewritten. Finally, in 1926 he completed the fourth and final draft. ' I went through four versions in four years, he wrote to E.M. Forster. 'I gave it all my nights and days till I was nearly blind and mad.'[36]

The title of *Seven Pillars of Wisdom* comes from the 'Book of Proverbs' 9:1: 'Wisdom hath builded a house: she hath hewn out her seven pillars.' Lawrence frequently used architectural metaphors of the house or citadel to describe his body and self, and *Seven Pillars* is primarily a reflexive narrative of his own identity. As Edward Said comments: 'Lawrence reduces the entire narrative of the revolt (its momentary successes and its bitter failure) to *his* vision of himself as an unresolved, "standing civil war".'[37] Like Said, the Arab scholar Suleiman Mousa has dismissed *Seven Pillars of Wisdom* as an apology of Western imperialism in the region: 'Lawrence had the advantage of the pen, while the Bedouin and Arab regulars enjoyed no such gift. And here lies the secret of his magnified stature, which he earned at the expense of others.'[38] Both Said and Mousa are right to express doubt about Lawrence's actual impact on the Revolt. *Seven Pillars* is a text in the European discourse of Orientalism, and consequently subject to its share of fantasy and fabrication. As a history which comes from the hand of its central protagonist it is invariably highly subjective in its account of events. Lawrence revelled in his legendary status and on one level the narrative of *Seven Pillars* actively colludes with Thomas's sensationalism. But he was also appalled and guilt-stricken by the spectacle of his fame: 'There was a craving to be famous', he pronounced, 'and a horror of being known to like being known.'[39] Lawrence turned to writing in an obsessive attempt to reconcile the past and to avoid mental breakdown. It was a similar fear which had driven him away from home and which lay behind his identification with the imperial mission. *Seven Pillars* provides the reader with an opportunity to explore the sexual and psychological vicissitudes of his English masculinity, and to unravel its fraught relationship with the ideals of Indirect Rule. The book is riven by a central contradiction, between its evocation of an imperial manliness and a secondary narrative of

Lawrence's personal 'standing civil war'. The latter weaves through the story of the Arab Revolt as a 'second note', becoming steadily more discordant and disruptive, until it finally undermines and destroys the mystique of Lawrence of Arabia as a heroic man of action.

The 'standing civil war'

T.E. Lawrence was born on 16 August 1888 in Tremadoc, Wales. His father, Thomas Chapman, had been an Anglo-Irish landowner in County Meath who had married a fanatically religious woman, Edith Hamilton. Their marriage was not a happy one and he began an affair with the governess of their four daughters, Sarah Jenner, also a deeply religious woman. The pair eloped, and after Edith refused him a divorce they took the name of Sarah's estranged and unmarried father, Lawrence. In 1896, after a period of constantly moving house, they settled in Oxford, passing themselves off as a respectable married couple with five sons. Lawrence claimed to have known about his own illegitimacy from the age of ten, and biographers have made a great deal of this stigma when explaining his motives and behaviour. At the time, it was also seen as a way of understanding his enigma. In 1927, King George V's secretary Lord Stamfordham sent Sir Reginald Wingate a private report on Lawrence's illegitimacy, part of which read: 'When they [the sons] were told that their mother was not married, it appears to have embittered their lives.'[40] Illegitimacy was a serious transgression of the Victorian bourgeois moral order, and it undoubtedly played a central role in shaping the psychodynamics of family life – particularly in the light of Sarah Lawrence's strict adherence to evangelical Christianity and her need to atone for her 'sin'. But to build an understanding of the relationship between Lawrence's sexuality and his practice of colonialism, guilt over his illegitimacy has to be seen as a condensation of another, more profound psychological drama – the 'standing civil war' which lay at the heart of his family life.

Lawrence spent his youth scouring the local churches for brass rubbings and immersing himself in romantic mediaeval literature. He cycled through France for successive summers, visiting mediaeval castles, and in 1909 embarked upon an epic one thousand mile journey through Syria for his thesis on the military architecture of the Crusades. Arnold Lawrence, his youngest brother, described this absorption in the past as 'a dream way of escape from Bourgeois

England.[41] It was also the opportunity to escape from a mother who, Lawrence considered, treated his father as a trophy of her power. 'My father was on the large scale, tolerant, experienced, grand, rash... My mother, brought up a child of sin ... then 'guilty' (in her own judgment) of taking my father from his wife ... remodelled my father, making him a teetotaller, a domestic man, a careful spender of pence.'[42] In much the same way as it affected Rupert Brooke, this perception of a dominating mother left Lawrence wary and suspicious of women and averse to female sexuality.

> Knowledge of her will prevent my ever making any woman a mother, and the cause of children. I think she suspects this: but she does not know that the inner conflict which makes me a standing civil war, is the inevitable issue of the discordant natures of herself and my father, and the inflammation of strength and weakness which followed the uprooting of their lives and principles.[43]

The conflict between his parents, and the feeling that he was obligated to repent for his mother's sinfulness, filled Lawrence with sexual guilt and a disgust of the body. In a letter to Lionel Curtis in 1923, he wrote: 'We are all guilty alike you know. You wouldn't exist, I wouldn't exist without this carnality ... isn't it true that the fault of birth rests somewhat on the child? I believe it's we who led our parents on to bear us, and it's our unborn children who make our flesh itch. A filthy business all of it.'[44] In Freudian psychoanalysis, a child's fantasy of its parents together forms the plot structure of the family romance (see p11) and it provides a starting point for an analysis of Lawrence's sexuality and its impact upon his public actions.

In his case study of the 'Wolf Man', Freud analysed a young man's dream about wolves which he deduced to be the condensation and displacement of his childish terror at the sight of his parents copulating.[45] Freud referred to this image as the primal scene. Rather than accept Freud's assertion that it is an actual event, it can be argued that the primal scene is a retrospectively constructed fantasy of the parents together, and the precondition of the oedipus complex. Freud depicts the scene as the father's sexual domination over the mother, conforming to his belief that the father is the preeminent psychological figure in the oedipus complex. The primal scene thus confirms the son's eventual heterosexuality and identification with the father. But Freud's evasion of the mother's psychological strength (see p12-13) continually downplayed her power to disrupt this neat heterosexual and patriarchal symmetry. An alternative scenario in the boy's psyche would depict the relative paucity of the father's presence and a psychologically powerful mother. The dominance of the maternal figure in his unconscious continually reactivates his repressed memory of her loss and his need for her (see p27). Lawrence's 'standing civil war' is his conflict between his identifications with his mother and his father (see p21). His 'filthy business' is his conception of a voracious mother who he feels has entrapped him in her power and denies him his identity. Like many Victorian and Edwardian middle-class men who were products of this gendered order, Lawrence took the path of other British imperialists and escaped from his family abroad.

In 1927, Lawrence described his feeling toward his mother to Charlotte Shaw, the wife of George Bernard Shaw: 'I think I'm afraid of letting her get, ever so little, inside the circle of my integrity: and she is always hammering and sapping to come in.'[46] In another letter he wrote of his terror of her knowing anything about his feelings, or way of life. If she knew 'they would be damaged, violated, no longer mine.'[47] His 'first rule of existence' was to avoid her. He told his biographer Basil Liddell Hart that he ran away from home at seventeen and enlisted in the Artillery. No records of this escapade exist, but he had been absent that summer, ostensibly on his first trip to France. When he returned, Lawrence's father had a small bungalow built for him in the garden, where he slept and undertook his university studies. That Christmas he refused to eat as a protest against 'the absurdity of all feasting'. Lawrence already had a predilection for acts of endurance and self-denial, but his morbid preoccupation with food and eating suggests the possibility that he developed a form of anorexia nervosa in order to exert control over his body and emotions. Lawrence's unresolved attachment to his mother led him to self-imposed starvation as a form of escape from her dominating regime of orderliness and compliance.

In his biography, Robert Graves, wrote at the instigation of Lawrence. 'He hates . . . spending more than five minutes on a meal. That is why he lives mainly on bread and butter. And he likes water better than any other drink. . . It is his occasional habit to knock off proper feeding for three days – rarely five – just to make sure that he can do it without feeling worried or strained.'[48] His fasting mimicked the monastic practices of the Middle Ages and he regarded eating as a morally and spiritually degrading activity . His asceticism expressed his growing aversion to his body. He claimed to fear animal spirits – sexuality, feelings, demonstrative acts – 'more than anything else in this world'.[49] He loathed any form of bodily contact and told Robert Graves that to be touched was to suffer 'a loss of integrity.'[50] A denial of his corporeality was a way of coping with his acute sexual anxiety. In 1924 he wrote to Sydney Cockerell, 'I'm frigid toward woman so that I can withstand her: so that I want to withstand her'.[51] The following year he told Charlotte Shaw, 'I'm too shy to go looking for dirt . . . I wouldn't know what to do, how to carry myself, where to stop. Fear again: fear everywhere.'[52]

As well as being a source of adventure and excitement, imperialism provided an escape route from his fear. His separation from his family, his acts of stoic solitude on his journeys, and his escape to Carchemish in 1910, were elements of his anorexic denial of his sexuality and the disavowal of his emotional dependency on his mother. The desert was a form of social exclusion from bourgeois familial culture and its sexualities: a 'spiritual ice-house' of personal renunciation and 'cleanness'. Lawrence cultivated his idealistic vision of monastic asceticism in the 'moral bareness' of the Bedouin. The desert confirmed Lawrence in his attempt at disembodiment through negation: 'The body was too coarse to feel the utmost of our sorrows and of our joys. Therefore, we abandoned it as rubbish.'[53] His vision of the 'moral bareness' of the desert embraced the 'fanatic Arabia' of his hero, the explorer Charles Doughty. 'We have all sometimes been weary in the desert' wrote Lawrence in the introduction to Doughty's *Arabia Deserta*, 'and some of us have been hungry there but none of us triumphed over our bodies as Doughty did.'[54] But negation did not bring with it the autonomous self-willed man he strove to be. His asceticism prohibited relationships with others and denied him the possibility of emotional development. Whatever evasive measures Lawrence took – his fortitude, his self-denial, his geographic distance – his mother remained, 'hammering and sapping to get in'.

As a boy, Lawrence developed fantasies of omnipotence to escape this predicament. Basil Liddel Hart recounts their significance in his youth:

> The idea of a crusade, the idea underlying it, revolved in his mind, giving rise to a dream crusade, which implied a leader with whom in a sense he identified himself yet remained as . . . a sympathetic observer. Naturally it would be a crusade in the modern form – the freeing of a race from bondage.[55]

In adulthood, Lawrence's daydreams remained conceived on an epic scale. He described his involvement in the Desert Revolt in omniscient terms: 'I wanted to feel what it was like to be the mainspring of a national movement, and to have some millions of people expressing themselves through me.'[56] Imperialism and the practice of indirect rule provided Lawrence with the opportunities to enact these fantasies. 'All men dream, but not equally . . . the dreamers of the day are dangerous men, for they may act their dream with open eyes, to make it possible. This I did.'[57] In psychoanalytic terms these delusions of grandeur can be described as an omnipotent defence against the hopelessness of an actual state of dependency. In his daydreams, Lawrence continually reenacted his 'standing civil war' in an attempt to resolve the contradictions of his sexuality and masculinity. His omnipotent fantasy of rescuing a race/son in bondage was the cathexis of his identification with the imperial mission and the inspiration behind his involvement in the Arab Revolt. It became personified in the figure of one, young boy.

Dahoum

Throughout the Arab Revolt, Lawrence carried a copy of Sir Thomas Malory's fifteenth Century epic, *Morte d'Arthur*. To Lawrence the desert was the reincarnation of the Age of Chivalry: 'steeped in an unfathomable pool of silence and past history . . . whose most sober story read like Arthur come again.'[58] The myth of King Arthur and the Knights of the Round Table, of manly love and its chivalrous codes of sacrifice, bravery and loyalty were romantic themes widely imitated by Victorian imperial manliness (see p4). Essential to the knightly code of honour in romantic, mediaeval literature was the cult of courtly love. A young knight pledged himself to the unobtainable love of his lord's wife. His valorous deeds and his suffering on the Crusades were performed in her name. Like the mediaeval knight, but with the sexual ambivalence of a Victorian imperialist, Lawrence too embodied his chivalrous quest for a nation's freedom in one eroticised figure.

Lawrence described his principle motivation in the Arab Revolt as an almost obsessive quest for a single individual: 'The strongest motive throughout has been a personal one, not mentioned here, but present to me, I think, every hour of these two years.'[59] *Seven Pillars* is dedicated to the cryptically named S.A., and opens with a poem in which

Lawrence declaims his passionate but posthumous love for this mysterious figure.

> I loved you, so I drew these tides of men into my hands
>   and wrote my will across the sky in stars
> To gain you Freedom, the seven-pillared worthy house,
>   that your eyes might be shining for me
>
>   When I came
>
> Death was my servant on the road, till we were near
> and saw you waiting:
> When you smiled, and in sorrowful envy he outran me
> and took you apart:
>
>   Into his quietness
>
> So our love's earnings was your cast off body to be held
> one moment
> Before earth's soft hands would explore your face and the
> blind worms transmute
>
>   Your failing substance.
>
> Men prayed me to set to my work, the inviolate house,
> in memory of you.
> But for fit monument I shattered it, unfinished: and now
> The little things creep out to patch themselves hovels
> in the marred shadow
>
>   Of your gift.[60]

In the name of his love for S.A., Lawrence embarked upon his quest for
the 'inviolate house'. On one level this refers to achieving victory in the
Arab Revolt. But it also refers to achieving victory in his 'standing civil
war' and securing a stable identity. But Lawrence discovers S.A. is dead
and so shatters this 'fit monument', leaving 'little things' and 'hovels' in
it's 'marred shadow'. Alongside the central narrative of the Revolt and its
betrayal, runs the 'second note' of Lawrence's growing disillusionment
with his role as a man of action. His attraction to Nietzsche and his belief
in the philosophy of the will to power had inspired his sense of destiny
and provided him with a reasoning for the ascetic management of his
body. He had imagined that through sheer will-power and self-enact-
ment he could achieve the 'inviolate house' of his self. But it delivered
only murder, extremes of hardship, his own deceitfulness toward the

Arabs, and eventually what he had always most feared: the breakdown of his self. The death of S.A. left him bereft of hope: 'I was tired to death of free-will... My will had gone and I feared to be alone, lest the winds of circumstance, or power, or lust, blow my empty soul away.'[61]

The S.A of the poem was a fourteen year old Arab boy, nicknamed Dahoum, whom Lawrence had befriended in Carchemish. His real name was Salim Ahmed and he was the first and only love of Lawrence's life. He died of typhoid in Damascus in 1918, months before Lawrence made his triumphal entry to 'rescue' him. During his years in Carchemish, Lawrence took great pleasure in flaunting his homoerotic attachment to the boy, and the local villagers were scandalised by the intimacy of their friendship. Lawrence repeatedly mentioned Dahoum in his letters home and in July 1913 brought him back to England to visit his family. There is no evidence of a physical sexual relationship with Dahoum; the boy embodied Lawrence's fantasy of the natural childlike simplicity of the desert Arab. In 1911, he wrote to his mother: 'The perfect hopeless vulgarity of the half-Europeanised Arab is appalling. Better a thousand times the Arab untouched.'[62] Dahoum was the boy Lawrence craved once more to be; unbesmirched by a corrupted bourgeois, parental sexuality. In Carchemish, Lawrence invented for himself a world of sociability, playfulness and sexual flamboyance. With the companionship of a young adoring boy and the reverence of the local population, he could allow himself to indulge in sexual reveries. His letters, describing his travels, his work and the Arabs he lived with, express a warmth and spontaneous pleasure in life. It was the happiest period of his life and laid the foundations of his love of the desert and his commitment to the Arab cause.

In *Seven Pillars of Wisdom*, the significance and meaning of the desert for Lawrence is described as a gift from Dahoum. 'But at last Dahoum drew me: "Come and smell the very sweetest scent of all", and we went into the main lodging, to the gaping window sockets of it's eastern face, and there drank with open mouths of the effortless, empty, eddyless wind of the desert, throbbing past... "This", they told me, "is the best: it has no taste".'[63] Dahoum leads Lawrence to what he most desires, the desire for negation, for what has 'no taste': 'My Arabs were turning their backs on perfumes and luxuries to choose the things in which mankind had had no share or part.'[64] The boy offers him a lyrical image which mirrors Lawrence's fear and denial of his own instinctual life; The 'cleanness' of the desert lay in its absolute lack of fecundity and its absence of women. It's sparseness and dryness were the antithesis of the imaginary maternal body with its enveloping softness and its fluids. Lowell Thomas accords Lawrence with saying: 'Perhaps that is one of the reasons why I am so fond of Arabia. So far as I know, it is the only country left where men rule.'[65] In the desert Lawrence imagined he could build his 'inviolate house' without fear that his task would be compromised by the proximity of female desire or his need of his mother; 'there was nothing female in the Arab movement,' he wrote, 'but the camels.'[66]

Lawrence eulogised the desert as a homoerotic world in which young men turned their backs on the 'raddled meat' of 'public women' and instead 'began indifferently to slake one another's few needs in their own clean bodies.'[67] In 1917, he recruited two boys into his bodyguard; 'Daud the hasty and his love-fellow, Farraj; a beautiful, soft-framed girlish creature, with innocent, smooth face and swimming eyes.'[68] When Lawrence encountered the two boys, they were about to be whipped for unruly behaviour. They appealed to Lawrence for clemency and offered to serve him: 'I took them both because they looked so young and clean'.[69] The chastisement of Daud and Farraj is a recurring theme in the pages of *Seven Pillars*. Despite describing them as 'two sunlit beings... the most gallant, the most enviable, I knew'.[70] Lawrence was not averse to administering his own punishments. On one occasion, he ordered that the boys receive 'a swinging half-dozen each' for playing a prank on him. On another they were forced to sit naked on scorching rocks. Lawrence subjected the Arab boys to his own sexual conflict, projecting onto them a mixture of love and hatred. Dahoum had personified Lawrence's narcissistic yearning for personal autonomy; Daud and Farraj personified his homosexual desire. His fascination with their bodies and their sexuality provoked in him an envious streak of sadistic cruelty.

Homosexuality and Masochism

The desert may have appealed to Lawrence's asceticism, but free of the European disciplinary codes of sexuality, it also provided him with the opportunity for homosexual encounters. The underlying drama of Lawrence's gradual disillusionment in *Seven Pillars of Wisdom* is the struggle between his will and his sexual desire. Sexual ecstasy is the antithesis of the will. Orgasm is without limit, it dissolves the ego and it breaks down the boundaries between self and other. Lawrence's fragile, incomplete 'inviolate house', already under siege from a mother 'hammering and sapping' to get inside, could not withstand the

WRECKED HOPES AND BROKEN DREAMS'

destructive impulse of sexuality. Only the will and its dictum of unquestioning obedience offered him security against his fear of break-down: 'Collapse rose always from a moral weakness eating into the body, which of itself, without traitors from within, had no power over the will.'[71] In his attempt to contain the destructive impulse of sexual-ity, Lawrence sought sexual pleasure in pain and denial, projecting his sadomasochistic fantasies onto the desert Arab. The sexuality that fascinated him, the luxuries he longed for in the bodies of young Arabs, were abnegation, renunciation and self-restraint: 'These lads took plea-sure in subordination; in degrading the body.'[72] At stake in such sado-masochistic fantasies is the repression of homosexual love. While there is no evidence for Lawrence's actual sexual engagement with individual Arab boys or men, he utilised the codes of Indirect Rule to take up the position of voyeur, revelling in the homoeroticism, and inflicting pain and humiliation upon himself and the Arab boys he controlled.

Chapter LXXX contains the pivotal scene in *Seven Pillars of Wisdom* in which the 'second note' finally shatters the mystique of heroic English manliness. Lawrence describes how he is caught on a scouting expedition into Deraa. Instead of being put in prison, he is taken to the bedroom of the Turkish Governor, where the older man attempts to seduce him. Lawrence resists and the Governor calls his guard for help. While the soldiers restrain him, the Governor beats Lawrence about the face with a slipper, bites him on the neck and kisses him. Finally he thrusts a bayonet into a fold of flesh over Lawrence's ribs. In his fear Lawrence breaks his silence. The Governor responds, 'You must under-stand that I know: and it will be easier if you do as I wish.' It is an enig-matic comment which might refer to Lawrence being who he is or may allude to the governor knowing about his secret masochistic and homo-sexual desires. Lawrence describes himself as dumbfounded and unable to trust himself to reply. The two men stare at one another in a mutual recognition. Eventually, Lawrence lifts his chin, the sign for 'No', and the Governor sits down, and half-whispers to the corporal that he should 'take me out and teach me everything.' Lawrence is pinned down and a corporal begins to whip him. When the man is exhausted, the other soldiers take turns and begin to sexually abuse and rape him. 'At last when I was completely broken they seemed satisfied.' The corporal begins kicking him to get him up. 'I remember smiling idly at him, for a delicious warmth, probably sexual, was swelling through me.' This sexual coquetry provokes the corporal to hack the whip handle into Lawrence's testicles. He begins to slash him with it. What follows sounds, in Lawrence's words, like an orgasm: 'A roaring, and my eyes went black: while within me the core of life seemed to heave slowly up through the rending nerves, expelled from its body by this indescribable pang.' Lawrence is dragged back to the Governor, but the man rejects him as 'too torn and bloody for his bed.' He is thrown into a shed, from which he manages to escape. The chapter ends: 'in Deraa that night the citadel of my integrity had been irrevocably lost.'

In a letter to Edward Garnet in 1922, Lawrence described his doubts about publishing the chapter; 'I put it into print very reluctantly, last of all the pages I sent to the press. For weeks I wanted to burn it in the manuscript: because I could not tell the story face to face with anyone.'[73] His reticence about revealing the chapter did not stop him revising it obsessively. In July 1925 he was rewriting it for the ninth time. Despite this preoccupation, the historical fact of the Deraa rape remains unproven.[74] The enigmatic confrontation with the Pilate-like Bey, the kiss of recognition, the spear in Lawrence's side and his flagellation draw heavily on the images of Christ's martyrdom and Christian iconography of homoeroticised male suffering. George Bernard Shaw wrote in the flyleaf of his wife's subscribers' copy of *Seven Pillars*: 'one of the chapters . . . tells of a revolting sequel to his capture by the Turks and his attraction for a Turkish officer. He told me that his account of the affair is not true. I forbore to ask him what actually happened.'[75] Whether it was an actual experience or a sexual fantasy, the masochistic ecstasy Lawrence experienced at his sexual humiliation represented the moment when he succumbed to sexual desire. In 1924 he told Charlotte Shaw that his fear of being hurt had led him to give away 'the only possession we are born into the world with – our bodily integrity':

> You may call this morbid: but think of the offence, and the intensity of my brooding over it for these years. It will hang about me while I live, and afterwards if our personality survives. Consider wandering among the decent ghosts hereafter, crying 'Unclean unclean!'[76]

Back in England after the war, exposed once again to its homophobic culture, Lawrence increasingly repressed his homosexuality in acts of self-degradation, and through a repetitive return to this scene of his sexual humiliation. He rejected the possibilities of careers in archaeology, scholarship, military service, colonial administration, government and politics, and instead sought anonymity in the RAF as an Aircraftman.

From T.E Lawrence to T.E Shaw

In 1921, before his enlistment in the RAF, Lawrence had been recruited by Winston Churchill into a newly created Middle East Department of the Colonial Office as a political adviser. During the year he was instrumental in creating the modern state of Iraq out of Mesopotamia, a region in the throes of anti-imperialist conflict. A number of nationalist revolts had been savagely repressed by the British army, but the cost of occupation was proving to be prohibitive – £38,500,000 in 1920 alone. Lawrence installed Feisal as head of government, but the problem of retaining civil order remained. Churchill persuaded him to work with Air Marshall Sir Hugh Trenchard for the deployment of air power in the region and together they transferred policing from the army to the RAF. Punitive raids – bombing villages – backed up by armoured cars, enabled a small, cheap, but technologically sophisticated colonial force to control vast territories. The scheme of air control was later adopted on the North West Frontier of India, the territory once ridden by Cust, Nicholson and the Lawrence brothers. Lawrence had once more reinvigorated the 'Punjab creed' and helped to usher in a new technological era of colonial domination.

By 1922 Lawrence believed that he had achieved a Middle East settlement to the satisfaction of the Arabs, the British government ànd himself. After a sustained effort to persuade Churchill to let him go, Lawrence enlisted in the RAF. On 28 August, with the connivance of Trenchard, he presented himself at the RAF recruiting office in Henrietta Street, near Covent Garden, as John Hume Ross. He was posted to the training depot at Uxbridge: 'I lay, sickly on my allotted bed. For a moment my bedfellow was perfect fear. Could a man, who for years had been closely shut up, sifting his inmost self ... could he suddenly end his civil war and live the open life, patent for everyone to read?'[77] The chronicle of his months at Uxbridge, published as *The Mint* (1955) indicate that Lawrence found the enforced company of others a trial of endurance. The book reads like a prison memoir, full of excruciating humiliation and degradation. 'I came in here to eat dirt,' he told Robert Graves, 'till its taste is normal to me.'[78] His vignettes of life as a new recruit are punctuated by perpetual anxiety at the physical stress he was forced to endure. 'The root-trouble is fear: fear of failing, fear of breaking down.'[79] However, Lawrence's enlistment was not simply the act of a man bent on self-destruction; as he told his mother, 'You know I always wanted to be in the R.A.F.'[80] It had been his ambition to join. In November, Lawrence used his contacts to secure a transfer to the RAF school of photography in Farnborough, where the regime was considerably less demanding. Farnborough confirmed his ambition – 'I grew suddenly on fire with the glory which the air should be'.[81] His intoxication with the RAF was part of a wider excitement about the possibilities of aviation in the 1920s and 1930s, when the conquest of the air opened up a new frontier spirit. In *The Mint* he wrote, 'The R.A.F. for me is now myself: a vocation absolute and inevitable beyond any question under the sky: and so marvellous that I grow hot to make it perfect.'[82] Unfortunately the *Daily Express* discovered his new career and on 27 December its headlines trumpeted; 'Uncrowned King As Private Soldier.' The RAF, anxious to quell the sudden storm of publicity, quickly discharged Lawrence, and he found himself homeless, aimless and without money. It was to take him two and a half years of hard lobbying, and a threatened suicide, before he managed to get himself readmitted.

Lawrence again drew on his connections in high places and in March 1923 he enlisted in the army's Tank Corps, under the name T.E. Shaw. He was sent to its training camp at Bovington in Dorset. In a series of letters to Lionel Curtis, Lawrence chronicled his acute depression and his belief that he had now reached the lower depths of humanity. He described the army camp as 'a cimmerian darkness with bog-lights flitting wrongly through its gas.'[83] In hut 12 he was forced into a close proximity with the carnality and animal spirits of his working-class fellow soldiers. On 14 May he wrote:

> The R.A.F. was foul-mouthed, and the cleanest little mob of fellows. These are foul-mouthed, and behind their mouths is a pervading animality of spirit, whose unmixed bestiality frightens me and hurts me ... I cried out against it, partly in self pity because I've condemned myself to grow like them, and partly in premonition of failure, for my masochism remains and will remain, only moral. Physically I can't do it: indeed I get in denial the gratification they get in indulgence... Everything bodily is now hateful to me (and in my case hateful is the same as impossible)... This sort of thing must be madness, and sometimes I wonder how far mad I am, and if the mad-house would not be my next (and merciful) stage.'[84]

In spite of his aversion to their coarse, sexualised language and behaviour, Lawrence recognised that these men had something he wanted. In a perverse way they were one of the reasons he had renounced the prospects of a bourgeois career for a life in the ranks. 'Sex is an integer in all of us, and the nearer nature we are, the more constantly, the more completely a product of that integer. These fellows are the reality. . . These fellows have roots. . . We call each other 'Brum' or 'Coventry' or 'Cambridge', and the man who hasn't a 'place' is an outsider.'[85] What the army lacked, but what the RAF provided, was a sense of mission.

Lawrence's life of self-imposed solitude had left him a permanent outsider. His identification with the Bedouin had been motivated by the allure of the male body and by his desire to secure for himself a sense of belonging. Now, in the forces, he wanted the 'sudden comradeship of the ranks – a sympathy born half of our common defencelessness against authority . . . and half of our true equality.'[86] Happiness had eluded Lawrence since his years in Carchemish. But it was once again a possibility if he could give himself in service to a higher cause and submit himself to the conformity of a group identity. He wrote in *The Mint*:

> I was trying to think, if I was happy, why I was happy, and what was this overwhelming sense upon me of having got home, at last after an inter-minable journey . . . word-dandling and looking inward, instead of swaying upright in the lorry with my pals, and yelling Rah Rah at all we met, in excess of life. With my fellows, yes: and among my fellows: but a fellow myself? Only when we obeyed some physical movement, whose pattern could momentarily absorb my mind.[87]

But this fellowship could only be achieved through obedience; 'for except under compulsion there is no equality in the world'.[88] The desert and the asceticism of the Bedouin had provided Lawrence with an enforced equality, a discipline of the body. His belief in the imperial mission was an outlet for actualising his fantasies of omnipotence. The RAF was a similar form of monastic existence. It offered him a routinised, militaristic culture of order and hierarchy which promised the controlled and disciplined proximity of the male body and service to the conquest of the air, another rich source of fantasy. In his transi-tion from abroad to home, Lawrence exchanged the imperial mission of his mentor, Hogarth, for Trenchard's new knights of the sky. Both regimes ensured his body would be disciplined, his sexuality tantalised but curtailed, his imagination allowed to soar. Hogarth was perceptive enough to recognise this need in Lawrence. 'Lawrence is not normal in many ways and it is extraordinarily difficult to do anything for him. . .

He will not work in any sort of harness unless this is padlocked onto him. He enlisted in order to have the padlocks riveted onto him.'[89] But like his previous mythical incarnation as a man of action, his ascetic attempts to renounce his sexual desire were played out in an environment purposely chosen for the proximity of male bodies. Surrounded by young men, the obscurity of the ranks could not ensure a state of sexual negation. To achieve this, Lawrence had to devise more extreme measures, and he took the bizarre step of hiring a eighteen year old Scot, Jock Bruce, to act out the incident at Deraa and administer him with beatings.

Bruce claimed to have met Lawrence early in 1922 at the house of a mutual acquaintance, shortly before he joined the RAF.[90] Through an intermediary Lawrence offered Bruce a retainer for services of a highly confidential and personal nature. It wasn't until July that he explained this cryptic offer. Lawrence told Bruce that he was illegitimate, that his father had died and left his money to a relative he referred to as 'The Old Man'. This was untrue – there was no 'Old Man' – but it was part of an extraordinary story Lawrence spun to ensure Bruce's allegiance. Lawrence explained he was heavily in debt and in need of a bank loan, and that he had gone to his relative to ask him to act as his guarantor. 'The Old Man' had agreed but only if he would submit himself to certain conditions. According to Bruce, Lawrence was deeply distressed and kept repeating, 'He called me a bastard, and meant it. How he must loathe us for my father's sins.'[91] Bruce asked him what he was expected to do, to which Lawrence replied: 'Have I not made it clear to you? I'm on the edge of a precipice crying for help, and you can help, I'm sure of that.' When pressed further, Lawrence declared, 'That depends on what the Old Man has in store for me... He will make me do everything I hate to do.'[92] When Lawrence enlisted in the Tank Corps, he persuaded Bruce to join him and it was in Bovington, in Clouds Hill, a small cottage rented by Lawrence, that the beatings began.

Some time in the autumn of 1923, Lawrence informed Bruce that 'The Old Man' had decided he had to be punished with twelve strokes of the birch. Bruce was to collect the birch, which had been dispatched to a nearby railway station, and was to write a report after the beating, describing Lawrence's demeanour and behaviour under punishment. The thrashing took place the same afternoon.

> He kept his trousers on and lay on the bed. He never murmured...
> Anyway, he went to see The Old Man the same afternoon. The Old Man

said it was not good enough and it was to be done with his trousers down. So I put rugs over his back and left only his small buttocks exposed. After I had given him the twelve he said; 'Give me another one for luck.'[93]

Bruce's testimony is corroborated by another, anonymous, independent witness, whom Lawrence asked to observe three beatings, between 1931 and 1934.[94] The witness described them as brutal, and delivered on the bare buttocks, and stated that Lawrence required them to be severe enough to produce ejaculation. In 1919 Freud wrote: 'It is surprising how often people who seek analytic treatment for . . . obsessional neurosis confess to having indulged in the phantasy: "A child is being beaten".'[95] It is clear from Freud's writing that these people are primarily men. Nevertheless, Freud designated the beating fantasy as a feminine trait, in which the individual 'is lingering on the "feminine line".' At stake in these fantasies is the male repression of homosexual desire. Masochistic fantasies work as a homophobic injunction against homosexual desire, but they also negate the patriarchal authority of the father: 'The boy evades his homosexuality by repressing and remodelling his unconscious phantasy: and the remarkable thing about his later conscious phantasy is that it has for its content a feminine attitude without a homosexual object-choice.'[96] Lawrence's masochism played with the tantalising proximity of his repressed homosexuality, embracing it and simultaneously denying it.

Men who harbour masochistic fantasies suggested Freud, 'develop a special sensitiveness and irritability towards anyone they can include in the class of fathers.'[97] The son's father is what he would like to *be* and also what he would like to *have*. What is beaten, ridiculed and humiliated in the masochist is the image and likeness of the father he desires to have. But it is the patriarchal father he aspires to *be*, who is beating him, and this invokes the son's grievance at his father's harsh and retributive behaviour toward his homosexual desire. This intense ambivalence toward father figures is a predicament of the son's unwillingness to identify with the position of the father in the oedipus complex. Lawrence's 'standing civil war' was not only his struggle to escape his dependency upon his mother; it was also his persistent and fruitless attempts to establish an identification with a father figure who would confirm his masculine identity. Throughout his life, he rebelled against conventional authority; but he made a number of older, charismatic men, like Hogarth, General Allenby, Winston Churchill and

Trenchard, into surrogate fathers, surrendering himself to their causes in the hope of being loved by them.

T.E. Shaw the Mechanic

The myth of Lawrence of Arabia, the ethos of indirect rule and the historical drama of the imperial mission, visibly embodied charismatic action and authority in the figure of a man. The myth gathered momentum in the inter-war years, but Lawrence's abject failure as a charismatic man of action, and his decision to become T.E. Shaw the mechanic, epitomised the historical redundancy of the autonomous, upper-class agent of imperialism. The myth of Lawrence of Arabia was a nostalgic defence against the uncertainties of imperial manliness and the decline of the British empire. The idealism of the imperial mission, with its self-deluding belief that power was embodied in the superior morality of English character, rather than their superiority of British weaponry, was about to be confronted by the transmutation of European imperialism into European fascism. Lawrence's transition from solitary hero abroad to subordinate ranker at home followed the logic of this transmutation. In his personal defeat, Rupert Brooke had turned to the reactionary values of pastoralism. Lawrence embraced the modern movement, the new sensation of speed and the impersonal power of machinery.

> the conquest of the last element, the air, seems to me the only major task of our generation; and I have convinced myself that progress to-day is not made by the single genius, but by the common effort ... it is the airmen and mechanics, who are overcoming the air ... as I said I went into the R.A.F. to serve a mechanical purpose, not as a leader but as a cog in the machine. The key word, I think, is machine.[98]

He drove his Brough 'Boanarges' motorbike – 'the steel magnificence of strength and speed' – at high speeds around the countryside.[99] 'My nerves are jaded and gone near dead', he told Lionel Curtis, 'so that nothing less than hours of voluntary danger will prick them into life.'[100]

Lawrence's transition came at a moment in European history when the imperial mission of its principal nations had peaked and had begun its turn back toward its neglected heartland of Europe, to embrace the masses and inject the 'modern movement' of Fascism and Nazism with its 'eternal stream' of history. In Britain, the idea of the exceptional

Englishman of Indirect Rule found a new incarnation, in the 'Thought-Deed Man' of Oswald Mosley's British Union of Fascists. The BUF was launched in October 1932, and to mark the occasion, Mosley published *Greater Britain*, a 40,000 word manifesto of the BUF. The title's allusion to Seeley's colonial nationalism was intentional. British fascism was the self-appointed heir to Chamberlain's mixture of nationalism, socialism and protectionist economic policies. Social imperialism formed a vital cornerstone in Mosley's conception of a fascist corporate state, as well as providing the BUF with an emotional appeal as the defender of Empire. William Joyce, one of its propogandists wrote: 'True Imperialism knows nothing of disintegration . . . true Imperialism knows nothing of surrender, true Imperialism knows nothing of injustice; and Fascism is true Imperialism.'[101] The early BUF represented a constituency of men who felt that their masculinity and their English ethnicity had been profoundly disempowered by a decadent postwar society, and imperial decline. Fascism would be a movement which looked to the future, reviving the imperial virtues of manliness, greatness and self-sacrifice: 'Fascism is the creed and the morality of British manhood. It is the creed of men who have determined that Britain shall live and again be great.'[102]

Although Lawrence had no direct involvement in the fledgeling fascist movement, his myth embodied this vision of British fascism. Lawrence himself had embraced being a 'cog of the machine'. His doctrine of equality under compulsion was echoed by Mosley in *The Greater Britain*: 'Voluntary discipline is the essence of the Modern Movement.'[103] And Lawrence's asceticism found its expression in the Fascist credo: 'In our ordered athleticism of life we seek, in fact, a morality of the Spartan pattern.'[104] His need to surrender himself to a higher cause prefigured the model Fascist individual who must run his life according to the fundamental principle; 'how can I serve the state?' And Lawrence's intoxication with air power was shared by many Fascists who alarmed the authorities by setting up their own air clubs in 1934. Mosley had flown with the Royal Flying Corps during the war and was an ardent supporter of air power. The journal *Aeroplane*, edited by C.G. Grey, was sympathetic to Fascism, and gave its enthusiastic support to German rearmament. With this symmetry of interests and sensibilities, Lawrence was approached by Fascists on a number of occasions, and asked to be a mentor for the BUF and a symbol of its dream alliance between a Fascist Europe and the British Empire. In May 1935, Henry Williamson, the well-known author of

Tarka the Otter, and a prominent member of the BUF, wrote to Lawrence suggesting they meet and discuss organising a large Fascist meeting of ex-soldiers in the Albert Hall. Williamson, who was a friend of Lawrence, believed he was the only man capable of uniting Europe. 'The new age must begin: Europe was ready for peace. Lawrence was the natural leader of that age in England. I dreamed of an Anglo-German friendship, the beginning of the pacification of Europe. Hitler and Lawrence must meet. I wrote this to him.'[105]

The Fascists were not the only ones who sought to draw Lawrence into an active, public political role as appeaser to Germany and defender of empire. He was feted by Nancy Astor and the 'Cliveden set', which included Lord Lothian (Phillip Kerr) and Lionel Curtis of the Round Table movement. The 'Cliveden set' was an informal political grouping which met at the Astor's country home, and which encouraged a policy of appeasement with Hitler. The Round Table had always recognised the power and threat of an imperial Germany to British interests and it had swung its influence behind Neville Chamberlain. Writing in *The Times* in 1935, Lothian argued that Hitler was sincere in his renunciation of war; 'what Germany wants is equality, not war.'[106] The *Round Table* of the same year expressed its support for Hitler against the more disagreeable elements amongst the old Prussian nationalists and 'wilder Nazis' who it considered were the main threat to European peace; 'Hitler is the leader. . . Never has he expressed himself more pacifically than now, never has he more clearly offered conciliation and compromise.'[107] On 7 May, Lawrence received a letter from Nancy Astor: 'I believe when the Government reorganises you will be asked to reorganise the Defence Forces.' She added, 'if you will come to Cliveden on Saturday, the last weekend in May . . . you will never regret it.'[108] Those present would include Lothian, Curtis and Stanley Baldwin, who was about to become Prime Minister. Lawrence replied; 'No: wild mares would not at present drag me away from Cloud's Hill.'[109]

On 13 May, Lawrence replied by telegram to Williamson's request to meet: 'Lunch Tuesday Wet Fine Cottage One Mile North Bovington Camp.' As he drove back from the Post Office to Clouds Hill, he swerved his motorbike to avoid two boys. He crashed and died in hospital six days later. Although Lawrence had not been seized by the ideology of Fascism, his life had been an exemplary practice of surrender to the eternal stream of history. In his masochism, in his denial of his body and sexuality, and in his longing to be no more than a 'cog of a machine', Lawrence had brought imperial manliness back home from abroad, to reveal that it had no belonging outside colonialism. The imperial mission was bankrupted. Only the ethos of surrender and discipline to a higher cause offered a valid form of life. Whether he would have embraced the cause of Fascism or retained his ethical principles is open to question.

> I'm 'out' of the R.A.F. and sitting in my cottage rather puzzled to find out what has happened to me, is happening and will happen. At present the feeling is mere bewilderment. I imagine leaves must feel like this after they have fallen from their tree and untill they die.[110]

Notes

1. John E. Mack (1977), *A Prince of our Disorder: The Life of T.E. Lawrence,* (Mack) Weidenfeld & Nicolson, p.281.
2. Lowell Thomas (1924), *With Lawrence in Arabia*, Hutchinson, p.13-14.
3. Ibid. p.16.
4. A.W. Lawrence, ed. (1937), *T.E. Lawrence by His Friends*, Cape, p.172-175.
5. Phillip Knightley and Colin Simpson (1971), *The Secret Lives of Lawrence of Arabia*, Panther, p.160.
6. Elaine Showalter (1985), *The Female Malady Women, Madness and English Culture*, 1830-1980, Virago, p.168.
7. Ibid., p.172.
8. Ibid., p.168.
9. Vera Brittain (1979), *Testament of Youth*, Fontana/Virago, p.143.
10. Sandra M. Gilbert (1983), 'Soldier's Heart: Literary Men, Literary Women, and the Great War' in *Signs: Journal of Women in Culture and Society*, vol.8, no.3, p.425.
11. David Jones (1979), 'In Parenthesis, Part 7.' in *The Penguin Book of First World War Poetry*, ed. Jon Silkin, Penguin.
12. Henry Williamson (1987), *The Wet Flanders Plain*, Geddan Books, p.19.
13. Martin Green (1992), *Children of the Sun: A Narrative of Decadence in England after 1918*, Pimlico.
14. Lowell Thomas quoted in Lawrence James, op.cit.. p.279.
15. Christopher Sykes (1969), 'Introduction' to Richard Aldington, *Lawrence of Arabia*, Penguin, p.14.
16. William M. Chace (1989), 'T.E. Lawrence: The Uses of Heroism' in *T.E. Lawrence: Soldier, Writer, Legend New Essays*, ed. Jeffrey Meyers, St Martin's Press, New York, p.132.
17. John Buchan (1940), *Memory Hold-The-Door*, Hodder and Stoughton

Ltd, p.218.

18. Charles Temple (1968), *Native Races and Their Rulers: Sketches and Studies of Official Life and Administrative Problems*, London, p.30.

19. Mack. p.106.

20. Ibid., p.89.

21. Ibid., p.98.

22. Lawrence wrote a guide for British officers serving in the Arab Revolt. Written in 1917, for the Arab Bulletin, 'Twenty-Seven Articles' offers a series of tips in leading the Arabs. What matters are not rules or procedures, but force of personality: 'Win and keep the confidence of your leader. Strengthen his prestige at your expense before others when you can. . . Live with him, that at meal times and at audiences you may be naturally with him in his tent. . . Your ideal position is when you are present and not noticed.' Success, he wrote, is achieved by combining authority with self-effacement; 'Wave a Sherif in front of you like a banner and hide your own mind and person. If you succeed, you will have hundreds of miles of country and thousands of men under your orders.' See T.E. Lawrence (1991) 'Twenty-Seven Articles (Arab Bulletin, 20th August 1917)' in *Secret Despatches from Arabia and other writing*, ed. Malcolm Brown, Bellew, London, p.154-155.

23. Mack. p.135.

24. Letter to G.J. Kidston (1919), Letters, p.169.

25. See Mary Bull (1963), 'Indirect Rule in Northern Nigeria 1906-1911' in *Essays in Imperial Government*, eds. Kenneth Robinson and Frederick Madden, Oxford.

26. Shortly after Lord Milner's death in 1925, a statement of his beliefs was discovered and published in The Times, under the editorship of Geoffrey Dawson. His 'Credo' was subsequently republished as a pamphlet and widely distributed to schools and other public bodies. The glue which would cement imperial union was race.

> I am British (indeed primarily an English) Nationalist. If I am also an Imperialist, it is because the destiny of the English race . . . has been to strike roots in distant parts. . . My patriotism knows no geographical but only racial limits. I am an Imperialist and not a little Englander, because I am a British Race Patriot. . . It is not the soil of England, dear as it is to me, which is essential to arouse my patriotism, but the speech, the tradition, the spiritual heritage, the principles, the aspirations of the British race.
>
> A.M. Gollin (1964), *Proconsul in Politics*, Antony Blond, p.129.

27. John E. Kendle (1975), *The Round Table Movement and Imperial Union*,

University of Toronto Press, p.51.

28. Cited in Hannah Arendt (1986), *The Origins of Totalitarianism*, Andre Deutsch, p.214.
29. W. Nimocks (1968), *Milner's Young Men: the 'Kindergarten' in Edwardian Imperial Affairs*, Duke University Press, p.155.
30. T.E. Lawrence (1920), 'The Changing East' first published in *The Round Table*, September Issue. Reprinted in A.W. Lawrence, ed. (1991) Oriental Assembly, Imperial War Museum.
31. Letter to G.J. Kidston, *Letters, op.cit.*
32. Letter to Vyvyan Richards (1918), *Letters*, p.150.
33. *Seven Pillars*, p.566. See also letter to Colonel C.E. Wilson (1917), *Letters*, p.112, in which Lawrence describes a meeting with Grand Sherif Hussayn in which the ambiguous message presented to the Arabs about the nature of the Sykes-Picot agreement was discussed.
34. *Seven Pillars*, p.30.
35. Mack. p.283.
36. Letter to E.M. Forster (1924), Letters, p.257. Lawrence produced a special subscriber's copy of *Seven Pillars* during his lifetime, but the full text was only published for the general public after his death in 1935.
37. Edward Said (1991), *Orientalism*, Penguin, p.242.
38. Suleiman Mousa (1966), *T.E. Lawrence: An Arab View*, trans. Albert Butros, Oxford University Press, p.262-263.
39. Eugene Goodheart (1989), 'A Contest of Motives: T.E. Lawrence in *Seven Pillars of Wisdom*' in *T.E. Lawrence: Soldier, Writer, Legend New Essays, op.cit.* p.204.
40. Knightley and Simpson, *op.cit.*. p.29.
41. Mack. p.41.
42. Letter to Charlotte Shaw (1927), Letters, p.325.
43. *Ibid.*, p.324-326.
44. Letter to Lionel Curtis (1923), *Letters*, p.233.
45. Sigmund Freud (1917[1916-17]), 'The Paths to the Formation of Symptoms' in *Introductory Lectures on Psychoanalysis*, PFL.1, p.418.
46. Jeffrey Meyers (1989), *op.cit.*, p.118.
47. Letter to Charlotte Shaw (1927), *Letters*, p.324.
48. Robert Graves (1991), Lawrence and the Arabs, Paragon House, p.43-44. See also *T.E. Lawrence to His Biographer Robert Graves* (1938), reprinted by Doubleday, New York, 1963. Lawrence was closely involved in the writing of Graves' book, as he was in the writing of Thomas's *With Lawrence in Arabia*. The passage quoted was supplied almost verbatim by Lawrence and simply copied out by Graves.

49. T.E. Lawrence (1962), *The Mint*, Panther Books, p.26.
50. Jeffrey Meyers (1989), *op.cit.*, p.121.
51. Mack. p.423.
52. Letter to Charlotte Shaw (1925), *Letters*, p.290. See also letter to F.L. Lucas (1929), *Letters*, p.408, in which he states that he has not experienced heterosexual intercourse.
53. *Seven Pillars*, p.28.
54. T.E. Lawrence (1993) 'Introduction' to Charles Doughty (1888), *Travels in Arabia Deserta*, reprinted in Harold Orlans, ed. *Lawrence of Arabia Strange Man of Letters: The Literary Criticism and Correspondence of T.E. Lawrence*, Farleigh Dickinson University Press, p.55.
55. Mack. p.37.
56. Letter to Kidston (1919), *Letters*, p.169.
57. *Seven Pillars*, p.23.
58. M.D. Allen (1991), *The Medievalism of Lawrence of Arabia*, Pennsylvania State University Press, p.85-86.
59. *Seven Pillars*, p.683.
60. The version published here is Lawrence's original which he sent to Robert Graves. Robert Graves edited it and it is the edited version which appears in *Seven Pillars*. For the original version see Knightley and Simpson, p.184-185.
61. *Seven Pillars*, p. 514.
62. Letter to his mother (1911), *Letters*, p.40.
63. *Seven Pillars*, p.38.
64. *Ibid.*
65. Thomas, p.149.
66. *Seven Pillars*, p.221.
67. *Ibid*, p.28.
68. *Ibid*. p.244.
69. *Ibid*.
70. *Ibid*. p.318.
71. *Ibid*. p.477.
72. *Ibid*. p.475.
73. Letter to Edward Garnett (1922), *Letters*, p.202.
74. See James 1993 and Knightley and Simpson 1971.
75. Mack. p.229.
76. Letter to Charlotte Shaw (1924), *Letters*, p.261.
77. *The Mint*, p.18.
78. Letter to Robert Graves (1923), *Letters*, p.221.
79. *The Mint*, p.18.

80. Letter to his mother (1925), *Letters*, p.298.
81. Letter to Lionel Curtis (1923), *Letters*, p.227.
82. *The Mint.* p.151.
83. Letter to Lionel Curtis (1923), *Letters*, p.233.
84. Letter to Lionel Curtis (1923), *Letters*, p.236.
85. Letter to Lionel Curtis (1923), *Letters*, p.324.
86. *The Mint*, p.22.
87. *Ibid.* p.22.
88. *Ibid.*
89. Knightley and Simpson, p.226.
90. See Knightley and Simpson and Mack.
91. Knightley and Simpson, p.202.
92. *Ibid.*, p.204-205.
93. *Ibid.*, p.223.
94. Mack. p.433.
95. Sigmund Freud (1919), 'A Child Is being Beaten' in *PFL*, 10, p.163.
96. *Ibid.*, p.187.
97. *Ibid.*, p.182.
98. Letter to Robert Graves (1935), *Letters*, p.420-522.
99. *The Mint*, p.186.
100. Letter to Lionel Curtis (1923), *Letters*, p.237.
101. D.S. Lewis (1987), *Illusions of Grandeur Mosley, Fascism and British Society 1931-1981*, Manchester University Press, p.182.
102. Stephen Cullen (1987), 'The Development of the Ideas and Policy of the British Union of Fascist, 1932-40' in *Journal of Contemporary History*, Vol. 22, p.124.
103. Nicholas Mosley, *op.cit.* p.221.
104. Cullen, *op.cit..* p.122.
105. Richard Griffiths (1980), *Fellow Travellers of the Right: British Enthusiasts for Nazi Germany*, Constable, p.136.
106. *Round Table*, No. 98, Vol. xxv, 1935, p.283.
107. *Ibid.* p.297-298.
108. Michael Yardley (1985), *Backing into the Limelight: A Biography of T.E. Lawrence*, Harrap, p.212.
109. Letter to Lady Astor (1935), *Letters*, p.537.
110. Letter to Bruce Rogers (1935), *Letters*, p.536.

5

ENOCH POWELL'S ISLAND STORY

In 1959, Enoch Powell wrote a review of Wilfred Thesiger's *Arabian Sands*, a chronicle of the author's solo journeys across the 'Empty Quarter' of Arabia. Described by Sir John Glubb in the *Sunday Times* as 'perhaps the last, and certainly one of the greatest, of the British travellers among the Arabs.' Thesiger epitomised the ascetic Englishman in search of an authentic native culture and the limits of his own will power and endurance.[1] As with Lawrence before him, Thesiger's hostile world was the modernity of his own society; his journeying an escape from its domesticity. And like Lawrence, Thesiger fashioned the desert and the Bedu into a simulacrum of his own homoeroticism and narcissistic longing for self-becoming. Powell was captivated:

> What is it about deserts that tugs at the hearts of men? Even those who have only touched the hem of the desert ... know what it was that Thesiger repeatedly sought and found in the centre of the Arabian emptiness, and they would, or think they would, go back again to get it if that were possible. . . The secret lies perhaps in the desert not as a mere environment, but as something travelled over, which seems to remove the purpose from journeying and substitute in its place a kind of timeless contentment, almost as though the soul were soothed by this emblem of its own metaphorical journey across the desert of the world. The desert is the true setting of the words: navigare necesse est, vivere non est necesse. [It is necessary to navigate but not necessary to live][2]

Powell's fascination with Thesiger lay in his own boyhood obsession with the desert travellers Burton, Blunt and Doughty. What these men held in common, and what Powell spent a lifetime attempting to emulate, was their journeying without a worldly purpose; their confrontation with the desert as symbolic of what Lawrence called 'death in life'. These men were the heirs of the seventeenth century pilgrims in search of a spiritual home, indifferent to the worldly and sensual. Fated, driven by the seduction of death and their need to subjugate their bodies, they pursued life to the centre of the desert, to the point at which its nature threatened to extinguish their cultural identities. It is here, Powell imagined, that they found their 'timeless contentment'.

Powell's own life was an attempt to reproduce this external compulsion of the desert, to construct an unyielding personal intellectual and theological order which would structure and contain his instinctual and emotional life. He once informed a journalist, 'I'm at home in an environment where rules are strict but external. . . Liberty of thought is consistent with willing submission, enthusiastic submission, to a formal ordered existence.'[3] In an interview in 1994, Terry Coleman asked him if he was a believing Christian.[4] He replied; 'I am an obedient member of the Church of England.' Loyalty and identification with the rules and rites of the institution were paramount; he would believe what he was commanded to believe. Sensing disingenuousness, Coleman pushed him to elaborate; 'what *did* he in conscience believe?' Powell replied; 'God knows what I believe: you only know what I'm saying.' For Powell, the formal syntax of his religious and political language was a protective carapace around the inner world of his beliefs and feelings. His play on the words 'God knows' suggests that what is there is an absence.

In 1943, Powell had the opportunity to discover the 'timeless contentment' of the North African desert. As a Lieutenant-Colonel and an intelligence officer he undertook a two week journey from Algiers to Cairo, travelling by lorry in the company of Major Michael Strachan. The experience was no metaphorical narrative of spiritual asceticism. The sandy wastes offered none of their mythic negation, only a frustrating tendency to sabotage the banal but necessary chores of daily life. Strachan later wrote a humorous account of Lieutenant-Colonel Powell's dangerous ineptitude as a driver and the shambles of his cooking.[5]

> The fire smouldered dejectedly until he teased it with a gill of petrol, and then it sprang up and singed his moustache; and when he assaulted the sausages the tin counter-attacked and cut his finger; the water refused to boil and while he was not looking tipped itself over into the fire. 'Oh the

malice – the cursed diabolical malice of inanimate objects!' muttered the Professor ferociously between clenched teeth. 'Here, let me help', I said. 'You keep away,' he snarled. 'If they want to be bloody-minded, I'll show them, by God I will,' booting the empty sausage tin into a cactus bush.

Strachan's light-hearted descriptions of 'cold and flabby' sausages and 'tea-leaves. . . on top of a grey, tepid liquid' mocked the serious-minded pretensions of Powell. But they also suggest an explanation for his later political career as an English nationalist. Powell was a man who was only ever to touch the hem of the desert. In his introduction to *Arabian Sands*, Thesiger wrote; 'I went to Southern Arabia only just in time. Others will go there . . . but they will move about in cars and will keep in touch with the outside world by wireless. They will . . . never know the spirit of the land nor the greatness of the Arabs.' History and the 'winds of change' were to rob Powell of empire and thwart his own imperial mission. If Powell imagined his heroes had discovered serenity in the centre of the desert, his own earthly quest uncovered nothing but a feeling of emptiness. More than any other figure of post-war Britain, he gave vent to this feeling of profound and irreconcilable loss; of Empire, of identity, of belonging. It was a loss he sought to resolve in his poetry, his religion and his political life. In the end, it was his mythologising of English nationalism which would form his imaginary, ascetic desert journey; his pursuit of 'death in life' – 'to have a nation to die for and to be glad to die for it-all the days of one's life.'[6]

The Hallucination of Empire

Before the outbreak of war, Powell had spent eighteen months as the Professor of Greek at Sydney University. On 4 September, 1939, the day after war was declared, he resigned and returned to England. He enlisted as a private in his father's old regiment, the Royal Warwickshires, but his period in the ranks was short lived. A Brigadier on an inspection asked him how he liked the work. Powell replied with a Greek proverb and found himself dispatched to an officer training programme at Aldershot, the first of a series of courses before being posted to North Africa in 1941. In Cairo he was assigned to the Intelligence and Plans Division as Secretary to the Joint Intelligence Committee, Middle East. The crucial factor in the desert war was U.S industrial-military power. Not only did Powell develop a contempt for the Americans' lack of finesse in military strategy, he felt a growing distrust of their geopolitical ambitions. 'By the end of 1942 it was clear to me. . . that for the survival of the British Empire what was over-whelmingly important was that the Far East – India and the Far East – Burma and the Far East – would be recovered by Britain before they were occupied by the United States.'[7] Powell's desert journey was his first move in securing a transfer to the war in the Far East. In August, 1943, he left Cairo for India, as Secretary to the Joint Intelligence Committee India and South East Asia. He harboured an ambition to be a part of the fighting and on his journey he approached Orde Wingate, with an unsuccessful request to join his Chindit campaign in Burma.

In *The Times* of 12 February, 1968, Powell recalled his two years in India. 'I fell head over heals in love with it. If I'd gone there 100 years earlier, I'd have left my bones there.' He taught himself Urdu, cycling from New Delhi to outlying villages to practise the language. 'It was one of the glories of the British Empire in India that they regarded it as desirable for officers up to the highest rank to identify themselves with the life and language of the country.' But his identification with India was a highly circumscribed affair. Powell avoided the Indian intelli-gentsia. It was the peasants and their archaic cultures of caste and reli-gion which attracted him. His loyalty lay with the fading glory of the Raj, its rigid codes of etiquette and the Pukkah Sahibs whose self-enhancing mystique of power ruled over the multitudes. The pomp and circumstance of the colonial hierarchy and the disciplined existence of army life provided Powell with his ideal world. When he told his biog-rapher Andrew Roth that the army was the happiest time of his life, it was more specifically the army in India. His conservatism and need for social conformity left him incapable of recognising the nationalist aspi-rations of the Indian people. The concept of self-determination, both personal and political had no place in Powell's mind's eye, nor in the parody of Late Victorian India he identified with. On a journey through Bihar, he was struck by a 'blinding revelation': 'I was the only Englishman within, thirty, forty, maybe fifty or sixty miles, and *that this was a part of the natural order of things*.'[8] Powell had imbued the myths of indirect rule. It was an attitude – arrogant, myopic, even unbalanced – that he brought to his administrative work.

By 1944, with the war effectively won in Europe, the British turned their attention to the political future of India. Powell was promoted to Brigadier and appointed Secretary to the Reorganisation Committee

responsible for deciding the future of the Indian army. He was a dominant figure on the committee and travelled extensively, garnering opinion and facts for its Final Report. He was also responsible for writing
one of the key chapters – recommending twenty-five years before the
Indian Army was ready for independence. The logic of Powell's argument was impeccable. The Indian army needed five thousand officers
with the right educational qualifications. Only three per cent of Indian
men with these qualifications held commissions in the army. A
committee had just reported that this number could only be increased
by two per cent a year. Therefore, Powell deducted, it would take
twenty-five years before the Indian army had its full officer corps.
Until then it must rely on British officers to command it. His argument
was meticulous, but it owed more to the academic analysis of a Greek
text than the real politic of British imperial rule; and he failed to recognise Indian antipathy towards the British as responsible for the low
level of recruitment to the army. Powell's failure to account for
contemporary political realities discredited other sections of the
Report and his recommendations were quickly dismissed as off the
mark. He did not appear to have been embarrassed by this setback.
India had prompted his Pauline conversion to imperialism and his
idealisation of the Raj left him floating in a dream world. He was now
about to manufacture himself as a man of destiny. 'I was determined to
do something', he told Roth, 'to stop the disintegration of the Empire
which seemed imminent.'[9] He would enter politics:

> I thought of how Burke had said 160 years earlier that the keys of India
> were not in Calcutta, not in Delhi, they were in that box – the Despatch
> Box at the House of Commons. I decided at that time that I must go
> there.[10]

Powell arrived back in England on 27 February, 1946. He was 33 years
old. He had already achieved the distinction of becoming a professor at
the age of 25 and the youngest Brigadier in the British army. With these
credentials he was quickly recruited into the Conservative Party, where
'Rab' Butler was endeavouring to organise its intellectual renaissance.
After an interview with David Clark, the Director of the Conservative
Research Department, Powell began work in the Conservative
Parliamentary Secretariat, alongside two other newcomers, Iain
Macleod and Reginald Maudling. He was made joint head of the Home
Affairs Department and Secretary of the Party's India Committee. In

1947, he was chosen as a by-election candidate for the safe Labour seat of Normanton in Yorkshire. His speech to the adoption meeting was an apocalyptic rallying cry for Empire: 'If there is a way for the Empire to survive . . . it can only be because through Britain is liberty and independence preserved. If that is not true, then we will perish in proving it otherwise.'[11] Seven months later, in August, India was partitioned. The central figment of his dream world was shattered. His reserved, disassociated comment; 'One's whole world had been altered' – offers little insight into his feelings, but the trauma compelled him to spend the night walking the streets. To Powell, the two hundred year long link with India *was* the empire; every other possession had been acquired for the sake of maintaining that link. India had gone, but he could not come to terms with its implications for the rest of the empire. He simply resolved to work harder for its preservation and unity.

Indian independence was the beginning of the end. Its immediate effect was a redefinition of the old concept of British citizenship as being based on being 'a subject of the King'. In 1948, the Labour government introduced the British Nationality Bill which would make a distinction between British subjects who were citizens of the United Kingdom and those who were Commonwealth citizens. The Bill ensured that the great majority of British subjects in the colonies and dominions would continue to have the legal right to settle in Britain. Their allegiance however, would no longer be to the British monarch. Powell and a number of other Tory imperialists tried to persuade the Conservative Party to vote against the Bill. He later explained his position in the *Birmingham Post* (6.11.52): 'the Crown is the great link which binds the Empire together in a common loyalty. But the British Nationality Act of 1948 took away allegiance to the Crown as the basis for British citizenship . . . citizens of the . . . Indian Union were expressly given all the rights and privileges of British subjects, though repudiating the King as their sovereign.' Powell failed to persuade the Party to vote against the Bill and, contrary to his own regressive opinions, the official party document, *Imperial Policy*, published in 1949, accepted the implications of Indian independence for the Commonwealth. The document became one of the intellectual cornerstones of One Nation Toryism and laid the ground for Harold Macmillan's 1960, 'winds of change' speech. Already the demarcation lines within the Conservative Party around the issue of race and nation were being drawn. Nevertheless, despite its permissiveness, The British Nationality Act represented the first step in the post-war racialising of immigration policy. As if to symbolise the moment, the SS *Windrush* arrived in May with 417 Jamaicans in search of work and a new life. It was they, rather than the hundreds and thousands of Irish and European immigrants, who signified the coming post-colonial struggle over the meanings of English ethnicity.

On 17 December, Powell was adopted as the candidate for Wolverhampton South-West. A reporter from the *Wolverhampton Express and Star*, interviewing the new candidate, described Powell's 'blinding revelation' of the 'tremendous force for good the Empire was.' On 23 February, he won the seat in the General Election, campaigning as an old fashioned imperialist. India, Pakistan, Burma and Ceylon were already independent nations, but he was determined to stem the retreat. His maiden speech in the House of Commons, two months after India had declared itself a republic, was emphatic in his refusal to contemplate the end of empire. Powell advocated the recruitment of a new colonial army which would replace the Indian army and defend 'His Majesty's Dominions as a whole throughout the world.' Indian independence had simply reinforced his dogged disregard for the emerging post-imperial world. The moment of reckoning arrived at the 1952 Commonwealth Prime Ministers' Conference. A number of heads of newly independent states objected to the Queen's formal title. It had an outdated and imperial ring to it: 'By the Grace of God of Great Britain, Ireland, and the British Dominions beyond the Sea, Queen, Defender of the Faith.' The Royal Titles Act of 1953 introduced a title which would account for the new Commonwealth sovereignties: 'By the Grace of God of the United Kingdom of Great Britain and Northern Ireland, and of her other Realms and Territories, Queen, Head of the Commonwealth, Defender of the Faith.' The semantics of the new title – the 'other Realms and Territories' – fractured the symbolic union of empire, and with it Britain's imperial preeminence. Powell rigorously opposed the Bill in a Parliamentary speech.

> That unity we are now formally and deliberately giving up, and we are substituting what is, in effect, a fortuitous aggregation of a number of separate entities. . . By recognising the division of the realm into separate realms, are we not opening the way for the other unity – the last unity of all – that of the person of the Monarch to go the way of the rest?

Unity, what he defined as a 'corporate identity' in which 'all the parts recognise that in certain circumstances they would sacrifice themselves in the interests of the whole', was the bedrock of his political beliefs. His venom was reserved for the Commonwealth leaders who had proved themselves incapable of such self-sacrifice. They were 'the underlying evil': 'We are doing this for the sake of those to whom the very names 'Britain' and 'British' are repugnant.' The linguistic entity of the British empire was dead, and the Suez crisis of 1956 would destroy the last vestiges of its moral and political legitimacy. The colonial peoples he had been willing to sacrifice his life for had rejected him. His shock at their 'ingratitude' was the decisive moment of his political career. That obscure and archaic play on semantics precipitated his turn to England as a new source of corporate identity. His bereavement, and the invasive, persecutory quality he ascribed to those who had disillusioned him, would later fuel his virulent, nationalist assault on her imaginary enemies. But by 1953, Powell was a man expelled to the hem of the desert, its meaning no more than badly made tea and burnt sausages.

The following year, Powell recanted his faith. On 12 July he presented a paper to the Conservative Political Centre Summer School entitled; 'The Empire of England.' In his meticulous style, Powell detailed the historical inevitability of the end of Empire. Seeley's ideal of imperial federation and the social-imperialism of Joseph Chamberlain, which had once inspired him, had been illusions: 'the unstable compromise of Imperial government by the Parliament of Great Britain could not in the long run endure.'[12] Parliament could not maintain its jurisdiction over peoples who owed their allegiances to other sovereignties. He concluded:

> the disintegration of that sovereignty which was known until some years ago as the British Empire is for the most part neither accidental nor due to the errors of policy or perversities of intention, but is the inevitable consequence of the political institutions of the United Kingdom and the character of its former and present dependencies.'[13]

The paper marks Powell's political and intellectual position on the end of Empire. Empire he states, 'was a self-delusion'. He had already adopted a similar terminology in his article for the *Birmingham Post* (6.11.52): 'To most of the world outside it seems that the British Empire, if it does not already belong to the past, has a short lease of life. Only here in England, like a nation of Rip van Winkles, do we live in a dream world of undisturbed complacency.'

Twelve years later, in April 1964, Powell turned once more to what he called the 'national hallucination' of empire. In a series of influential articles in *The Times*, he set out a Conservative, political agenda which was to anticipate the Thatcher revolution. In his second, 'Patriotism Based on Reality Not on Dreams', he condemned the Commonwealth as a 'gigantic farce', and appealed for a clean break with Britain's imperial past.

> The change in Britain's relative power and position in the world since 1939 has imposed a colossal revision of ideas on Britain . . . which draws most strength and inspiration from that position and power. In the course of this revision, self-deception has been employed on the grand scale and has served a purpose. Now the wounds have almost healed and the skin formed again beneath the plaster and the bandages, and they come off.

It is hard not to conclude that Powell was speaking about his own damaged psyche. The following year he declared that his own wounds were irreparable.

> One can never resolve in the span of a human lifetime that kind of a revolution [the end of empire] without the marks being left of a struggle. I confess to you that for all that I write, for all that I think, for all that I try to demonstrate to myself and others I shall go to the grave with a conviction at the back of my mind that Her Majesty's ships still sweep the oceans of the world in case there should be any hostile warships which it might be necessary to sink. That hallucination will be there when the mind stops.[14]

In 1968, in a book review, Powell referred to this hallucination as an 'English sickness'. 'One feels like a doctor sitting in the middle of an epidemic with the sovereign vaccine on his shelves, and the population will not take it.'[15] He concluded: 'so the psychoanalysis through which lies the cure for Britain's sickness has to be twofold: first we must identify and overcome the mythology of the late Victorian empire; then we must penetrate to deeper levels and eradicate the fixation with India from our subconscious.' The review was published five months after Powell's 'rivers of blood' speech had catapulted him into public consciousness, and into the print columns of political commentary. Drawing upon his recent visit to the United States and his perceptions of its racial conflict, Powell predicted that the mass immigration of

New Commonwealth citizens to Britain would result in a racial war: 'As I look ahead, I am filled with foreboding. Like the Roman, I seem to see "the river Tiber foaming with much blood".'[16] A period of fifteen years had passed between the collapse of his idealisation of empire and this apocalyptic vision. His championing of racial incommensurability unleashed an ethnic populism –Powellism- which launched a frontal assault on the class paternalism of post-war Toryism and helping to pave the way for Thatcherism. To understand this transition and the virulence of the politics in which it culminated, we can follow his own advice. But it is not only the patient who needs to be examined. The doctor is also in need of attention.

Jack's Clarinet: 'It doesn't do to awaken longings that can't be fulfilled.'[17]

John (Jack) Enoch Powell was born on 16 June, 1912 in a semi-detached house in Flaxley Lane, Stechford, near Birmingham. His father, Albert Powell, was the son of a general merchant from Staffordshire. In 1909, at the age of 35, he had married Ellen Breese, fourteen years his junior and the daughter of a Liverpool policeman. Both were primary school teachers and products of the Victorian artisan class. Albert Powell had earlier divested himself of the moral strictures of its fundamentalist Methodism, by converting to Anglicanism. Powell described his father as having an 'agreeable temperament', 'a warm presence . . . and another boy around the place.'[18] In contrast, his mother was a Tory and a puritan, with a Victorian drive for education and self-improvement. Despite her atheism, she held to the basic principles of her class culture, imparting its moral sobriety and its rigid codes of conduct to her only son, for whom she possessed a driving ambition. After his birth, she gave up her job and devoted herself to his care and his education. 'My childhood is very much my mother. . . She was also my first teacher. . . from the very beginning, right up to the sixth at grammar school, she took a part in my learning, encouraging me and helping me and very much working with me.'[19]

Powell's mother was the dominating presence in the household. Her financial economies and emotional austerity ruled the household with a parsimonious rigour. 'My mother used to quote St Paul: eat what is set before you asking no questions.'[20] As a schoolgirl she had taught herself Greek and she set out to cultivate the same assiduous attention to detail in her son. She began with the alphabet when he was two and had taught him to read in a year. 'My earliest recollections are of my mother putting up the alphabet round the kitchen wall so that I could learn it – and my saying the most elementary lessons to her standing on a chair in the kitchen, while she worked at the stove or the sink.'[21] By the time he was four he was reading Harmsworth's encyclopaedia. His precocity earned him the nickname of 'The Professor'. Patrick Cosgrave, one of Powell's biographers, recounts the story of a local girl who used to visit the eight-year-old, Jack Powell. He would invite her to choose a book and return it the following week. 'This I did, and to prove that I *had* read it he would ask me a lot of questions about it. I was four years older, and it was terrible if I couldn't answer the question correctly.'[22] According to Cosgrave, the eight-year-old Powell organised a debating society amongst local children and in one session argued that Bacon, and not Shakespeare, had written *Henry V* and *A Midsummer Night's Dream*. His mother's tuition not only determined his leisure activities. It ensured that he became, in his words, a ' "prize-scholarship winning, knowledge-eating" being.'[23]

Powell won a scholarship to King Edward's School in Birmingham, where he was remembered as a loner. An old classmate recalls, 'he was really unlike . . . any other schoolboy one had known. He was austere. One seldom, if ever, had seen him standing against a wall with his hands in his pockets, just talking. He didn't play games... He was either at his books or he was walking purposively from A to B with a goal in mind, with either his books or his clarinet under his arm.' At 17, he won a scholarship to Trinity College Cambridge. Here he established a personal regime of unremitting austerity. He locked himself away in his room and worked from 5.30 am to 9.30 pm, venturing out for lectures, meals and visits to the library. His only pleasure was a daily evening walk to the train station – 'I simply picked a place to walk to, and back from. The station seemed a good destination.' Powell's social autism ensured him the majority of the classics prizes and no friends. The local head of the 'Old Edwardians' paid him a social call: 'as I remember it there was no fire, there were no pictures, Powell was sitting in his overcoat with a rug across his knees and . . . he was surrounded by eighteenth century folios... I said: "Hello Powell, would you like to come to tea?" and he said "No." I'd never met this response before... I walked over to his mantelpiece and leant on it and took out a cigarette and he said "Would you mind not smoking!" And so I left.'[24] Powell's own version of his reclusiveness is less acerbic. 'I didn't know [there was anything else to do . . . the social life of a college was a social life completely unfamiliar to me – even the sheer mechanics of it, of how to tie a bow tie, were unknown to me.'[25]

Powell's childhood revolved around books and words and the acquisition of knowledge. Years later he wrote: 'For all my life has been about words: manuscript words, printed words, spoken words. Thinking, loving, fighting, striving have always revolved around words – not mere words, but words, because apart from words men are but as brutes.'[26] Biographical accounts of his childhood (Lewis 1979, Roth 1970, Cosgrave 1986, Pedraza 1986) make no reference to play – emotion and desire appear entirely absent from his early years. Powell's own distinction between words and brutishness suggests that he used language and learning to set himself apart from feelings and bodily impulses. His love of the clarinet offers the only glimpse of a life other than one of strenuous scholasticism. At fifteen, he wanted to be a composer or conductor and to sit a scholarship for the Royal Academy of Music. The clarinet was an instrument of the disciplined and formal structures of classical music, but for Powell it also featured in band music, suggestive of more anarchic, emotional rhythms. His parents (but perhaps chiefly his mother) argued that book learning was more important and dissuaded him from pursuing a career in music. 'Cambridge it had to be, and I put my clarinet away for the last time: I've never looked at a sheet of music since.' Fifty years later, asked why he rarely listened to music, he answered: 'I don't like things which interfere with one's heart strings. It doesn't do to awaken longings that can't be fulfilled.'[27] There was to be no more illicit fantasies of band music. Powell's nascent exuberance was firmly suppressed beneath the intensive, singular activity of reading, fuelling an overweening ambition to become a classical scholar.

Powell's disavowal of pleasure was in the name of ambition – 'This was how one got on and up.' But it left the problem of how to manage his emotional life. At Cambridge, he adopted the poet and classics scholar A.E Housman as his role model – another outsider, ill at ease amongst the ruling classes. 'Here was someone who for whole decades had survived the heart-chilling loneliness of Cambridge. Could I not manage to resist it with the same stony manfulness?'[28] Powell followed the poet's advice;

> Courage, lad, 'tis not for long:
> Stand, quit you like stone, be strong.'[29]

It was Housman's 'moral fervour', and his ability to teach; 'Patiently, resolutely, with the power and precision of a steel machine,' which inspired Powell.[30] 'Not the least part of my good fortune was to encounter early ... the enduring inspiration of A.E. Housman's courage in the "mental fight".'[31] Powell had already been introduced, at the age of fifteen, to the 'mental fight', through the work of Thomas Carlyle. Housman confirmed Carlyle's ideal of manliness – earnest, high-minded, chaste and driven by ambition and a sense of duty.

> there was the detonation of *Sartor Resartus*: I still hear, when I recall the first reading of those intoxicating pages, the gentle hissing of the incandescent gas mantle above the table where homework was done, and the tone of my father's voice saying that I would find Carlyle as great an experience as he had done at the same age.[32]

Carlyle's promotion of self-denial reflected his own contradictory feelings about being a writer – an activity his father considered unmanly and domesticated. His solution was to redefine the status of intellectual work: strenuous mental effort replaced physical labour as the sign of a man's innate quality. In contrast, abandoning this struggle for a life of ease and pleasure was to fall into the feminising realm of idleness. Powell's puritanical work ethic and self-denial emulated Carlyle's heroic and manly intellectual. His intellectualism confirmed his masculinity; it was retentive and industrious rather than imaginative and creative, involving painstaking analysis and criticism of ancient Greek texts. In later years, to read and listen to Powell is to be aware of his meticulous attention to detail, his carefully chosen sentences and exacting syntax, the precision of his diction and the preeminence he gives to logic. His discourse acts like a procrustean defence against desire and emotional need, controlling language into a flattened intonation imbued with an exaggerated display of rationality. As Housman's poem concludes:

> And I stepped out in flesh and bone
> Manful like the man of stone.

Powell learnt to sculpt his language into a hard protective shell.

His reading of Carlyle had introduced him to German culture and a passion for Nietzsche. His infatuation with the transcendental world of German Romanticism prefigured his later love of India. It provides an illustration of the relationship between his inner world of feelings and the outer realm of language.

> The year in which I opened a German grammar for the first time was 1927... I knew that something had happened in my life and would go on happening. It is trite to say that it was the language of which I had dreamt. But it conveys exactly what I experienced at the time. It was to me as if this language had waited all this time to be discovered just by me and to be absorbed by me. I dived into it like a familiar body of water and I could swim right away.
>
> This linguistic experience was accompanied by 'all possible romantic and exciting feelings'. It was the discovery of a dual world; 'of fantasy and romantic magic and a world of mental strength and philosophical courage.'[33]

German was 'sharp, hard, strict, but with words that were romance in themselves, words in which poetry and music vibrated together.'[34] It was a language of firm boundaries, which both expressed and contained his unfulfilled longings. Such identifications became the idiom of his life. In adulthood, the external compulsion of institutions, regulated and disciplined his body and sexuality. His loyalty to concepts like 'The Crown' and 'Empire', and his fundamentalist religion, displaced his sensuality into an abstracted higher cause. He pursued bourgeois propriety to the point of parody because it emphasised convention and code over spontaneity and feeling. Powell feared his longings were potentially boundless and needed the security of clearly defined limits. Nevertheless he literally lost himself in his immersion into German culture and his 'head over heals' love affair with India. Melanie Klein has argued that these kinds of unrealistic idealisations, spring from 'the instinctual desires which aim at unlimited gratification'.[35] Powell's description of empire as an hallucination was psychologically correct; in its denial of reality it symbolised the illusion of gratification.

Powell's love for music, for German culture and for empire were attempts to resolve the split between his self-denying world of language and his emotional life; to bring words to repressed, unconscious feelings. This relationship between language and feeling is the key to understanding Powell's metaphor of the desert as symbolic of a lost unity of 'timeless contentment'. It can also explain why, in pursuit of this unity, he was drawn to the 'corporate identity' of empire; it explains too, the intense struggle, the sensibility of fanaticism, which he brought to its defence. Freud has defined an identification as 'the earliest expression of an emotional tie with another person.'[36] The shape and the feel of later political and cultural identifications have their genesis in this emotional tie to the mother. Like hallucination, idealisation is a defence against the fear of her absence; and Powell's idealised India, like his fantasy of the desert, was a sublime symbol of the continuity of his mother's presence. Independence destroyed its possibility, and symbolised his abandonment, in a place which he had no language to describe. Because language comes to replace attachment with the mother and to represent the child's own instinctual life, an unresolved attachment means there is a failure of linguistic representation. Loss and separation can be felt, enacted and dreamt, but it cannot be spoken about or thought because it exists anterior to language. This crisis of self does, however, find its way into representation through metaphor, in particular it seeks expression through the adoption of political and cultural identifications. Powell's identifications with Germany and later with India were metaphorical attempts to transfer unconscious predicaments into a familiar language and assimilate them into the ordered structure of his intellectualised world. But when these identifications failed him, when his idealised world was shattered, he was confronted with that wordless original loss: a loss of meaning.

In 1934, Powell was elected a fellow at Trinity and began work on his lexicon of Herodotus. His first academic essays were printed in German journals and he began travelling to Europe, to visit libraries. Hitler had become Chancellor in January 1933 and there were already documented reports of pogroms, arrests and German bellicosity. But his passion for German culture did not extend to any recognition or consideration of this political climate. On 30 June, 1934 Hitler launched his attack on the Brownshirts in the Night of the Long Knives.

> I cannot escape the impression that the decisive date was for me the first of July 1934, which was when the news of the Rhoehm massacre reached England. I still remember clearly how I sat for hours in a state of shock, shock which you experience when, around you, you see the debris of a beautiful building in which you have lived for a long time. . . So it had all been illusion, all fantasy, all a self-created myth. Music, philosophy, poetry, science and the language itself – everything was demolished, broken to bits on the cliffs of a monstrous reality. The spiritual home-

land had not been a spiritual homeland after all. . . Overnight my spiritual homeland had disappeared and I was left only with my geographical homeland.'[37]

Like his clarinet before and empire after, Powell's renunciation was
total: '1934 was also the year in which I recognised it would come to
war. . . The enemy was to be Germany and at stake was the freedom of
England. From then on Germany, although still an abstraction, was for
me the enemy. . . All the aspects which had seemed to me so wonderful and lovable took on a new appearance . . . a new pattern which let
one recognise the threatening danger and illuminate it.'[38] What was
loved became hated. 'Germany' (and this pattern was later to be
repeated with the Commonwealth leaders) became the source of persecutory feelings which threatened to destroy him. His spiritual homeland was reduced to meaningless lines of cartography; he was living on
the hem of life, devoid of a centre. Fated by this meaninglessness he
sought his recompense in war. 'I was, if you like, fatalistic. There was
nothing I could do to change the course of events, nor their outcome.'[39]
It was a war Powell did not expect to survive. It offered him the solace
of death.

Without a sense of purpose or belonging, Powell turned to poetry to
give voice to his 'painful emotions'. It was an activity he would pursue
intermittently for the next sixteen years – a form of internal dialogue
with himself. In his Foreword to his *Collected Poems*, he recalled how
his personal pain demanded an outlet, 'In Tennyson's and Housman's
Cambridge I was not ashamed to break off my work on Greek
Lexicography to "cry out" in the vein they had made available.'[40] His
first book of poetry, published in 1937, has a succession of images of
'youth doomed to die', threnodies which also express his own death
wish:

> As clear as light, sharp as a knife,
>   A truth springs in my breast:
> There are but two things, death and life,
>   And death of these is best (p50)

Of the two final poems addressed to his mother, the first begins like
Brooke's 'The Soldier'

> When I am gone, remember me
> Not often. But when in the east

Grey light is growing, and the mind
With fears and hope is clouded least,
Then, in the hour I love best,
And where I still reflected find
All that I ever sought to be,
I will return to you as one
New risen from the grave, as clear
As now you seem, and as dear
As when I slept beneath your breast
   Before I saw the sun (p51)

The second concludes with the unconscious wish behind his idealisation of Germany and later of empire and nation.

Mother, with longing ever new
   And joy too great for telling
I turn again to rest in you
   My earliest dwelling (p52)

This search for meaning of life in an undifferentiated union with his mother was an impossibility. But, like Rupert Brooke before him, he rediscovered meaningfulness in war. In contrast to the wistful, sometimes tortured, melancholy of his other poems, he celebrates the beginning of war with an exuberant, sexual imagery. War is a bride that he embraces.

Their faces all, both man and boy,
   With a lover's flush are fired:
They haste with swinging steps of joy
   To meet their long-desired;

And every eye is glistening
   With hope no more denied;
For now the marriage-morn will bring
   The bridegroom to the bride (p65)

She is also the harbinger of death:

O thou that takest
The hearts thou makest,

120

And them thou breakest,
Behold I die (p66)

But Powell, of course, did not die. To his everlasting shame he survived the war and sought to repay his debt in service to the nation.[41]

Enoch Powell's Island Story

In the early summer of 1950, Powell wrote his final book of poems; *The Wedding Gift*. It had been inspired by his love for an unnamed woman: 'Like a powerful hallucinatory drug, it unsealed again the necessity and the capability to write poetry. Dawn after dawn the stuff rose in my throat and would have choked me, had I not got it down and licked it into shape.'[42] But his love was unrequited and the romantic tenor of the early pages is overtaken by a fatalistic religious imagery. The final two lines of the last poem are a dramatic turn to God; 'I rise, and take the bitter sop, and go, / Whispering, 'Lord, 'tis I!' (p189) With the end of the Indian empire and now his failure in love, Powell was in need of a new, metaphorical home. Previously a militant atheist, he made another Pauline conversion and found a home in the Church of England. 'I was proud enough and English enough to see that it was a goodly inheritance from which, like a prodigal son, I had so long deliberately exiled myself.'[43] For Powell this 'ancestral home' was not just the national church; it extended to what he called the 'Church Universal'. It was an identification, like his attachment to empire, that provided him with a metaphor of wholeness of which he was a small part. 'I had been compelled to acknowledge a truth that is corporate, and when I had done so, I noticed that the loyalties I had lived with in war and peace had been corporate too.'[44] Unlike empire, the church could offer him a logos which would never abandon him. With this ontological security, he adopted a Christianity of punishing and unremitting harshness, dismissing more liberal theology as a 'sugary, romantic, cosy religion, suitable to match the Welfare State.'[45]

The post-war period was one of change and consolidation in his life. In January 1952, to the surprise of his colleagues, Powell – who had given all the appearances of being a confirmed bachelor – married Pamela Wilson, the daughter of an Indian army Lt-Colonel. In May of the following year his mother died after a long illness. In 1954 his first daughter was born and at Christmas a year later his father died. Powell ceased to write his poetry. What had been a compulsive need to express his feelings vanished: 'One cannot be content just to answer: "It stopped".... The vision, once experienced, cannot be dismissed. If there was a river, the river went underground; but underground it must have been flowing still. The metaphor helps.'[46] His need to 'cry out' was to resurface in his nationalist politics: 'The words, and the compulsion to utter them, are drawn, I suspect, from the same source, though long since hidden underground, as the poetry.'[47] But it was a river that was still meandering across the plains; in the meantime, he was getting on with making a political career for himself. After the victory of the Conservatives in the 1955 General Election, Anthony Eden made Powell Secretary to the Ministry of Housing, where he worked on the 1956 Rent Act. In 1957 Eden resigned and Harold Macmillan emerged as the new Prime Minister. Powell was appointed Financial Secretary to the Treasury, alongside Nigel Birch as Economic Secretary. Peter Thorneycroft was made Chancellor of the Exchequer. The team were the forebearers of economic monetarism. A year later, after serious disagreements with Macmillan over the control of inflation, all three men resigned. Powell had established himself as a rising star who would not let loyalty to the party leadership stand in the way of his principles. Over the next two years, writing in periodicals such as *The Stock Exchange Gazette* and *The Banker*, he developed his monetarist economics. His temperament and upbringing were well-suited to its promotion of the retentive control of the money supply and its moral approbation of the work ethic and thrift.

By 1958, the question of immigration from the colonies and Commonwealth had moved in from the fringes of political debate. The summer had witnessed a series of white pogroms against black immigrants in Notting Hill, Dudley and Nottingham. In the House of Commons, the Tory MP Sir Cyril Osborne demanded immigration controls in order to safeguard the white population from the prospect of a 'chocolate coloured Afro-Asian mixed society'. In the House of Lords, Lord Salisbury called for controls to safeguard the 'English way of life'. Osborne approached Powell for support in organising an anti-immigration group within the Tory Party. Powell declined to give it – but not because he opposed control in principle. In 1956, in his first published comment on immigration, he had distanced himself from the crude bigotry of Osborne. Speaking to the Wolverhampton Branch of the Institute of Personnel Management, Powell defined the problem of immigration as a problem of citizenship. What was needed was a redefinition of citizenship determined by a person's place of birth.[48] It was a language which evaded the old imperial rhetoric of racial inferiority in favour of the incommensurability of cultural differences. To Powell, the origins of the problem of immigration lay in the capitulation of successive governments to the demands of Commonwealth leaders, whose unreasonable demands were epitomised, in his eyes, by the Royal Titles Act of 1953. In 1959, there were 4000 immigrants, mainly rural Jamaicans, living in Wolverhampton; but Powell showed no interest in making an issue out of their presence, prepared to bide his time for the right moment. In the following year, his appointment as Minister of Health coincided with the expansion of the NHS and recruitment of overseas ancillary workers, doctors and nurses. Powell praised their contribution. When the newly formed British Immigration Control Association met him after a meeting held in Wolverhampton, he politely opposed their views.

In 1961 the Conservative Government responded to the anti-immigration campaigners and introduced the Commonwealth Immigrants Bill. It was a half-hearted affair; a number of Ministers were lukewarm in their support and press commentary was unfavourable – *The Times* of 14 November, declared it a 'bad Bill' and for a brief moment the *Daily Express* supported the Labour opposition. But the following year, despite a minority of Tory MPs opposed to it, the Bill became law. It upheld the distinction between citizens of Britain and its colonies and citizens of independent Commonwealth countries. The latter were now subject to immigration control unless they were born in Britain, held passports issued by the British Government, or were included in passports held by persons in either of these two groups. Other Commonwealth citizens seeking to enter Britain were divided into three categories and had to apply for an employment voucher. Category A was for those with a specific job to come to; Category B was for those with a recognisable skill or qualification in short supply. Everyone else came into the last category, C, preference being given to those who had fought in the war. The law served a similar function to the Aliens Act of 1906, introduced to control the entry of Jewish immigrants fleeing persecution in Eastern Europe. Even the most vigorous campaigners for this earlier Bill, had refused to admit in public they were motivated by anti-semitism. English racism had adopted a fastidious manner of denying its prejudices, and supporters of the 1962 law issued similar loud protestations against accusations of racism. Nevertheless, despite their claims to the contrary, the main clauses of the Commonwealth Immigrants Act were designed to control the entry of black Commonwealth citizens into Britain .[49]

Powell's reticence about publicly articulating an anti-immigration politics began to change in 1963. Macmillan, his health bad, had resigned and Alec Home, in a Machiavellian series of manoeuvres, had beaten 'Rab' Butler to the premiership. Powell, believing Home's behaviour had been corrupt, refused to serve in the cabinet and began to distance himself from the Party hierarchy. In July, he served notice on the political orthodoxies of the party leadership. He told an audience in Bromsgrove that an era was passing and it was time for the Conservatives to reassert themselves as the party of free market capitalism.[50] In April 1964 his three articles appeared in *The Times*, advocating the centrality of the market, attacking the economics of the welfare state and calling for the privatisation of the nationalised industries (see p123). At stake was the soul of the Conservative Party and the future of the nation:

> Tacitly almost, the Conservatives had agreed to drop their distinctive badge: you can almost feel them wince when they sing 'Land of Hope and Glory' at the Albert Hall. It hurts more than the union jack in which the speaker's table at meetings of the faithful always has to be swathed. It hurts- and pain is a symptom of something still amiss.

Powell was preparing to go over the heads of the Tory leadership, making a political turn to his own petit bourgeois values of patriotism, economic self-sufficiency and hard work. Nationalism was the ideological cement which would bond these values into a cross-class appeal to 'the people'.[51] On 22 April, in a speech to the Royal Society of St George, he proclaimed his vision of England.[52] The power and the glory of the empire had gone, but in the midsts of the 'blackened ruins' there remained; 'like one of her own oak trees, standing and growing, the sap still rising from her ancient roots to meet the spring, England herself.' It was the task of his generation to reclaim their English heritage, to rediscover that earlier generation of Englishmen who had lived before the 'expansion of England', and had been untainted by empire. In language reminiscent of his most bathetic poetry, Powell led his audience back to the 'brash adventurous days of the first Elizabeth': 'there at last we find them ... in many a village church, beneath the tall tracery of a perpendicular East window and the coffered ceiling of the chantry chapel.' He asks these imaginary Englishmen a rhetorical question:

Tell us what it is that binds us together; show us the clue that leads through a thousand years; whisper to us the secret of this charmed life of England, that we in our time may know how to hold it fast.'
What would they say? (p145)

His own answer lapses into pastoral excess:

They would tell us of that marvellous land, so sweetly mixed of opposites in climate that all the seasons of the year appear there in their greatest perfection; of the fields amid which they built their halls, their cottages, their churches, and where the same blackthorn showered its petals upon them as upon us (p145)

This sentimental, rustic wonderland is embodied in three enduring principles of Englishness; its unity under the Crown in Parliament, its historical continuity and its racial homogeneity. The political institutions of England have evolved out of this pastoral idyll, like works of nature.

The deepest instinct of the Englishman – how that word 'instinct' keeps forcing itself in again and again! – is for continuity; he never acts more freely nor innovates more boldly than when he most is conscious of conserving or even of reacting.

From this continuous life of a united people in its island home spring, as from the soil of England, all that is peculiar in the gifts and the achievements of the English nation (p145)

And what binds and symbolises this 'continuous life' is the 'English kingship'. This, Powell declares, is England's unalterable truth which no 'Hanoverian' or 'Headships of Commonwealths' can undermine.

Powell had embarked upon his version of Britain's island story; narrativising 'the people' into a renewed 'corporate identity' of 'The Nation'. In a speech in Dublin, on 13 November, he argued that such stories and myths were essential to the meaning of nationhood: 'All history is myth. It is a pattern which men weave out of the materials of the past . . . what I am saying is that a nation lives by its myths. . . The greatest task of the statesman therefore is to offer his people good myths and to save them from harmful myths.'[53] Good myths represent the corporate imagination of the people and form the essence of their well-being:

As with individuals, so it is with that mysterious composite being, the
nation: or – to speak less figuratively and more accurately – as it is with
individuals in their personal lives, looking inward, so it is with them in
their corporate lives, when, looking outward, they see themselves as a
larger entity, and feel in their own persons the ups and downs of fortune,
the hopes and fears, the regrets and aspirations, which they attribute by
an act of imagination to the nation, as though it were a sentient, living
being (p136)

This myth of nation parallels Powell's own personal quest for a corporate identity and his compulsive need to idealise the object of his identification. 'Old England' – 'sentient and living' – is 'the timeless
contentment' of maternal love he yearns for. Powell's island story is the
product of his search for symbolic equivalents of this love, an attempt
to secure his precarious hold over it and establish a language which
might speak of his own longing and despair. This internal narrative
immures his imaginary nation in a golden age which will come again.
The more his Messianic narrative evokes the panacea of a golden age,
the more impossible becomes its closure around a future moment of
national self-becoming. Because it is the projection of a wish for a plenitude which has never existed, it can never be actualised and it continuously deconstructs the historical and racial continuity it is supposed
to promote. The future is collapsed into a nostalgic longing for a mythical past and breeds an irrational politics of struggle and reaction which
can never realise its ends. In danger of becoming a narrative of self-
immolation it must translate its pursuit of its idealised object into an
attack on imaginary enemies who thwart its rebirth.

On 10 October, in the *Wolverhampton Express and Star*, Powell
identified the enemies of 'Old England':

> No doubt, like other groups, the immigrants will often wish to retain for
> a long time some of their distinctive customs and beliefs; but the idea of
> them as an unassimilated element of our society, living apart in certain
> districts and following only certain occupations, is insupportable.

His description of immigration adopted two critical images which were
to become persistent features of his anti-immigration speeches.[54] The
first was a fixation on numbers:

> In 1963, the only complete calender year since control came into force,
> there was a net admission of 50,000 coloured immigrants. Surely no one

can imagine that, with a million already here, this country is capable of assimilating a further twenty million coloured immigrants every twenty years.

The second was his fear of their concentration into small, unassimilable areas – 'It is the ten per cent and more of the considerable areas of population which present the real problem.' His language evokes an image of potentially endless, teeming fragments which enter the 'sentient, living being' of England, coagulating and hardening into nuggets which block and threaten her instinctual life. In his essay on paranoia, Freud argued that an individual's internal conceptions of reality can be suppressed and distorted and enter consciousness as external perceptions.[55] Powell's twin imagery of invasive fragments and unassimilable lumps are the representations of his own infantile defence mechanisms against the dread of his mother's absence. If such a feeling of dread is too great for the infant's immature ego to contain, it is attacked and broken into pieces. Such a predicament has, if any, only the rudiments of linguistic representation. Consciousness of the reality of her absence has been denied and repressed, but it remains a psychical reality. The fragmented sounds and images that constitute the only mental representations of this predicament in the boy's psyche return him always to that wordless non-signifiable dread. He is fated: without separation there can be no language and without language there can be no resolution to this predicament. The black and Asian immigrants who had once constituted the anonymous, passive backdrop to Powell's idealisation of empire, and who, through his splitting and projection became the persecutory cause of the loss of his loved empire, have now come to symbolise the return of the repressed. Fragments which coalesce into that life-denying, unassimilable emptiness.

In October 1964, Labour narrowly won the General Election and Harold Wilson became Prime Minister. Despite the successful racist campaign fought by the Tory candidate Peter Griffiths in nearby Smethwick, Powell's election references to immigration were mild. Race was now becoming a significant public, political issue in the country. In January 1965 the annual report of the Medical Officer for Health for West Bromwich noted the high birth rate amongst immigrants. It followed on from the 1963 annual report made by Dr Galloway, the Medical Officer of Health for Wolverhampton, which claimed that Commonwealth immigrants had produced 22.7 per cent of all births and 30.4 per cent of hospital confinements.[56] The Labour government, reversing its previous liberalism, signalled its support for tighter restrictions on immigration with a white paper on 'Immigration from the Commonwealth'. The 1962 law had exempted a large number of East African Asians from immigration control and they now began to arrive in Britain, creating a focus for the growing racial antagonism. On 3 February, Alec Home, Leader of the Opposition, called for tighter immigration controls, assisted repatriation and the vigorous pursuit of illegal immigrants. Two days later, Sir Cyril Osborne placed a motion on the order paper in the House of Commons calling for the banning of all future immigration. One hundred and sixty two Conservative MPs, including Powell, supported him.

In March, a group of Wolverhampton councillors met with Powell to bring his attention to the medical reports and to register their fear that white people in the Midlands could become a racial minority. On 21 May, Powell ended his reluctance to speak out on immigration. In a speech to the women's branch of his constituency association he warned of the threat posed by the birth rates of resident immigrants. This new outspokenness was probably linked to the coming election for a new Conservative leader. Three men were seeking to replace Home: Edward Heath, Reginald Maudling and Powell himself. A firm stand against immigration could win him votes from the right wing of the Party. On 21 July the results brought a conclusive victory to Heath; Powell only managed fifteen votes. His growing authority within the Party had been severely dented; but despite this, Heath made him Shadow Secretary of State for Defence. For the next two years, Powell maintained a low level but persistent interest in the politics of immigration. Then, in early 1968, the Labour government introduced the second Commonwealth Immigrants Act, designed to limit the numbers of East African Asians entering Britain to 1500 annually. On 9 February, in a speech to the Walsall Conservatives, Powell launched a vehement attack against the Government's immigration policies. The tenor of his rhetoric had undergone a dramatic change; it sounded personal.

> There is a sense of hopelessness which comes over people who are trapped or imprisoned, when all their efforts to attract attention and assistance bring no response. This is the kind of feeling which you in Walsall and we in Wolverhampton are experiencing in the face of the continued flow of immigrants into our towns.[57]

Meanwhile, the liberal Home Secretary, Roy Jenkins had introduced the Race Relations Bill. Powell had been inundated with letters of support after the publicity of his Walsall speech and he was anxious to try another, more potent anti-immigration speech. There was now a growing rift between himself and Edward Heath and, following in the footsteps of his forebear, Joseph Chamberlain, he wanted to build himself a Midlands, power base. The Shadow Cabinet met on 11 April to discuss the Bill and race relations and immigration in general. Powell was due to give a speech in Birmingham, to the West Midlands Area Conservative Political Centre on 20 April. He left the meeting assured that what he planned to say was consistent with party policy.

There were only 85 people in the audience, but the Birmingham speech was headline news the following morning. It transformed Powell from an interesting politician of the Tory Right into a national figure. His erstwhile colleague, the MP Angus Maude, described it as 'a sensation unparalleled in modern British political history... With a single entrance last April, Mr Powell succeeded in upstaging all the leading politicians of the day, and he has remained ever since firmly up-centre with the limelight full on him.'[58] Powell was probably correct in his belief that his speech fell within the accepted policies of the Conservative Party. What created the furore was its tone of unrepentant rage. Having begun in a sober vein he quickly adopted a personalised style.[59]

> A week or two ago I fell into conversation with a constituent, a middle-aged, quite ordinary working man employed in one of our nationalised industries. After a sentence or two about the weather, he suddenly said: 'If I had the money to go, I wouldn't stay in this country.' I made some deprecatory reply, to the effect that even this government wouldn't last forever; but he took no notice, and continued: 'I have three children, all of them been through grammar school and two of them married now, with family. I shan't be satisfied till I have seen them settled overseas. In this country in fifteen or twenty years' time the black man will have the whip hand over the white man' (p129-30).

With a rhetorical flourish, Powell had conjured up the archetypal 'Englishman' of the skilled working class – a class fraction who were on the cusp of transforming British politics with their turn to Conservatism in the 1970s. It was they, not he, who had identified the problem of immigration. It was his duty to speak out for them – 'I simply do not have the right to shrug my shoulders and think of something else.' Powell extrapolated current numbers of immigrants to claim that by the year 2000 there would be, 'in the region of 5-7 million – whole areas, towns and parts of towns across England will be occupied by different sections of the immigrant and immigrant descended population.' What had to be done, he claimed, was official Conservative Party policy, was to stop the 'inflow' and promote ' the maximum outflow'.

> It almost passes belief that at this moment twenty or thirty additional immigrant children are arriving from overseas in Wolverhampton alone every week – and that means fifteen or twenty additional families of a decade or two hence... It is like watching a nation busily engaged in heaping up its own funeral pyre (p131)

Powell then turned to the impact of immigration on the white English population: 'For reasons which they could not comprehend ... they found themselves made strangers in their own country.' And, with a liberal interpretation of the two Midlands medical reports, themselves of dubious integrity, he claimed: 'They found their wives unable to obtain hospital beds and their children unable to obtain school places, their homes and neighbourhoods changed beyond recognition, their plans and prospects for the future defeated.'

But, worse still, the white Englishman found himself a persecuted minority in his own land. People were afraid to speak out:

> what surprised and alarmed me was the high proportion of ordinary, decent, sensible people, writing a rational and often well-educated letter, who believed that they had to omit their address because it was dangerous to have committed themselves to paper to a Member of Parliament agreeing with their views I had expressed, and that they would risk either penalties or reprisals if they were known to have done so (p134).

Finally, Powell challenged political liberalism: 'integration' of New Commonwealth immigrants was a 'dangerous delusion'. They would never give up their cultural heritages. But more than this, there was a growing force acting against integration: 'vested interests in the preservation and sharpening of racial and religious differences, with a view to the exercise of actual domination, first over fellow-immigrants and then over the rest of the population.' This was the true source of the problem – the liberal establishment, the politicians and journalists and intellectuals who had abrogated their duty to uphold the integrity of the nation, the welfare professionals who were promoting the language of multiculturalism and the Race Relations Bill – 'the very pabulum they need to flourish'. Powell's underground river carrying the language of his unfulfilled longings had reached its apocalyptic full flood: 'As I look ahead, I am filled with foreboding. Like the Roman, I seem to see 'the River Tiber foaming with much blood'.

The following day, Powell, who claimed to be taken completely by surprise at the turn of events, was the subject of blanket press coverage. Heath immediately sacked him from the shadow cabinet and the majority of the press and political commentators heaped opprobrium on his head. In the Monday edition of *The Times* , the editorial was headed, 'An Evil Speech'. The Conservative MP Humphry Berkeley accused Powell of being a new Oswald Mosley (something he later retracted in his biography of Powell). The *Spectator* carried an attack on Powell by Auberon Waugh, who made the perceptive comment that what had upset the political establishment more than his racial language, was his refusal to play the game; 'the prophet has not been behaving like a gentleman.'[60] Powell had destroyed his chances of ever rising in the Conservative Party, but he had succeeded in establishing himself as a spokesman for 'the people'. On Monday morning, 45,000 letters arrived at his London home. Within days he had received 100,000 letters. Overwhelming in their support, they came from people of all classes. Only a small minority employed a language of racist abuse. The majority emphasised the cultural incommensurability of New Commonwealth immigrants and the threat this posed to their national identity. For example:

> No Briton wants to see his traditional way of living, the country he has loved and fought for, lose its identity, and particular character through the over great acceptance of too many peoples of quite different cultures and ways of life.[61]

Both the *Daily Express* and the *News of the World*, with a combined readership of 11.3 million, had supported him. On 23 April, meat porters at Smithfield market struck in sympathy with Powell. In the afternoon, thousands of London dockworkers marched on Parliament demanding 'free speech' for Powell and an end to his victimisation. A delegation of dockworkers emerging from a meeting with him, told the waiting press; 'it made us proud to be British.'[62]

Powell now believed himself a tribune of the people. On 16 November, in a speech to the Bournemouth Rotary Club, he declared that his Birmingham speech had; 'revealed a deep and dangerous gulf in the nation . . . a gulf between the overwhelming majority of the people throughout the country on the one side, and on the other side a tiny minority with almost a monopoly hold upon the channels of communication, who seem determined . . . to blind both themselves and others.'[63] Few on the Left could make sense of this new phenomenon of Powellism. The standard commentary was to dismiss him as an 'unbalanced' and 'dangerous' demagogue. But Tom Nairn, in an incisive analysis, published in *New Left Review* in 1970, recognised Powellism as 'a preliminary ground breaking exercise', presaging a potential new phase of authoritarian government.[64] Even he could not foresee Margaret Thatcher's historic routing of the Left in 1979. It was one of the intellectual architects of the coming, right wing hegemony, the historian, Maurice Cowling, who understood Powellism as the first major assault on Britain's post war, welfare consensus. Writing in the Personal Column of The *Spectator*, he identified the main target as the permissive, metropolitan, liberal intelligentsia. Powellism represented; 'the struggle to destroy the insufferable moral condescension characteristic of certain sections of the British ruling elite when it addresses the English people.'[65]

On 18 May, 1970, Harold Wilson announced a General Election. During the election campaign Powell was at the height of his political influence. On 13 June, in a speech in Northfield, Birmingham, he declared that Britain was under attack from an enemy within. The enemy was manifested in terroristic students, demonstrators, the Civil Rights Movement in Northern Ireland , but most of all in race.

> The exploitation of what is called 'race' is a common factor which links the operations of the enemy on several different fronts . . . 'Race' is billed to play a major, perhaps a decisive, part in the battle of Britain, whose enemies must have been unable to believe their good fortune as they watched the numbers of West Indians, Africans, and Asians concentrated in her major cities mount toward the two million mark.[66]

It was a speech of paranoid delusions and a contempt for notions of fairness and justice, and democratic politics generally. To Powell, these were merely ruses employed by a minority, whose 'devilish' techniques of media control and brainwashing had rendered the majority passive and helpless, abandoning England to those who hated her. Answerable to nobody but himself, he pulled British politics in his direction. The Conservatives won an unexpected victory in the election. For Maurice Cowling, Powell played a decisive part by drawing in new classes of support and changing the climate of opinion.[67] The Conservatives had promised there would be 'no further large-scale permanent immigration'. In 1971, they introduced the Immigration Act confining the right of abode to citizens of Britain and the colonies who were patrials. The new Act scrapped the old system of vouchers. Anyone who was not a patrial had to obtain a work permit which could be renewed annually, effectively turning them into migrant labourers. At the same time, by qualifying the notion of citizenship to place of parental and grandparental birth, the Act progressively took away the right of black Commonwealth immigrants to settle in Britain. When the Thatcher Government, elected in 1979, introduced the 1981 British Nationality Act, the Conservatives cemented the racially discriminatory immigrations laws into a new definition of citizenship. Powell's loathed 1948 Nationality Act was finally buried.

Powell's political legacy is similar to the underground stream of his metaphor. It continues to flow, quietly, unobtrusively, its adherents content not to make too public a show of their political debt to a man who went beyond the pale.[68] To end, I want to return to a key image in Powell's 'rivers of blood' speech. He has just described how the white English are becoming a persecuted people in their own land. He chooses one illustration. It is a letter written to him by a woman in Northumberland, concerning an elderly woman who is living in his constituency.

Eight years ago in a respectable street in Wolverhampton a house was sold to a negro. Now only one white (a woman old-age pensioner) lives there. This is her story. She lost her husband and both her sons in the war. So she turned her seven-roomed house, her only asset, into a boarding house. She worked hard and did well, paid off her mortgage and began to put something by for her old age. Then the immigrants moved in. With growing fear, she saw one house after another taken over. The quiet street became a place of noise and confusion. Regretfully, her white tenants moved out.

The day after the last one left, she was awakened at 7am by two negroes who wanted to use her phone to contact their employer. When she refused, as she would have refused any stranger at that hour, she was abused and feared she would have been attacked but for the chain on the door. . . She is becoming afraid to go out. Windows are broken. She finds excreta pushed through her letterbox. When she goes to the shops, she is followed by children, charming, wide-grinning piccaninnies. They cannot speak English, but one word they know. 'Racialist', they chant. When the new Race Relations Bill is passed, this woman is convinced she will go to prison (p134-135).

Questioned about the veracity of this story, Powell has never produced the letter as evidence.[69] Whether a figment of his or someone else's imagination, this is Powell's island story – the imperial 'black peril' brought home. A white mother, his mother, the signifier of all her son's unfulfilled longings, besieged by black males, persecuted, her life slowly being extinguished. Racial difference confronts him with the paranoia that he will lose his precarious hold on the maternal object. His concern is narcissistic if he allows the maternal object to die, his own sense of aliveness will whither. The son must save his mother/nation, even at the risk of his own life. If he is fated never to leave her, then he must be prepared to defend her, for she holds the key to his life; in the end all he can do is die for her.

Notes

1 Quote from frontispiece to Wilfred Thesiger (1984), *Arabian Sands*, Penguin.
2 Enoch Powell (1959), 'Escape to the Void' in *National and English Review*, December issue, p.199-200.
3 Andrew Roth, (1970), *Enoch Powell Tory Tribune*, Macdonald, p.7.
4 Terry Coleman, *The Guardian*, Aug. 27th, 1994.
5 Michael Strachan (1952) 'Educating the Professor', *Blackwood's Magazine*, February issue.
6 Berkeley, p.128.
7 Patrick Cosgrave (1989), *The Lives of Enoch Powell*, The Bodley Head, p.81.
8 Cosgrave, p.87.
9 Roth, p.41.
10 Berkeley, p.51.
11 *Ibid.*, p.52.

12 Enoch Powell (date not known), 'The Empire of England' in *Tradition and Change Nine Oxford Lectures*, Conservative Research Department, p.49.

13 *Ibid.*, p.53.

14 Quote taken from Cosgrave, p.59.

15 Enoch Powell (1968), 'Imperial Sickness', the *Spectator*, 13 September. Review of Colin Cross, *The Fall of the British Empire, 1914-1968*, Hodder and Stoughton.

16 The full text of the April 20th, Birmingham speech is in Berkeley, p.129-137.

17 Howard Pedraza (1986), *Winston Churchill and Enoch Powell*, London, p.81.

18 Roth, p.12.

19 Cosgrave, p.31.

20 *Ibid.*, p.37.

21 Roth, p.11.

22 Cosgrave, p.37.

23 Roth, p.12.

24 Cosgrave, p.43.

25 Roth, p.18.

26 Enoch Powell (1986), in Alvilde Lees-Milne and Derry Moore, eds. *The Englishman's Room*, Viking, p.118-121.

27 Pedraza, p.81.

28 Enoch Powell (date not known), 'A Personal Recollection of A.E. Housman', *Housman Society Journal*, Vol. 1, p.27.

29 From poem LI of 'A Shropshire Lad', by A.E. Housman.

30 Enoch Powell (1990), 'A.E. Housman' in *Housman Society Journal*, Vol.16, p.48.

31 *Ibid.*, p.49.

32 Enoch Powell (1962) 'Thin but Thorough' in *The Times*, 27 September.

33 Roth, p.17.

34 Roy Lewis (1979), *Enoch Powell Principle in Politics*, Cassell, p.15.

35 Melanie Klein (1946), 'Notes on Some Schizoid Mechanisms' in Juliet Mitchell, ed. *The Selected Melanie Klein*, p.182.

36 Sigmund Freud (1921), 'Group Psychology and the Analysis of the Ego' in *PFL*, Vol.12, p.137.

37 Roth, p.24.

38 *Ibid.*

39 Cosgrave, p.53.

40 Enoch Powell (1990), 'Foreword' to *Collected Poems*, Bellew Publishing, p.vii.

41 Powell made these comments in Sue Lawley in Radio 4's *Desert Island Discs* in the mid-1980s.

42 Powell (1990), p.ix-x.

43 Berkeley, p.32.

44 *Ibid.*, p.32-33.

45 *Ibid.*, p.37.

46 Powell (1990), p.191.

47 *Ibid.*, p.191-192.

48 Paul Foot (1969), *The Rise of Enoch Powell*, Penguin, p.32-33.

49 See John Solomos (1993), *Race and Racism in Britain*, Macmillan.

50 See John Wood (1965), *A Nation Not Afraid The Thinking of Enoch Powell*, Hodder and Stoughton, p.24-29.

51 As with so many of Powell's varying political loyalties and identities, his shift to populism involved the idealisation of an object or person. In 1977, Powell's biographical study; Joseph Chamberlain was published (Thames and Hudson). His political manoeuvring follows a remarkably similar pattern to Chamberlain's career and suggests that he emulated the myth of the heroic outsider who sought political power by appealing to the people over the heads of corrupted party machines. Powell's subsequent resignation from the Tory Party over their pro-European politics in 1974 and his appeal to voters to support Labour can be partly explained by Chamberlain's own behaviour – 'Three times . . . he was the agent of defeat and even of destruction to the political party in which he lived and worked.' (p.151)

52 John Wood. *op.cit.*, pp.143-146.

53 *Ibid.*, p.136-143.

54 For example, see Powell's speech in Wolverhampton on 11 June, 1970 which is consumed with his concern over numbers and their concentration: 'So – number is of the essence, and geographical concentration is of the essence, and each multiplies the effect of the other.' John Wood, (ed) (1971), *Powell and the 1970 Election*, Elliot Right Way Books, 1971, p.101.) Powell described the consequence of this effect to a public meeting of the Hampshire Monday Club in Southampton on 9 April, 1976. 'The nation has been, and is still being, eroded and hollowed out from within by the implantation of large unassimilated and unassimilable populations – what Lord Radcliffe once in a memorable phrase called 'alien wedges' – in the heartland of the state.' Richard Ritchie, (ed), *A Nation or No Nation? Enoch Powell*, Elliot Right Way Books, 1978. In the 27 September issue of the *Spectator*, 1968, Quintin Hogg, MP took issue with Powell's use of numbers, quoting T.E. Utley's *Enoch Powell: The Man and his Thinking*,

William Kimber. See also, Paul Foot 1969.
55 S Freud, (1911c[1910]), 'Psycho-Analytic Notes on an Autobiographical Account of a Case of Paranoia (Dementia Paranoides)', *PFL*, Vol.9.
56 See Paul Foot *op.cit.*.
57 Cosgrave, p.242.
58 Angus Maude MP (1968), 'Enoch Declares War' in the *Spectator*, 22 November.
59 Berkeley, p.129-137.
60 Auberon Waugh (1968), 'Black Powell' in the *Spectator*, 26 April.
61 See Diana Spearman (1968), 'Enoch Powell's Postbag' in *New Society*, 9 May. Also see Diana Spearman (1971), 'Enoch Powell's Election Letters' in John Wood (ed), *Powell and the 1970 Election*, *op.cit.*.
62 C.C. Aronsfeld (Circa 1970), 'Challenge to Socialist brotherhood British dockworkers and coloured immigrants' in *Patterns of Prejudice*, Institute of Jewish Affairs, Vol. 2, No.4, July Aug.
63 Text of the Speech appears in Enoch Powell (1969), *Freedom and Reality*, B.T. Batsford Ltd.
64 Tom Nairn (1970), 'Enoch Powell: the New Right' in *New Left Review*, No.61, May-June.
65 Maurice Cowling (1968), 'There's been a revolution here, too.' in the *Spectator*, 24 May. For a discussion of Cowling and the Peterhouse New Right and their relationship to Enoch Powell see Gill Seidel (1988), 'Culture, Nation and 'Race' in the British and French New Right' in *The Ideology of the New Right*, Ruth Levitas (ed), Polity Press.
66 The full text of the speech is reprinted in John Wood, (ed), (1971), *Powell and the 1970 Election*, Elliot Right Way Books, p.104-112.
67 Maurice Cowling (1971), 'Mr Powell, Mr Heath, and the Future' in John Woods, *ibid*.
68 In 1993, Powell gave the third Ian Gow Memorial Speech to a little known organisation called the Friends of the Union, a group of right-wing intellectuals dedicated to the preservation of the Union and who operate in a similar fashion to the prewar Round Table organisation *The Guardian*, 4 February, 1995). In recent years a number of right-wing historians have adopted a Powellite, nationalist interpretation of postwar British geopolitics. Two in particular herald an attempt to assert a right-wing hegemony over the history of post war Britain: John Charmley in *Churchill's Grand Alliance: The Anglo-American Special Relationship, 1940-57*, 1995, and Andrew Roberts in *Eminent Churchillians*, 1994. This right wing intellectual offensive parallels the fortunes of the Tory right, and its future within the Conservative Party hangs in the balance. In the 1995 Conservative

Party leadership election, Roberts (a principal member of Friends of the Union) was a close aide and spokesman for John Redwood. Another Powellite connection to the leadership contest was Greville Howard, Powell's personal assistant from 1968 to 1972 , who made his house available to Michael Portillo as a campaign HQ (*The Guardian*, 3 July, 1995). Powell's official biography, in the hands of Simon Heffer, will reflect the perceptions of right wing Conservatism. But there has also begun a wider rehabilitation of his reputation. Robert Shephard, whose previous biography of Iain Macleod gave intellectual weight to the more liberal wing of the Conservative Party has produced a biography of Enoch Powell, published in 1996 (Hutchinson). As Powell nears the end of his life, there will be, no doubt, an attempt to construct him as the great statesman we never had.

69 See Paul Foot *op.cit.*

6

MR NICE (AND MR NASTY)

The Mr Nice and Mr Nasty of the title are the two archetypal responses of white men to racial difference. This final chapter brings me to contemporary Britain and to the ways in which white middle class men's masculinities are shaped by English ethnicity and the legacy of empire. In particular I want to focus on white men's relationship to black men, a relationship which is a potent source of white racial antagonism and fear and which is closely connected to men's uncertainties about their gender roles and identities.

In 1994, the film production company 'Working Title' launched its low budget film, *Four Weddings and a Funeral*. Despite the lack of critical acclaim, it was a popular success in the US and Britain, and a vehicle for a new, unlikely, English hero. The film transformed Hugh Grant from a nice, middle class boy into an ambassador of English manliness. His swept back hair, his good looks and his image of harmless, bumbling, repressed ex-public school boy had a remarkable resemblance to that other doyen of mythologised homoerotic boyishness, Rupert Brooke. Grant was well aware of the Edwardian origins of his own particular appeal.

> They love me in Japan. But unfortunately I don't want their love. I want their money. I was cooking up schemes to try and get it. I thought I might write some sensitive poetry because they all think I'm sensitive and poetic [and publish it] with a nice big picture of me perhaps dressed as Rupert Brooke on the front.[1]

Unlike the muscle bound action heroes of Hollywood who had dominated popular cinema in the 1980s, Grant's appeal lay in his understated masculinity; his slender body, his Bermuda shorts and unathletic legs. Despite, or perhaps because of, his ineptitude in love, women were sympathetic to him. As he mumbled and fumbled beneath the cool and appraising gaze of his co-star, Andie MacDowell, English manliness found its renaissance in a compliant, self-deprecating boyishness. *Four Weddings and a Funeral* is all about a man too nice to be manly.

Grant plays Charles, who along with his upper-middle class circle of friends, is a frequent attender of posh weddings. Saturday mornings appear as an endless ritual of oversleeping and late arrivals at weddings located in pastoral landscapes and wealthy London venues. The weddings symbolise the cultural reproduction of an English, *haute bourgeois* way of life. Whether in Somerset, London or the Highlands of Scotland, the rituals of conjugation are associated with the symbols and landscapes of the British Union: sexual reproduction and patrimony are closely entwined with a sense of place and nation. The problem for Charles is that he has never attended his own wedding; his personal crisis is his inability to connect with the right women and find true love. Charles, as the saying goes in the film, is a serial monogamist who cannot make the commitment of marriage and so cannot inherit his place in a patrilineal culture. The film's celebration of marriage and its associated culture of grand houses, gardens and pastoral scenery is an attempt to recover a one nation Toryism; an image of England as muddled, romantic and at ease with itself. Through Charles' emotional incompetence and eventual success in love, it seeks to allay the sexual insecurities of an English middle-class masculinity, offering the prospect of success in the pursuit of that elusive quality, manliness. Being nice and sensitive will pay the dividend of a woman and patrimony.

Hugh Grant epitomises a masculinity which has adopted the social tactics of niceness, compliance and liberal tolerance in response to the rising aspirations and assertiveness of women. Both in his public persona and in his fictional character of Charles, his hesitant speech and self-effacement appear to leave him incapable of asserting himself. But this foppish play-acting is designed to preserve his narcissism. In *Four Weddings*, Charles' pursuit of true love is a quest for his masculine and heterosexual prowess in marriage. However, confirmation of his manliness has been continually thwarted by a heterosexual world where true love appears to be lacking. In the end of course, he commits himself to leading lady Carrie. Weddings, masculinity, heterosexual union and the English way of life, all appear to be confirmed as they kiss beneath an umbrella and the credits roll. But the film leaves behind a frisson of instability in this representation of male heterosexual love. In spite of its preoccupation with marriage, it is the relationship of

Charles' two gay friends, Gareth and Matthew, which embodies true love. Both men are assimilated into the heterosexual culture of weddings and appear at first to be tokens of the film's liberalism. In spite of the ideal they symbolise, their relationship exists outside the symbolic and legal structures of patrimony. In this respect they offer neither a threat nor a viable alternative to the happy ending. But the significance of their relationship in the film destabilises its conventional narrative of romance. Their love for one another reflects the unresolved sexual insecurities of heterosexual men and their ambivalence toward women.

Gareth's demise from a heart attack precipitates the funeral of the film's title. Unlike the idyllic surrounds of the weddings, it takes place in an industrial area, close to his working-class, childhood home. While the various heterosexual unions are in symbolic locations of nationhood and its continuity, homosexuality is located 'outside'. The funeral is markedly different from the exclusive upper-class ambience of the weddings: the camera lingers on young gay men and one young black man, as well as older white working-class men and women. This representation of difference defines homosexual love as tolerated but extraneous to 'England'. It cannot be allowed representation or public recognition in a wedding. Instead it is expressed in terms of a profound sense of loss. After the funeral, Charles walks with Tom, the film's dimwit aristocrat, who admits that the only true love in his life was a dog he once owned. Charles doubts he will ever find love at all. Both acknowledge Gareth and Matthew as role models of men who can love. This is Charles's dilemma. What he desires to emulate is the antithesis of the English heterosexual manliness he aspires to. He gives expression to that recurring difficulty of upper and middle class, heterosexual Englishmen – loving women. Women are necessary to confirm a man's masculinity and to continue the patrilineal culture of the nation. But the film's representation of homosexual love as something lost suggests that Charles must renounce the homoerotic origins of his desire. He succeeds in securing a woman through the efficacy of sensitivity and niceness. But the doubt remains that what he was loving was more his own desire (for himself, for other men) than a woman.

The significance of *Four Weddings and a Funeral* is not its celebration of Englishness, but what it reveals about the loose threads in the fabric of English male heterosexuality and ethnicity. Its insistent celebration of the niceness and compliance of its hero and his culture of weddings only serves to highlight the contemporary crisis in the relationship of middle-class masculinities to marriage, home and family. During the 1990s there has been an increasing willingness amongst liberal middle-class men to reject the benign masculinity associated with the New Man and to re-assert their personal and political interests against those of women.

Behind the painted smile

In the post-feminist era of the 1990s, there has been a growing disaffection amongst middle-class men with the ideal of sexual equality. The massive expansion of part-time jobs for women and the pattern of women divorcing men, have created a new wave of doubt and uncertainty in men's private lives. Organisations like 'Families need Fathers', campaigning against the divorce laws and for men's right to custody of their children, had already carved out a political space for a men's anti-feminist politics during the 1980s. Middle class men began to experience a relative loss in their social prestige and economic status. An era of economic insecurity has been precipitated by globalisation, technology driven job losses and economic recession. Careers are being superseded by short-term contracts, freelancing, part-time work and piecework at home. For growing numbers in full-time employment, conditions of work are too insecure and idiosyncratic to be called jobs. Throughout the golden age of post-war consumer capitalism, full-time, tenured employment underpinned the middle-class nuclear family and its twenty-five year mortgage. By the year 2000 it will have become a minority form of work.[2] In apparent contradiction to this trend, negative equity and falling salaries have propelled men into working longer hours. The impact of this new work order on a generation of thirty and forty something men, who inherited their fathers' expectations of a career for life, threatens to undermine their role of head of household. At the same time it is destroying work as the principle source of their masculine self-esteem and personal integrity.

The decline in male jobs has been accompanied by changing masculine sensibilities, as increasing numbers of men invest more time in domestic life and their children. However this turn to the home has served to heighten male insecurity as women's increased independence has led to their greater willingness to leave men. By 1993, two and a half times more divorces were granted to women than to men.[3] It is a state of affairs which led David Thomas to declare in his book *Not*

Guilty: In Defence of the Modern Man: 'The fact is, people are in pain. And right now, the ones who wear trousers and stand up to piss don't seem to count for much when it comes to being healed' (p7). But this notion that men are the new victims has little grounding in social and economic reality. In August 1993, The National Child Development Study, which had been following the lives of 11,500 men and women born in one week in March 1958, presented a report to the annual British Association meeting in Keele. It argued that, 'Marital break-downs are creating a new underclass of women who are trapped in a downward economic spiral.' It added; 'There are few signs that men had metamorphosed into the caring and labour-sharing breed that the media was trumpeting in the early 1990s.'[4] In December 1993 the market research group Mintel published *Women 2000*, a survey of 1500 men and women.[5] It came to similar conclusions. Only one man in a hundred, it claimed, did his 'fair share of the housework'. While two men in ten said they took an equal share in the cooking, only one in ten women thought they did. Over half of the women interviewed had full time jobs, but they were paid, on average, 29 per cent less than men in comparable jobs and were significantly less likely to have a company pension. Only 20 per cent of the working women claimed their male partners equally shared any single domestic task. Mintel's consumer manager Angela Hughes told *The Guardian*: 'Men seem to set out with good intentions to share the domestic chores but the catalyst appears to be the arrival of children. At this stage, the man appears to abdicate responsibility for his share, regardless of whether his partner is work-ing.'[6] The surveys indicate that the downturn in men's fortunes are unrelated to any tangible increase in female equality. Men may be doing badly, but women are still worse off.

The most publicised anti-feminist diatribe was published in 1992 by a journalist, Neil Lyndon. His book, *No More Sex War: The failures of feminism*, argued that the women's liberation movement had been 'fundamentally false in logic, thoroughly false in history and poisonous in effect.'[7] Lyndon's career as a spokesman for a male backlash against feminism began with an article in the *Sunday Times Magazine* in 1991. 'It is hard to think,' he declared, 'of one example of systemic and insti-tutionalised discrimination against women in Britain today.' He argued that the liberation of women in the past twenty-five years had been a consequence of the new technologies of contraception and the right to abortion. Feminism had merely served to entrench gender stereotypes and promote antagonism and sex war between men and women. The effect of this revolution on his own life can be gauged by an article written by his wife, Deirdre Lyndon, which appeared in the *Daily Mail* on 21 September, 1992 (reprinted in *The Guardian*, the following day). Her opening sentence – 'This is the book that killed my marriage' – summed up the consequence of what had become her husband's obsessive loathing of feminism: 'I kept urging Neil to temper his arguments. . . "It's not feminists you're attacking," I would say. "Surely it's only militant feminists?" But it became clear that it was indeed all feminists and that, to some extent, the war was indeed being waged on women.' Lyndon moved out of the family home and began a relationship with another woman who had been acting as his part-time secretary. In trying to understand her husband's 'politics of hatred', Deirdre Lyndon suggested he had moved out because 'he needed to shred all the strands of domesticity to write this book.' She added: 'In some ways I think Neil wants to strip women of motherhood.'

Deirdre Lyndon had put her finger on the primary target of anti-feminist rhetoric. Men's confusion over their role in society and feelings of impotence have encouraged the search for a scapegoat in mothers and motherhood. For Lyndon, society's neglect of the needs of men is epitomised in men's exclusion from their own homes and children: 'If our society is a patriarchy, why does it allow no statutory right to paternity leave?'[8] For anti-feminists, the problem men face, and the predicament of society and culture, is the declining authority of the father and the subsequent prevalence of female-led one-parent families. 1992 witnessed the emergence of another symptom: male reaction to the apparent feminisation of society; the 'Wild Men', an import from the US, inspired by Robert Bly's book, *Iron John*. This 'mytho-poetic' men's movement was the first popular development in men's sexual politics since 'Men against Sexism' began in the 1970s. While the latter had taken its inspiration from the Women's Liberation Movement – men rejecting the masculinity of their fathers and embracing their more 'feminine' feelings – the 'Wild Men' were intent upon reclaiming their fathers and their own male potency. The caring and sharing New Man of the mid-1980s, a product of its consumer boom, had reflected the changing sensibilities of post 1960s middle-class masculinities. But for Bly, the archetypal 'soft' man only proved that men had lost touch with their inner virility. Men's waged work outside the home had broken the bond between father and son. Boys raised exclusively by their mothers learnt to see their father through her eyes: 'If the son learns feeling primarily from the mother, then he will probably see his own masculinity from the feminine point of view as well' (p25). According to Bly, modern men are mother's boys. Unable to grow up and relate to women as adults, they become trapped in compliant relationships leaving them feeling powerless and manipulated. The New Man of the 1980s is Bly's 'naive man'. He can be receptive, can feel the other's pain, but he cannot say what he wants, he is too frightened to say 'no'. The 'naive man' has no resolve. Bly argues that beneath his nice exterior is a man full of misogynistic anger.

Bly declares this unmanliness to be a crisis of men's relationship with their fathers: 'Not seeing your father when you are small, never being with him, having a remote father, an absent father, a workaholic father, is an injury' (p31). Abandoned to their mothers, boys do not acquire the self-preservating aggression which sustains the boundaries of selfhood. 'A grown man six feet tall will allow another person to cross his boundaries, enter his psychic house, verbally abuse him, carry away his treasures, and slam the door behind; the invaded man will stand there with an ingratiating, confused smile on his face' (p146). The purpose of the Wild Men movement was to rediscover the father within and tap his power. Groups of men attended weekend gatherings in the countryside, using ritualised dancing, drum banging and male bonding to make cathartic, primeval attempts to harness their 'masculine free spirit'. Despite widespread but mostly sceptical British press interest, Bly's simple assertion that men had a fundamental problem in being men found a ready constituency amongst a middle-class disoriented and demoralised by the new work order and the erosion of traditional masculine certitudes. The journalist Andrew Anthony, attended one gathering. The profile of the one hundred men attending was remarkably homogeneous; 'Aged between late twenties and early fifties, they are all – with only one exception – white, heterosexual, overwhelmingly middle-class, highly educated, articulate and socially aware.'[9] Anthony described the pro-feminist commitments many of the men professed, but noted how little time was spent talking about wives and girlfriends. However, men were not so reticent to talk about their mothers. 'When one fortysomething man confesses his anger at his mother's incessant demeaning of his absent father and half-jokes: "You can't hit a 75-year-old woman, even if she is your mother," the laughter and palpable sense of endorsement is universal and just a little disturbing.'[10]

Bly stressed that blame for men's failure to be manly did not lie with women. The problem lay with fathers not doing their job of parenting.

But the mytho-poetic movement he spawned, focusing on men's feelings of humiliation and shame and seeing these as a consequence of a mother dominated family, inevitably fed into the language of women blaming. In spite of his progressive intentions, Bly provided one impetus for a growing masculine language of complaint, directed at female power and authority in the home. Men's childhood experience of the domestic power of their mothers, refracted by a culture which disparaged male emotional dependency, readily fuelled the rhetoric of anti-feminism amongst otherwise liberal men.

Liberal men and sexual conservatives

Both Lyndon and Thomas are middle-class men whose lives have been shaped by the cultural freedoms and social permissiveness ushered in by the 1960s. They are a part of the revolt of Bly's 'naive man'; reacting against their own niceness and compliance towards women with an aggressive defensiveness which polarises men as victims and women as persecutors. Like Lyndon, Thomas's grievance against feminism is most strongly felt in his discussion about the personal injuries done to divorced and separated fathers denied access to their children – 'Whichever way you roll the dice, the game of parenthood is more viciously loaded against men than the meanest crap shoot in Vegas' (p236). He likens the separation of a child from its father to the crime of rape. On the basis of this rough straw poll he claims that 'coercive sex with an acquaintance . . . is less traumatic than the loss of one's children' (p234). But only rape is a crime: 'Any man who assaults a woman runs the risk of severe punishment under the criminal law. Any woman who denies a man access to his own children runs . . . no risk'(p235). Morgan suggests that this may sound paranoid, but asks us to view his statistical data, which demonstrates that: 'an absolute minimum of 20 per cent of all fathers. . . will be permanently separated from their own flesh and blood' (p236). His willingness to use such an extraordinary and inappropriate analogy is indicative of his animosity toward feminism.

Neil Lyndon traces the cause of his angry reaction to feminism back to his student days in the 1960s: 'I think that modern feminism was rooted in the totalitarian attitudes of the late Sixties when, in its search for a "class enemy", the New Left in America and the rest of the West appropriated the axioms of Black Power about white "honky" culture and applied them to sexual politics.'[11] In his book he locates the origins of the new social movements in the New Left of the 1960s. He argues that the biggest problem faced by the white middle-class student radicals was to identify a class enemy and a revolutionary agent of change. Black Power provided the answer. With the 'bludgeon and cleavers of totalitarianism', it persuaded white students that black people were the revolutionary agents and that white people were the enemy. According to Lyndon, the 'nincompoop generation', eager to prove themselves guilty, happily swallowed this logic. Unable to explain this act of political masochism, he speculates that it assuaged young whites' feelings of exclusion and powerlessness and made a confusing world comprehensible on a personal level. Personal psychology was more manageable than the complex realities of geopolitics, and it provided white students with something concrete to do: they could work on themselves and their relationships to exorcise their racism. Lyndon refutes the idea that feminism invented the term 'the personal is political'. He claims that this 'particular spark of unreason' originated with the Black Panthers. Adopted by the wider white political movement, it ensured the 'instantaneous collapse of liberal principle' and provided the central tenet of the offspring of Black Power and Marxism: feminism.

Lyndon's book has been dismissed as the rantings of an embittered maverick. However, his wild overestimation of the influence of Black Power on the lives of young middle-class whites and his analysis of the new social movements – anti-rational and socially destructive – shares the New Right perspective which began with Enoch Powell and his 1970 speech 'The Enemy Within'. Powell described the enemies of society as multifaceted and potentially everywhere. But he was quite clear on their social origin: they began with the influx of 'Negroes' into the northern states of America, which flung them into the 'furnace of anarchy' and created 'Black Power'. Powell described 'race', as the common factor linking the operations of 'the enemy' on several fronts.[12] 'Race' was the signifier of difference or 'otherness', subsuming the social antagonisms of the youth revolt, women's protest and class conflict under its rubric (see Chapter 4). Powell was emphatic: 'Race' would 'play a major, perhaps a decisive part in the battle of Britain.'[13] Powell's 'enemy within', originating in the culture and politics of African Americans, signified blackness as a threat to white English ethnicity and its way of life. Lyndon has appropriated Powell's argument to legitimise his casting feminism beyond the boundaries of respectable white society. In effect, Lyndon constructs feminism as a metaphorical form of 'blackness'. His anti-feminism redirects Powell's discourse of 'race' to signify an attack on white patrimony; on his own paternal role and manliness. And he has not been alone in doing this. The themes of race, the undermining of fatherhood and the family, and the racial and gendered treachery of the liberal intelligentsia have been the key preoccupations of new right social discourse since the 1980s.

In their introduction to *Family Portraits*, a collection of right-wing essays on the family, Digby Anderson and Graham Dawson identified 'brands of feminism which are deeply hostile to the family, most especially to the role of fathers.'[14] Patricia Morgan's contribution develops this theme. Her essay, 'Feminist Attempts to Sack Father: A case of unfair dismissal', prefigured Lyndon's anti-feminism and echoes the language of Robert Bly, albeit in a different political register. She begins: 'If there is a "war over the family",' then one of its principal battle fronts is whether homes need fathers' (p38). In recent years, she claims, 'fathers have faced not only the dismissal, but a positive denigration of their role. Informed by Marxism feminism and a more thorough-going collectivism, a strong lobby now exists to disestablish men's ties to the family' (p39). She argues that the absence of fathers and exclusive feminine nurture condemn young males to a life of violent crime and underachievement at school. Her political crusade is to defend 'the home', its 'cultural heritage and the "middle class values" which it, and thus the family, is felt to harbour and transmit' (p61). To defend the home, it is necessary to defend the father. He is the principal socialiser and educator of these values and consequently the prime target of the feminist detractors of the family:

> What we can predict with certainty is that any rise in the number of boys without close ties to males with socially acceptable standards of behaviour is the very thing which is virtually guaranteed to generate a brutalised and violent masculine style... Sexual identification is best facilitated in relationships where the father is affectionate, nurturant and extensively participates in child-rearing (p53).

Morgan dismisses the statistics which reveal the paucity of men's involvement in household chores: 'the range of household tasks a father undertakes does not necessarily reflect his involvement with the children ... it becomes quite inappropriate to measure any parental contribution to child-rearing in terms of practical caretaking' (p54). What the father provides is his stabilising role of breadwinner and his ability to maintain and furnish the home; these activities construct the psychological and material parameters of family life and foster a 'more coherent, constructive and responsible world view which itself tends toward higher aspirations, good performance and low criminality' (p 55). The father might not be concretely present for his children, but his formal attachment to the household serves as a transcendental signifier of good order and stability.

Morgan uses her idealised model of paternal participation as a yard-stick to judge lower working-class and black British families whom she sees as sources of social dislocation and disruption. She draws on a study of different ethnic groups in a Midlands town, which revealed a 41 per cent level of paternal absenteeism in families of West Indian origin, as opposed to 7.5 per cent in white families.[15] She is unwilling to explore the cultural, economic and historical reasons for this differen-tial level of female-run households. Instead she infers that black fami-lies in which the father is absent are a primary source of the 'prolifera-tion, diversification and accentuation of violence as an individual and group phenomenon' (p58). A society without fathers, she argues, would degenerate into a state of 'rootlessness – where there are no heritage or ties and people have no place or past, but simply wander about the face of the earth . . . a world without responsibilities in which relationships are thin and transitory' (p60). Her eloquent paranoia about the destruction of a patrilineal society is both racial and gendered in character. For Morgan, the ideological function of the father is to enforce social discipline and to represent the moral, ethical and social foundations of culture; its symbolic law. It is an opinion she has reiter-ated in her 1995 booklet *Farewell to the Family*: 'Fatherhood, that "creation of society", exemplifies the rule-making and rule-following without which no culture is possible'.[16]

The perception of a causal relation between absent fathers, social disorder and the ties of national-racial identity articulated by the New Right in the 1980s, reflected the chronic uncertainties about the mean-ings of English ethnic identity. Paternal authority reaches beyond the realm of gender to embrace the social order as a whole; the Law of the Father is seen to protect the racial continuity and homogeneity of the family and of the nation. Anxieties aroused by the imagined failure of white patrimony create a desire for the reassertion of the symbolic function of the White Father, to guard against miscegenation and to propagate a white ethnic patrilineality. This Law of the Father is expressed by politicians and political commentators in that ubiquitous

and ambiguous phrase, family values. As long as it remains predomi-
nant, white men can aspire to the dream of a patriarchal authority. But
masculinity is an identity built on illusions: white men can never satisfy
the demands of the idealised Father, and because a patriarchal authority is an impossibility white men project their own shameful, patrimo-
nial failure into a racialised contempt for black patrimony. White
masculinity teeters between an abstracted superiority over the black
man, and a sense of its own failed manliness. To achieve some degree of
stability in its identity, white ethnicity and white masculinity projects
its dilemmas onto black people. The fatherless black family becomes a
symbol of social breakdown, and the most potent source of white fear
and desire, the young black man is fantasised as a sexually dangerous
threat to the white familial order.

Racial Difference, Masculinity and Absent Fathers

In the early 1990s this self-perpetuating racial economy of stereotypes
and fantasies adhered itself to the black hyper-masculinity of gangsta
rap. Rappers like Snoop Doggy Dogg, Dr Dre and the late Tupac
Shakur echo the anger of young, poor African American men who have
been structured out of the mainstream economy and made reliant on
drugs and gangs for financial and personal survival. Self-defined as the
CNN of the ghetto, gangsta rap 'reflected the nihilism of the gun
culture of the black ghetto and its language of violence, male heterosexual prowess, misogyny and hopelessness. Snoop Doggy Dogg, on
trial as an accessory to murder in October 1995, exemplified this trend
by releasing a song about his forthcoming trial and using the killing of
20 year-old Philip Woldemariam to promote his street credibility. As
Paul Gilroy has put it, 'an amplified and exaggerated masculinity has
become the boastful centrepiece of a culture of compensation that self-
consciously salves the misery of the disempowered and subordinated.'[17] The gangsta rappers who have celebrated the AK 47, black-
on-black murder and drive-by shootings, and employed an abusive
sexual language of 'ho's and 'bitches' have personified the white stereotype of a sexually violent and dangerous black masculinity. An image –
eagerly commodified by corporate America – which tended to over-
shadow the pleasure and excitement of the music itself.

By the mid 1990s rap's popularity transcended divisions of class,
race and gender. Its elements of machismo and misogyny attracted the

emulation of white teenage boys who appropriated the signifiers of black, hyper-masculinity as symbols of social prestige. White boys adopted significations of blackness to enhance their masculinity: it might be a turn of phrase or swing of the body, reversing their baseball caps or wearing their jeans on their hips. The popular teen band of the early 1990s, East 17, was a prominent example of this appropriation. Their use of rap iconography defined their difference – their bad boy, working-class street image – from the more feminised, soulful masculinities of their then rivals, Take That. Les Back, in a study of working-class, white boys' adoption of black popular culture, confirms its preoccupation with masculine prowess: 'For young white men, the imaging of black masculinity in heterosexual codes of "hardness" and "hypersexuality" is one of the core elements which attracts them to black masculine style.'[18] Amongst middle-class boys too, identification with black hyper-masculinity has been a way of rebelling against their mothers and the 'soft' masculinities bestowed on them. Representations of the black male body in rap culture exemplified forms of body management and display which offered an antidote to their feelings of lack. For white boys, masquerading blackness is part of a (short-lived) adolescent revolt, a means of asserting themselves against parental authority and stabilising an uncertain masculine identity. For black boys, the impact of rap stereotypes can trap them in the representational economy of the dominant white society, which reproduces and reinforces restricted and unrepresentative images of black masculinity.

Gangsta rappers undoubtedly played on stereotypes of black masculinity to provoke white racial fears. But their posing has been a part of a real problem in which young black men themselves are the chief victims. A growing black commentary, both conservative and liberal, has identified young black men and black masculinity as being in a state of crisis. Its language of failed paternity and deserted sons is similar in its modality to white male concern with patrimony.[19] Trevor Phillips, writing in *The Weekly Journal*, in June 1992, declared, 'Thank God my children are girls.' His article catalogues the appalling social prospects for young black men: they are 16 per cent of the prison population, they fill the law courts, they are three times as likely as anyone else to land up in jail; they are excluded from school, and they fail academically. In contrast, in spite of racial discrimination and sexism, young black women are doing a lot better. Phillips asks, 'So what happened to boys?' He answers his rhetorical question by asserting that 'very many young black men' are raised in families without discipline and ambition: 'They have to grow up without even the idea of a father, and with mothers struggling to make ends meet.' The result is young black men who don't respect themselves or black women. He concludes his article with the comment; 'our girls need to find partners, not sexual lodgers'.

The theme of fatherless black boys is the subject of *fatheralong*, by African American writer John Edgar Wideman.

> Ideas of manhood, true and transforming, grow out of private, personal exchanges between fathers and sons. Yet for generations of black men in America this privacy, this privilege, has been systematically breached in a most shameful and public way. . . Generation after generation of black men, deprived of the voices of their fathers, are for all intents and purposes born semi-orphans. . . Fathers in exile, in hiding, on the run, anonymous, undetermined, dead. . . The power to speak, father to son, is mediated or withheld; white men and the reality they subscribe to, stand in the way' (pp64-65).

Wideman feels impelled to examine his relationship with his own father in order to historicise his black identity. He extrapolates his private drama to include the predicament of African American culture which he likens to a second Middle Passage: 'young people feel rootless, deserted, adrift in a world no one has prepared them to understand. A void behind, a void ahead' (pxxiii). This economic and social catastrophe is the consequence of historical racism; Wideman addresses it as an issue of racial patricide – 'Who wants me dead? Who has expended such enormous energy killing my fathers? I've wanted answers to these questions my entire life' (p78). Despite his alarm at the impact of white racism on black lives, Wideman asserts the liberal belief that 'race' is a social fiction, that ethnic differences need not be mutually exclusive and that their exists a diversity of racial identities. But the search for an African American identity, and the crisis of its masculinities, has also encouraged the growth of an essentialist, separatist politics of black nationalism. In its desire to reassert the patriarchal authority of the black male, the politics of black nationalism calls for the regeneration of an black African patrimony which was destroyed by slavery. In so doing it rejects the possibilities of racial amalgam.[20]

In 1995, black nationalist activists announced a 'Million Man March' in Washington on 16 October. Benjamin Chavis, one of its coordinators and an associate of the organiser, Louis Farrakhan and the separatist Nation of Islam, described the march as a response to the deteriorating conditions in the United States of black people in general and black men in particular.[21] While black men were asked to atone for taking drugs, beating their wives and abandoning their children, the march organisers called upon black women to stay at home, look after the children and abstain from shopping and work. In an interview with *The Guardian* journalist, Jonathan Freedland, Farrakhan said:

> The endangered species among us are black men. If you look at the fratricidal conflict that rages in our community, at the jails filled with men – we are in bad, bad shape. If 68 per cent of the homes in the black community are headed by a woman and there are children there, we did not get these children by osmosis: a male was involved. But the male is not involved in the teaching and mentoring of that child.[22]

Farrakhan's prestige in African American politics had risen dramatically by the mid 1990s, but the radicalism of his rhetoric disguised a conservative politics which located the cure of a discriminatory and racialised political economy in the individual behaviours of black men. It is an analysis which can end up blaming the victim for causing his own economic redundancy, exclusion and oppression. The fundamentalist politics of identity encouraged by the Nation of Islam mirrors white, right-wing discourses on gender and race. The way it promotes black self-affirmation essentialises black people under a singular and homogeneous 'Black' identity.[23] While this strategy provides an alternative to the narrow stereotypes perpetuated by white society, it mimics its racist discourse by denying the heterogeneity, diversity and pluralism of black culture and identities. Similarly, because it has used gender as the idiom of its politics of racial purity, its ideal of wholesome manliness mirrors its Manichean universe of polar opposites. There is no room for gender ambiguities or sexual ambivalence. It promotes a masculinity which is homophobic, while it uses its fundamentalist interpretations of Islam to segregate women and enforce a strict sexual division of labour. Consequently it ends up perpetuating what it is attempting to eradicate, but fatally caught up in; the binarism and double bind of 'race'.[24]

Because of the conservatism of this fundamentalist politics of identity, Cornel West has called for black cultural workers to interrogate the other of Blackness/Whiteness. 'One cannot deconstruct the binary oppositional logic of images of Blackness without extending it to the contrary condition of Blackness/Whiteness itself.'[25] Whiteness and blackness are not racial categories of intrinsic, self-contained meaning. They are not biologically determined. They are social and cultural distinctions, founded upon physiological differences, whose meanings are dependent upon their relationship to one another. The pursuit of a racial purity as a solution to racial oppression has an appealing simplicity, but can only ever be a destructive illusion. Racial difference has multiple boundaries determined by class, sexuality and gender. In the US, unlike in Britain, race is the principle faultline dividing the country because of its history of slavery and economic exploitation of black labour. Automation of US industries in the 1950s and 1960s resulted in massive redundancies amongst black unskilled workers, destroying the precarious economies of black communities and creating the conditions for today's exclusion of large numbers of black men from the mainstream economy. Britain has similarly reproduced its old colonial relations within its borders. As the economy was rationalised and deregulated in the 1980s, a growing number of black men were excluded from work and educational opportunities. However Britain has a markedly different history of race relations to the US. Its relatively mixed geographical distribution of ethnic groups has so far prevented the development of racial segregation and ghettos.[26]

As the riots on peripheral housing estates indicate, young working class white males are facing a similar, if less intense, structural economic redundancy. This has given rise to media images of enforced idleness, a perception of a lack of steady sexual relationships, a self-destructive culture of drug misuse, an increase in criminality and a masculinity seen as irresponsible, violent and burdensome on local communities. On the positive side it has seen the burgeoning of an informal economy which has encouraged ingenuity in the art of getting by. These are behaviours and social trends which have been attributed to black masculinities and associated with black communities in the past. Their association with young white-working class males suggests they are not the product of a man's ethnicity but a response to economic redundancy and deprivation and the subsequent loss of meaning for men's roles and masculine identities.[27] Differences do divide, not least in the way cultural differences have been racialised in the last decade, but political economy suggests that much is also shared and that issues like gender and class create shared experiences across ethnic groups. The contemporary insecurities of masculinities is one example. The crisis of black masculinities, while of a different historical order and severity to white masculinities, has led to a similar desire to promote the authority of the father. In the process it has encouraged a more polarised gender order.

Mr Nice (and Mr Nasty)

The black cultural critic and writer bell hooks has argued for caution in the controversy surrounding violence and misogyny in rap which, she believes, has become an 'elaborate form of scapegoating.' Similarly, other black cultural critics have attempted to establish a critical stance against rap's homophobia and treatment of women, without at the same time letting themselves be positioned alongside white conservatives and racists.[28] Because gangsta rap has been so popular amongst the children of the white middle class it became for a while, a litmus test of white liberal attitudes towards black people. White liberals remained guarded in their opinions. The fear of becoming embroiled in a racist discourse or being challenged by black critics for covert racism ensured that white liberalism maintained its strategy of resolving its guilty feelings about black people by being nice. It is a response which submerges the white interlocutor in a welter of platitudes which leave the polarised dichotomy of 'race' relatively untouched. In effect it imposes a cultural silence around issues of racial difference. In recent years there has been a marked retreat from the 1970s language of anti racism and multi culturalism which are perceived to have failed as strategies for racial integration. White liberalism has abdicated responsibility for race relations in favour of an ethnic exclusivism; the separating off of ethnic groups into their own social and cultural spheres.

Jared Taylor, author of *Paved with Good Intentions*, and a white supremacist, characterises this unspoken liberal position with his comment:

> Most whites are basically indifferent to blacks, but they are certainly not trying to oppress them or hold them down. If the US has a real problem, it is not whites hating blacks. It is more a problem of blacks hating whites.[29]

A similar proposition can be made for the British experience of race relations. This reversal of racism, from being a white problem to being a problem of black people, reflects the wider political failure of white liberalism to develop a language of self-reflection on the meaning and dynamics of whiteness. Longstanding resentment towards black people has been disguised by the white liberal fascination with 'ethnic cultures' and commodities. The white person's inappropriate smile to a black person and the willingness – founded on guilt – to give uncondi- tional approval to black people, regardless of what they might do or say, simply because they are black, has given way to a growing indif- ference or even hostility. As Frantz Fanon has commented on this apparent reversal of feeling: 'the man who adores the Negro is as "sick" as the man who abominates him.'[30] As increasing numbers of black people move into white suburbs and display the trappings of relative prosperity and as they compete with the white middle classes for jobs and university places, the middle class sense of civic duty toward a deprived community gives way to a new perception of black people as competitors: potential usurpers who are unfairly aided by undeclared policies of positive discrimination. Once the fascination with otherness has been exhausted and once the guilt has been expiated by what is perceived as a recidivist black underclass, 'race' for the white liberal becomes a no-win situation. On the one side is the unacceptable real- ity of white racism and reaction, on the other is the fact and fantasy of black anger, resentment and ambition.

Jared's disingenuous self-appointment as uninvolved and bewil- dered bystander is the classic stance of white liberalism in a difficult predicament. The liberal failure of nerve around race has created the political space for the right to construct a new language of racial antag- onism. Charles Murray's *The Bell Curve*, a bible of the American Right, employs a socio-biological argument to claim that the poor educational performance of blacks is due to their innate inferior intel- ligence.[31] This recurrence of scientific racism is a part of a broader assault on the liberal politics of multiculturalism and racial tolerance. Dinesh D'Souza's *The End of Racism: Principles For a Multiracial Society* takes the abdicatory logic of Jared Taylor to its conclusion, arguing that white discrimination against blacks is a rational response to the anti-social behaviour of black people and the pathologies of black culture. For D'Souza the liberal hope of multiculturalism has given way to liberal despair as increasing numbers of whites become scornful toward black demands for what they perceive as preferential treatment. In the face of this New Right assault on the basic principles of racial justice and equality, white liberalism has buckled. At the

Labour Party conference in Brighton in 1995, Tony Blair spoke of the British as 'Decent People. Good people. Patriotic people . . . these are "our people". . . It is a new Britain. One Britain: the people united by shared values and shared aims.' His populist language of one nation represented a cultural homogeneity which denied the plurality of ethnic identities which make up British culture. It is a rhetoric which evades the racial antagonisms which exist between ethnic groups and downplays the continuing racial discrimination against ethnic minorities. His communitarian principles of individual responsibility towards, and cultural deferral to, an ill defined notion of community, has much in common with the social conservative tactics of 'colour blindness' and no special favours for any ethnic group. Blair's emphasis on a national collectivity denies racial diversity and is symptomatic of the liberal retreat from race.

In contrast to the racial abdication of white liberalism, John Wideman offers a place to begin exploring the complex web of fear, shame, hatred, confusion and recrimination which divides, and intimately intertwines, black and white men. In his book, Wideman describes his journey with his father to his father's birthplace, a Southern small town called Promised Land, where he meets a white ex-college professor, Bowie Lomax. Over the following few days, Lomax teaches him the history of the local area and Wideman recalls: 'I enjoyed his company, benefited incalculably from his patient tutelage. . . I was grateful, even fond, of this elderly man who shared himself, his insights and craft, so unreservedly with a stranger' (p113). But this gratitude, part of what Wideman calls a reciprocicity of niceness, disguises less pleasant feelings. One day, he is retrieving some metal boxes full of historical documents from a high shelf in Lomax's private library. As he passes them down to the older man he is suddenly consumed with an intense hatred;

> I was surprised, shocked even, by the ice-cold wave of anger, the fury compressed into one of those if-looks-could-kill looks I found myself flashing down at the back of his thin bald skull. . . It was Professor Lomax's skull I envisioned shattering, spilling all its learning, its intimate knowledge of these deeds that transferred in the same 'livestock' column as cows, horses, and mules, the bodies of my ancestors from one white owner to another. . . Didn't . . . the power and privilege to tell my father's story, follow from the original sin of slavery that stole, then silenced, my father's voice (pp114-115).

Lomax signifies the White Father, the symbolic law which has destroyed black patrimony and left its sons adrift and at the mercy of white men and their racial hatred. Wideman's emotional openness and reflexive language recalls the personal pain and distress of Frantz Fanon's similar existential confrontation with 'the white man':

> On that day, completely dislocated, unable to be abroad with the other, the white man, who unmercifully imprisoned me, I took myself far off from my own presence, far indeed, and made myself an object. What else could it be for me but an amputation, an excision, a haemorrhage that spattered my whole body with black blood. But I did not want this revision, this thematization. All I wanted was to be a man among other men.'[32]

Both Wideman and Fanon bear witness to their distress in this racial confrontation, but the white man remains silent. This silence reflects the discourse of racism which reinforces whiteness as the dominant and universal norm, allowing for the continuation of an unquestioned and undivided, white self-consciousness. By dehumanising its victims, racism protects whites from culpability, and recognition of black people as different, but also similar to themselves. Similarly, its dominant emotions of hatred, ignorance, fear, pity and indifference militate against a language of self-reflection and empathy. Perhaps it is this failure of language which has ensured that a white liberal politics of race has avoided interrogating whiteness and has remained stuck at the level of contrition.

In *Black Skin White Masks*, Fanon explores how the racial alterity of Self and Other has been constructed and how it has effected him as a black man. In the process, he offers white masculinity a language of self-reflection.[33] His analysis draws upon the work of Jean Paul Sartre. In *Being and Nothingness*, Sartre argues that the existence of other people can be defined as the Other; the self which is not one's own self.[34] The Other is 'indispensable... to my consciousness as self-consciousness' (p235). An individual can only be for him or her self through another; but at the same time; ' it is only in so far as each man is opposed to the Other that he is absolutely for himself.' (p.236) The Other is simultaneously the origin of self-consciousness and the source of its destruction. To be looked at, or recognised by, the Other, is to become an object of his world, an event which undermines the self-consciousness of one's own world. Sartre's philosophical structure of

Self and Other relies on Hegel's dialectic of recognition, which structures alterity as a relationship of domination and struggle – only through the domination of the Other can an individual achieve an identity (for self-knowledge, self-preservation and self-mastery). Following this logic, Sartre's relation to the Other mimics the binarism of 'race'. Like Hegel's epistemology it offers a powerful descriptive insight into what it is like to live within the binarism of 'race', but it cannot provide a language to deconstruct its binarism and establish the basis of a dialogue between Self and Other.[35] Fanon attempts that dialogue.

Fanon tempers Sartre's duality of Self and Other by introducing a psychoanalytic model of human relations. In his essay, 'Fact of Blackness', he describes a confrontation between himself, a small white boy and the boy's mother. Whether it was a real life event or invented, the confrontation serves a metaphorical function as the imaginary scene of racial difference; a triangular, homosocial relationship which fixes him in the discourse of 'race'.[36] Fanon is caught in the look of the small boy: 'Mama, see the Negro! I'm frightened' (p112). This misrecognition defines his blackness.

> My body was given back to me sprawled out, distorted, recoloured, clad in mourning in that white winter day. The Negro is an animal, the Negro is bad, the Negro is mean, the Negro is ugly; look, a nigger, it's cold, the nigger is shivering, the nigger is shivering because he is cold, the little boy is trembling because he is afraid of the nigger, the nigger is shivering with cold, that cold that goes through your bones, the handsome little boy is trembling because he thinks that the nigger is quivering with rage, the little white boy throws himself into his mother's arms: Mama, the nigger's going to eat me up (pp113-114).

It is a misrecognition which also defines the boy's whiteness and in this respect the scene serves as a metaphor for white men's relationship to their black Other. Fanon's triangle of man, mother and son is a representation of Freud's primal scene and introduces the gendered, oedipal nature of this confrontation. In his case study of the 'Wolf Man', Freud analysed a young man's nightmare about being eaten by wolves, which he argued was the condensation and displacement of his childish terror at the sight of his parents copulating (see p87).[37] The young man conceived the act as an aggressive assertion of his father's sexual power over his mother. The boy's fear of his father – being eaten by the wolves – represents the threat of castration which will annihilate his attachment to his mother. However, while the young man's dream signifies his desire to escape the oedipal tyranny of his father, it also represents his desire both to succumb to and have his father's sexual power.

> It seems, therefore, as though he had identified himself with his castrated mother during the dream, and was now fighting against the fact. 'If you want to be sexually satisfied by Father', we may perhaps represent him as saying to himself, 'you must allow yourself to be castrated like Mother; but I won't have that.' In short, a clear protest on the part of his masculinity.[38]

Despite Freud's depiction of the boy's masculine protest, his analysis reveals the son's identification with the father as ambiguous and never fully secured: should he be like his father or to retain an identification with his mother.[39] Freud's small boy stands before his father in much the same way as Fanon's small white boy stands before his black Other; incapacitated by the uncertainty of his own identity and shamed by his incompleteness. It is the childhood legacy of adult men. As Sartre writes: 'I am ashamed of myself as I appear to the Other. . . Shame is by nature recognition. I recognise that I am as the other sees me. . . Thus shame is the shame of oneself before the Other. . . But at the same time I need the Other in order to realise fully all the structures of my being' (p222).

Fanon, like Freud, heralds the arrival of Otherness in the form of a frightening male figure. Confronted with this black father figure, he places the boy in a feminised position, seeking an identification with the mother. This identification contains the vestiges of his pre-oedipal relationship; his immature ego is undifferentiated from the maternal object and his meaning resides in the mind and body of his mother. In this pre-oedipal state, the struggle for recognition and mastery over the Other is absent, but so too, is self and identity. In the moment he throws himself into his mother's arms, he turns his back on the Law of the Father and with it his gendered subjectivity. In oedipal terms, the boy's identification with his mother reverses the male trajectory through the oedipus complex; he becomes his father's daughter. Even as the black man trembles in his own fear, the white boy learns that the site of racial difference is the potential undoing of his own masculine identity.

This imaginary scene of racial difference confronts the white man with the limits of his masculinity. To secure his place in the patrimony and diminish the threat of the black Other, he must destroy the paternal function of black masculinity which threatens him with castration. To defend himself he has two archetypal strategies. The first is to defend his own internal boundaries, to reassert his masculine independence from his mother and aggressively align himself with the existing polarities of 'race' and the heterosexual gender order. This way lies racial paranoia and the struggle for domination: the black man is the threatening Other who covets 'his' mother/woman. His domination over the black Other is an integral part of his desire, to inherit the patriarchal mantle of the white father figure; to repress his mother love, subordinate women and pursue the illusion of an undivided masculine plenitude. But he can never fully achieve patriarchy's idealised symmetry of gendered antinomies. Behind his militant reaction, his own fear of the Other ignites his repressed wish for union with his mother. Humiliated by the Other's recognition of his lack, he redoubles his hostility towards the black man. The self-perpetuating cycle of fear, shame and hatred escalates until the obvious solution presents itself – castrate the black man metaphorically, and if necessary literally. Once unmanned, the black father can no longer sit in judgment over the white man's infantile choice of castration in that primal confrontation with the Father/Other. With the destruction of the black father, black men in the white man's imaginary, are reduced to his own level of permanent adolescence. But the fantasy of castration eroticises the black man, his mutilated body signifies its willingness to be penetrated. Each confrontation with his black Other ignites the white man's repressed homoerotic desire. His racial paranoia is fuelled by his homophobia and spirals into an ever increasing brutality as he attempts to subjugate and destroy his unmanly and illicit desires. 'Race' becomes a sexual war in which the body of the black man functions as the involuntary screen onto which the white man projects his oedipal dilemmas.

Against this backdrop of racial hatred, and its historic practices of lynching and sexual mutilation, is counterposed a second strategy, one which is associated with a white liberal politics of race. This second strategy is designed to evade the troubling and potentially dangerous confrontation with Otherness; to negate it, to reduce difference to sameness, to love the Other in an attempt to place him outside the sphere of mastery. The black man is de-structured as an Other and refashioned as the same as the white man. What unites them in the mind of the white man is a shared enemy, the White Father. It is the fantasy of the rebellious white son in search of potential allies – a brotherhood of the dispossessed. But the white man's open embrace, his social tactic of niceness and of compliance with the Other, repeatedly pushes him into a masochistic position. As Sartre wrote: 'Masochism is characterised as a species of vertigo . . . before the abyss of the Other's subjectivity.'[40] In spite of his apparent good intentions and pleasant words, this white man is even more afraid of his black Other than his paranoid brother. While the latter struggles to defend his ego boundaries by whatever means necessary, the nice man is unable to lock anyone out. He feels constantly under threat of invasion. To retain the integrity of his boundaries in the face of his own eagerness to give them up, he hones a language of evasion, abstracting black men into an amorphous victimhood. He can champion victims, but he cannot conceive of the black man's own separately defined integrity and manliness. His niceness is essentially a narcissistic attack on the Other, designed to disarm difference and render the Other pliable and benign. Because he fears black men as he fears his own father, he fosters fantasies about black women brutalised by black men and neglected by black fathers. Like his own mother, they need his protection and care.

The archetypes of Mr Nice and Mr Nasty are not mutually exclusive terms. They are responses of white masculinity to the dilemma of Otherness, and their relative disposition and expression in individual men is determined by social, cultural and historical factors. The furore in the British press when Hugh Grant was caught with a prostitute in Los Angeles and charged with lewd conduct, revealed the extent to which these two archetypes are seen as incompatible and polar opposites. Grant's 'seedy sex' momentarily shattered the mythology of the essentially decent, sexually innocent English gentleman. 'What will the girl with the prettiest boyfriend in Britain decide to do?' asked Jane Green in the *Daily Express*. Her helpless answer spoke less for Grant's girlfriend, Liz Hurley than for England; 'Certainly she will scream "How could you Hugh?"'[41] While the majority of the papers commiserated with Liz Hurley and ran features on the psychology of men's infidelity, the *Daily Mail* published an article by Anthony Lejeune on 'Whatever happened to the English gentleman?'. Lejeune, in his desire to resurrect a fallen idol, turned to Britain's religious past and the ghost of Cardinal Newman. 'The classic definition [of a gentleman] comes from Cardinal Newman. . . "It is almost a definition of a gentleman to say that he never inflicts pain. His great concern being to make everyone feel at ease and at home".' But this genteel host who invites even strangers to feel his magnanimity is at a loss when his claim to the exclusive ownership of the home is challenged. At such a moment, when the white English gentleman is confronted by the political demands and ambitions of women or black and Asian British people, the only readily available alternative to his apparent niceness is an aggressive, defensive reaction.

The purpose of this essay has been to explore a third way to respond to racial difference: one in which white, middle-class Englishmen stop pretending to be the considerate host and recognise the relations of power and subordination such a role is built upon. In the white liberal politics of race such a recognition has often been followed by a state of contrition and self-effacement; a denial of identity and self-interest which all too often culminates in an angry if covert backlash. Disowning white English ethnicity has done little towards understanding our intimate, emotional connections to it. A third way has to avoid self-deception and recognise that the archetypes of Mr Nice and Mr Nasty are both elements of our racialised subjectivities. It means acknowledging the contradictory, often confused nature of our feelings about, and reaction to, black and Asian British people. The white liberal politics of race has celebrated the shared humanity of ethnic groups and avoided engaging with the incommensurabilities of racial difference. Consequently it has failed to develop a language which can speak of racial antagonisms, conflicts of interest and cultural values, personal anxieties and fears. Faced with these, language withers into racial stereotypes and prejudice. The celebratory language of multi-culturalism has tended to reproduce Asian and black British people as Other simply because it never took white English ethnicity, as a problematic. Similarly white anti-racism in its disavowal of whiteness and English ethnicity ignored or denigrated white peoples' emotional attachments to their ethnicity. Neither strategy provided the space to analyse whiteness and English ethnicity and make it a subject of debate. We need that critical self-reflection because the alternative is to continue to resurrect the old imperial dream of English manliness, and to hinder still further the protracted process of decolonising and deracialising the post-colonial English home. The consequence of doing nothing will be the same collective self-deception as the film, *Four Weddings and a Funeral*. It will put white England back to sleep with Mr Nice and allow the long dream to continue . . .

Notes

1. Paul Mungo (1995) 'Hugh me?' in *GQ* magazine.
2. From Will Hutton (1995), 'Why the poor remain silent' in *The Guardian*, 30 October.
3. Social Trends 1996, p.59.
4. Report in *The Guardian*, 31st August 1993.
5. Report in *The Guardian*, 21st December 1993.
6. *Ibid.*
7. Neil Lyndon, 'Feminism's fundamental flaws' in the *Independent on Sunday*, 29th March 1992.
8. *Ibid.*
9. Andrew Anthony (1992), 'Wild at Heart' in *The Guardian*, October 17th.
10. *Ibid.*
11. Neil Lyndon, *op.cit.*
12. Enoch Powell (1970), 'The Enemy Within' in *Powell and the 1970 General Election*, ed. John Wood, Elliot Right Way Books.
13. *Ibid.*, p 107.
14. Digby Anderson and Graham Dawson 'Popular but Unrepresented: the Curious Case of the Normal Family' in *Family Portraits*, eds. Anderson and Digby, Social Affairs Unit 1986, p.11.
15. Sandra Scarr, Barbera K. Caporulo, Barnardo M. Ferdman, Roni B. Tower and Janet Caplan, 'Development Status and School Achievements of Minority and Non-Minority Children from Birth to 18 years in a British Midlands Town', *British Journal of Developmental Psychology*, No. 1, 983.
16. Patricia Morgan (1995), *Farewell to the Family?*, Institute of Economic Affairs, p.153.
17. Paul Gilroy (1993), *The Black Atlantic: Modernity and Double Consciousness*, Verso, p.85.
18. See Les Back (1994), 'The 'White Negro' revisited: race and masculinities in South London' in *Dislocating Masculinities Comparative Ethnographies*, eds. Andrea Cornwall and Nancy Lindisfarne, Routledge.
19. For example, in 1995, a black US educational psychologist, Dr Spencer Holland, visited London to discuss Project 2000, an in-school mentoring scheme in Washington DC, specifically designed to support black boys. His visit was filmed by the Frontline programme (Channel 4, 13 September). His preoccupation with absent fathers and his dismissal of the value of women as mentors and role models for boys, closely resembled the predominantely white Wild Men movement. See *The Guardian Education Section*, 26 September, 1995, for two opinions on Holland's

ideas and methods.

20. See Hortense J. Spillers (1987), 'Mama's Baby, Papa's Maybe: An American Grammar Book' in *Diacritics*, Vol. 17, No.2.

21. *The Guardian*, 16 September, 1995.

22. Jonathan Freedland (1995), 'Demon at the Heart of America' in *The Guardian*, 14 October.

23. For critiques of the politics of black nationalism see the work of Cornel West, eg. 'The Postmodern Crisis of the Black Intellectuals' in *Cultural Studies* (1992), eds. Grossberg, Nelson and Treichler, Routledge; 'The New Cultural Politics of Difference' in *The Cultural Studies Reader* (1993), ed. Simon During, Routledge. The essays of Paul Gilroy (1993), *Small Acts*, Serpent's Tail; also the writing of bell hooks. Black female rap artists have challenged the discourse of black hyper-masculinity, as have the mixed band, *Arrested Development*. Amongst others, rap artists, *De La Soul* have offered an alternative sensibility for black masculinity.

24. The separatist and gender exclusive Million Man March, came within a month of the conclusion of the O.J Simpson Trial; an event of historic significance which has revealed the racial polarities of American society. Opinion polls revealed that before the trial, 80 per cent of African Americans believed Simpson to be innocent of murdering his wife and her friend. In contrast, 70 per cent of white Americans believed him to be guilty. By the end of the trial this polarised perception remained unchanged. In *The Guardian*, Jonathan Freedland reported the support given to Farrakhan by the mainly white militia movement ('White far right courts blacks', 20 October, 1995). Norm Olson of the Michigan militias said: 'His message is the very same message as my message. We've got a nation of black wimps and white wimps and we've got to change that.' Gerald Gruild of the racist Aryan Nations was more to the point. 'He wants an all-black nation with the total extermination of all whites and we would want just the other side of the coin.' In 1986, after Louis Farrakhan was barred from entering Britain, he found support from the National Front whose posters proclaimed; 'Louis Farrakhan speaks for his people. We speak for ours.' In spite of Farrakhan's loathing of white supremacism (his long speech at the march reiterated his belief that the main enemy of black equality was white supremacism), his politics of separatism offers a mutually compatible common ground with the far right.

25. Cornel West (1993), 'The New Cultural Politics of Difference' in *The Cultural Studies Reader*, ed. Simon During, Routledge, p.212. In the *New York Times*, Cornel West wrote of the the Million Man March; 'Coming after the O.J. Simpson verdict, the march promises to be a pivotal moment

in our nation's history' Quoted from Jonathan Freedland's report in *The Guardian*, October 16th, 1995. See also, Manning Marable 'A black tie occasion' in the same issue.

26. I don't wish to overstate this argument. However it does raise the hope that US style ghettos will not develop in Britain, even if racial segregation gathers apace in other social, cultural and economic forms. However a study of the geographic distribution of Britain's ethnic minorities by David Owen has challenged the belief that Britain is a multi-cultural society. His report, published in *Population Trends* No. 78, (1994), published by HMSO, uses the 1991 census to show the segregated nature of many ethnic minority communities. Owen told *The Guardian*, 'In much of Britain, people from the white ethnic group may only occasionally come into contact with people from ethnic minority groups. But where minority ethnic groups tend to concentrate, the white ethnic group may only just form the majority of the population.' ('Ethnic map shows racial isolation', *The Guardian*, 14 December, 1994).

The Government report *Social Focus on Ethnic Minorities* confirms that black and Asian people remain disadvantaged on most main social and economic indicators. Ceri Peach, author of the Office of National Statistics report *Ethnicity in the 1991 Census* describes the black Caribbean population as working class, waged labour, state educated and council housed. *Social Focus* reports that Black and Asian people have jobless rates three times as high as whites. But race is not the sole determinant of these trends, class also plays its part. The black British newspaper *New Nation* conducted a NOP survey on black people for its first edition. Its report began: 'A countrywide poll of a representative sample of black Britons aged between 18 and 35, found that 45 per cent are in the higher income brackets, 30 per cent are owner-occupiers and 56 per cent own at least one car' ('Official figures prove creation of middle class' in *New Nation* 18 November 1996).

27. Onyekachi Wambu, writing in *The Voice* ('Marching for men' 24 October, 1995) also makes this link when he writes; 'The Million Man march was the beginning of this Black male discourse, and in time it will spread to White males as well. Our fight for civil rights and equality unleashed the women's and gay movements... Similarly, now the definition of a new male longing for spiritual and economic contentment amidst the huge industrial and technological changes which we have recently undergone has kicked off with the Black male defining the terrain.'

28. Quote taken from Sharon Krum (1995), 'Now hear this' in *The Guardian*, 12 September. See also Michael Eric Dyson (1996), *Between God and*

Gangsta Rap, Oxford University Press, and Helen Kolawole (1996), 'sisters take the rap ... but talk back' in *Girls! Girls! Girls! Essays on Women and Music*, ed. Sarah Cooper.

29. Quote taken from Martin Walker (1995), 'America's great divide widens' in *The Guardian*, 2 September. See also Jonathan Freedland (1995), 'Exclusive: white and wronged' in *The Guardian*, 23 September.

30. Frantz Fanon (1986), *Black Skin, White Masks*, Pluto Press, p.10.

31. Murray's book *The Bell Curve: Intelligence and Class Structure in American Life* (1994) is a throwback to the Victorian pseudo-science of eugenics. He was invited to Britain by the *Sunday Times* in 1989 and again in 1993. On each visit he wrote for the *Sunday Times Magazine*. His ideas about the emergence of a British underclass have been published by the right wing Institute of Economic Affairs. See Murray's, *The Emerging British Underclass*, 1990 and *Underclass: The Crisis Deepens*, 1994, available from the Institute of Economic Affairs.

32. Frantz Fanon, *op.cit.*, p.112.

33. Fanon's failure to address gender makes his work of more limited value in debates around sexual difference and black and white femininities.

34. Jean-Paul Sartre (1986), *Being and Nothingness*, Methuen and Co.

35. Sartre's central tenet that human culture and society is founded upon the antinomies of Self and Other derives from Hegel's account of the 'independence and dependence of self-consciousness' (see *The Phenomenology of Spirit*). For a discussion on the similarities between Hegel's dialectic of recognition and the discourse of 'race' see Robert Young (1990), *White Mythologies Writing History and the West*, Routledge. For example: 'Hegel articulates a philosophical structure of the appropriation of the other as a form of knowledge which uncannily simulates the project of nineteenth-century imperialism; the construction of knowledges which all operate through forms of expropriation and incorporation of the other mimics at a conceptual level the geographical and economic absorption of the non-European world by the West.' (p3) Perhaps the single aim of post colonial theories has been to find an alternative to the Hegelian dialectic of recognition which can avoid the exclusionary practice of identity. But given that the nineteenth century epistemologies of psychoanalysis and Marxism are themselves rooted in Hegelian philosophy, the problem of finding another way to speak of racial and sexual difference remains unresolved.

36. There are two intellectual origins of this scene. The first can be found in Sartre's section on 'The Look' (p252) where he describes the experience of looking through a keyhole and being caught in the act (pp259-160). The scenario introduces a third figure into his equation of Self and Other; the

voyeur, the subject behind the door and the person who catches the
voyeur. In this moment of discovery and humiliation, Sartre reproduces
Freud's scenario of masochism in 'A Child is Being Beaten' (1919) (see
PFL, Vol.10). The second is Jacques Lacan's essay, 'The mirror stage as
formative of the function of the 'I' as revealed in psychoanalytic experience' (Lacan 1949). Lacan argues that the infant establishes its ego identity
(its 'I') through a misrecognition of its wholeness in a mirror image of
itself. This mirror stage inaugurates identifications with other people and
forms the psychoanalytic foundations of relations between Self and Other.

37. S. Freud (1918b[1914]), 'From the History of an Infantile Neurosis (The
    'Wolf Man')', *PFL*, Vol.9.

38. *Ibid.*, p.280.

39. In his essay 'The Ego and the Id', Freud describes the 'more complete
    Oedipus Complex' with its 'positive and negative' trajectories. He writes:
    'one gets the impression that the simple Oedipus Complex is by no means
    its commonest form, but rather represents a simplification or schematiza-
    tion..' see *PFL*, Vol. 11, p.372.

40. Jean Paul-Sartre (1972), *Being and Nothingness*, Methuen.

41. Jane Green (1995), 'Hurt by a lover's need for seedy sex' in the *Daily
    Express*, 29 June.

BIBLIOGRAPHY

Abdullah, Achmed and Compton Pakenham, T. (1930), *Dreamers of Empire*, Harrap and Co. Ltd.

Adams, Michael C.C (1990), *The Great Adventure: Male Desire and the Coming of World War 1*, Indiana University Press, USA.

Allen, M.D (1991), *The Medievalism of Lawrence of Arabia*, Pennsylvania University Press.

Alston, Leonard (1907), *The White Man's Work in Asia and Africa*, Longmans, Green and Co.

Arendt, Hannah (1973), *The Origins of Totalitarianism*, Andre Deutsch.

Avery, Gillian (1965), *19th Century Children: Heroes and Heroines in English Children's Stories 1780-1900*, Hodder and Stoughton.

(1975), *Childhood's Pattern: A study of the heroes and heroines of children's fiction 1770-1950*, Hodder and Stoughton.

Benjamin, Jessica (1978), 'Authority and the Family Revisited: or, A World Without Fathers', *New German Critique*, Winter, p.48.

Berger, Mark, T (1988), 'Imperialism and Sexual Exploitation: A Response to Ronald Hyam's "Empire and Sexual Opportunity"' in *Journal of Imperial and Commonwealth History*, 17, 1. pp.83-89.

Berkeley, Humphry (1977), *The Odyssey of Enoch: A political memoir*, Hamish Hamilton.

Best, Geoffrey (1975), *The Victorian Public School*, Simon, Brian and Bradley, Ian (eds), Gill and Macmillan.

Bhabha, Homi, K (1983), 'Difference, Discrimination and the Discourse of Colonialism' in *The Politics of Theory*, Francis Barker et al (eds), The University of Essex, Colchester.

(1983), 'The Other Question', *Screen* 24:6.

(1984), 'Of Mimicry and Man: The Ambivalence of Colonial Discourse', *October*, 28.

(1985), 'Signs Taken for Wonders: Questions of Ambivalence and Authority under a Tree Outside Delhi, May 1817', in *Europe and its Others*, 2 volumes, Francis Barker et al (eds), University of Essex, Colchester.

(1986), 'Foreward: Remembering Fanon: Self, Psyche and the Colonial Condition', in Frantz Fanon, *Black Skin White Masks*, Pluto Press, London.

(1990), 'DissemiNation: time, narrative, and the margins of the modern nation', in *Nation and Narration*, Homi K. Bhabha (ed), Routledge.

Birkin, Andrew (1979), *J.M. Barrie and the Lost Boys*, Constable, London.

Bollas, Christopher (1987), *The Shadow of the Object: Psychoanalysis of the Unthought Known*, Free Associations Books.

Boyd, Kelly (1991), 'Knowing Your Place The tensions of manliness in boys' story papers, 1918-39' in *Manful Assertions; Masculinities in Britain since 1800*, Michael Roper and John Tosh (eds), Routledge.

Bratton, J.S (1986), 'Of England, Home and Duty: the image of England in Victorian and Edwardian juvenile fiction', in MacKenzie (ed), *Imperialism and Popular Culture*, Manchester University Press.

Bristow, Joseph (1991), *Empire Boys Adventures in a Man's World*, HarperCollins, London.

Buchan, John (1940), *Memory Hold the Door*, Hodder and Stoughton.

Carpenter, Humphrey (1985), *Secret Gardens: A Study of the Golden Age of Children's Literature*, George Allen and Unwin.

Carr, David (1991), *Time, Narrative, and History*, Indiana University Press, USA.

Carter, Violet, Bonham, *Winston Churchill As I Knew Him*, Eyre and Spottiswoode.

Chace, William, M. (1989), 'T.E. Lawrence: The Uses of Heroism' in *T.E. Lawrence: Soldier, Writer, Legend New Essays*, Jeffrey Meyers (ed), St Martin's Press, New York.

Colley, Linda (1994), *Britons Forging the Nation 1707-1837*, Pimlico.

Colls, Robert and Dodd, Phillip (1986), *Englishness Politics and Culture 1880-1920*, Croom Helm.

Colquhoun, Archibald, R. (1906), 'A Link of Empire: The Royal Colonial Institute' in the *Royal Colonial Institute Report of Proceedings 1906-07.* pp.119-124.

Connolly, Cyril (1973), *Enemies of Promise*, Andre Deutsch.

Cosgrove, Patrick (1989), *The Lives of Enoch Powell*, Bodley Head.

Cullen, Stephen (1987), 'The Development of the Ideas and Policy of the British Union of Fascists, 1932-40' in *Journal of Contemporary History*, Vol. 22, p.124.

Cust, Robert (1899), *Life Memoir*, Robert Needham, London.

Davidoff, Leonore and Hall, Catherine (1987), *Family Fortunes: Men and Women of the English Middle Class 1780-1850*, Hutchinson.

Dawson, Graham (1991) 'The Blond Bedouin: Lawrence of Arabia, imperial adventure and the imagining of English-British masculinity' in *Manful Assertions Masculinities in Britain since 1800*, Michael Roper and John Tosh (eds), Routledge.

(1992) 'The Public and Private Lives of T.E. Lawrence: Modernism, Masculinity and Imperial Adventure', in *New Formations*, No. 16, Lawrence & Wishart.

Delaney, Paul (1987), *The Neo-Pagans: Friendship and Love in the Rupert Brooke Circle*, Macmillan.

Dunbar, Janet (1970), *J.M. Barrie: The Man Behind the Image*, Collins.

Dunae, Patrick, A (1980), 'Boy's Literature and the Idea of Empire', in *Victorian Studies*, 22. 2, pp.133-150.

Egan, Michael (1982), 'The Neverland of Id, Peter Pan, and Freud' in *Children's Literature*, Vol.10.

Etherington, Norman, A (1978), 'Rider Haggard, Imperialism, and the Layered Personality' in *Victorian Studies*, Vol. 22, No.1.

Fanon, Frantz (1986), *Black Skin White Masks*, Pluto Press.
(1990), *The Wretched of the Earth*, Penguin.
Foot, Paul (1969), *The Rise of Enoch Powell*, Penguin.
Field, John, H (1982), *Toward a Programme of Imperial Life: The British Empire at the Turn of the Century*, Clio Press, Oxford.
Foucault, Michel (1991), *The Order Of Things: An Archeology of the Human Sciences*, Routledge.
Freud, Sigmund (1900a), 'The Interpretation of Dreams', *Pelican Freud Library*, Vol.4.
(1909), 'Family Romances', *PFL*, Vol.7.
(1910h), 'A Special Type of Object Choice Made by Men', *PFL*, Vol.7
(1911c[1910]), 'Psycho-Analytic Notes on an Autobiographical Account of a Case of Paranoia (Dementia Paranoides)', *PFL*, Vol.9.
(1912d), 'On the Universal Tendency to Debasement in the Sphere of Love',*PFL*, Vol.7
(1914c), 'On Narcissism: An Introduction', *PFL*, Vol.11.
(1915c), 'Instincts and their Vicissitudes' , *PFL*, Vol.11.
(1916[1915-16]), 'Dreams', *PFL*, Vol.1.
(1917[1916-17]), 'The Paths to the Formation of Symptoms', *PFL*, Vol.1.
(1917e[1915]), 'Mourning and Melancholia',*PFL*, Vol.11.
(1917 [1916-17]), 'General Theory of The Neuroses', *PFL*, Vol.1.
(1918b[1914]), 'From the History of an Infantile Neurosis (The 'Wolf Man')', *PFL*, Vol.9.
(1919e), 'A Child is being Beaten', *PFL*, Vol.10.
(1919h), ' "The Uncanny"', *PFL*, Vol.14.
(1920g), Beyond the Pleasure Principle, *PFL*, Vol.11.
(1921c), Group Psychology and the Analysis of the Ego, *PFL*, Vol.12.
(1924c), 'The Economic Problem of Masochism', *PFL*, Vol.11.
(1924d) 'The Dissolution of the Oedipus Complex', *PFL*, Vol.7.
(1925j), 'Some Psychical Consequences of the Anatomical Distinction between the Sexes', *PFL*, Vol.7.
(1926d[1925]), 'Inhibitions,Symptoms and Anxiety', *PFL*, Vol.10.
(1927c), 'The Future of an Illusion', *PFL*, Vol.12.
(1930a), 'Civilization and its Discontents', *PFL*, Vol.12.
(1940e[1938]), 'Splitting of the Ego in the Process of Defence', *PFL*, Vol.11.
Garthorne-Hardy, Jonathan (1979), *The Public School Phenomenon*, Penguin, London.
Gollin, A.M (1964), *Proconsul in Politics*, Antony Blond.
Goodhart, Eugene (1989), 'A Contest of Motives: T.E. Lawrence in Seven Pillars of Wisdom' in *T.E. Lawrence: Soldier, Writer, Legend New Essays*, Jeffrey Meyers (ed), St Martin's Press, New York.
Graves, Robert (1991), *Lawrence and the Arabs*, Paragon House.
Green, André (1986), *On Private Madness*, Hogarth Press, London.
Green, Martin (1980), *Dreams of Adventure Deeds of Empire*, Routledge & Kegan Paul.
(1992), *Children of the Sun: A Narrative of Decadence in England after 1918*, Pimlico.

Green, Michael (1981), 'The Charm of Peter Pan' in *Children's Literature*, Vol.9.

Griffiths, Richard (1980), *Fellow Travellers of the Right: British Enthusiasts for Nazi Germany*, Constable.

Harris, Pippa (ed), (1991), *Song of Love: The Letters of Rupert Brooke and Noel Oliver*, Bloomsbury.

Harrison, J.F.C (1990), *Late Victorian Britain 1875-1901*, Fontana Press.

Hassall, Christopher (1972), *Rupert Brooke: a biography*, Faber.

Hill, Christopher (1970), *God's Englishman: Oliver Cromwell and the English Revolution*, Weidenfeld and Nicolson.

Hyam, Ronald (1988), ' "Imperialism and Sexual Exploitation": A Reply' to Mark T. Berger in *Journal of Imperial and Commonwealth History*, 17, 1. pp.90-98.

Hyam, Ronald (1992), *Empire and Sexuality: The British Experience*, Manchester University Press.

Ingram, Edward (1986), 'The *Raj* as Daydream: The Pukka Sahib as Henty Hero in Simla, Chandrapore and Kyauktada' in *Studies in British Imperial History*, Gordon Martel (ed), Macmillan.

Jack, R.D.S (1990), 'The Manuscript of Peter Pan' in *Children's Literature*, Vol.18.

James, Lawrence (1993), *The Golden Warrior: The Life and Legend of Lawrence of Arabia*, Paragon House.

Kendle, John F. (1975), *The Round Table Movement and Imperial Union*, University of Toronto Press.

Keynes, Geoffrey (ed), (1967) *The Letters of Rupert Brooke*, Faber and Faber.

Kiely, Robert (1971), 'Adventure as Boy's Daydream: Treasure Island' in *The Victorian Novel: Modern Essays in Criticism*, Ian Watt (ed), OUP.

Klein, Melanie (1928), 'Early Stages of the Oedipus Complex' in *The Selected Melanie Klein*, Juliet Mitchell (ed), Penguin.

(1930), 'The Importance of Symbol Formation in the Development of the Ego' in *ibid*.

(1937), 'Love, Guilt and Reparation' in *Love Guilt and Reparation and Other Works 1921-1945*, Virago (1991), London.

(1940), 'Mourning and its Relation to Manic Depressive States' in Juliet Mitchell, *op.cit.*

Knightley and Simpson (1971), *The Secret Lives of Lawrence of Arabia*, Panther.

Knoepflmacher, U.C. (1992), 'Female Power and Male Self-Assertion: Kipling and the Maternal' in *Children's Literature*, Vol.20.

Lacan, Jacques (1949), 'The mirror stage as formative of the function of I as revealed in psychoanalytic experience', in *Écrits: A Selection* (1989), Tavistock/Routledge, London.

Lawrence, A.W. (ed) (1937), *T.E. Lawrence by His Friends*, Cape.

Leed, Eric (1979), *No Man's Land: Combat and Identity in World War 1*, Cambridge University Press.

Lehmann, John (1980), *Rupert Brooke His Life and His Legend*, Weidenfeld and Nicolson.

Lewis, D.S. (1900), *Illusions of Grandeur: Mosley, Fascism and British Society*

172

1931-1981, Manchester University Press.

Lewis, Helen B. (1987), *Sex and the Superego: Psychic War in Men and Women*, Lawrence Erlbaum Associates, London.

Lewis, Roy (1979), *Enoch Powell Principle in Politics*, Cassell.

Low, Gail Ching-Liang (1989), 'White Skins/Black Masks: The Pleasures and Politics of Imperialism' in *New Formations*, No.9.

(1990), 'His Stories?: Narratives and Images of Imperialism' in *New Formations*, No.12.

Lynch, Michael (1985), ' "Here is Adhesiveness": From Friendship to Homosexuality' in *Victorian Studies*, Vol.29, No.1.

MacDonald, Robert, H. (1989), 'Reproducing the Middle-class Boy: From Purity to Patriotism in the Boy's Magazines, 1892-1914' in *Journal of Contemporary History*, Vol.24, No.3, Sage, London.

MacKenzie, John M, (1984), *Propaganda and Empire The Manipulation of British Public Opinion 1880-1960*, Manchester University Press.

(1987), 'The imperial pioneer and hunter and the British masculine stereotype in late Victorian and Edwardian times', in *Manliness and Morality: Middle-Class Masculinity in Britain and America, 1800-1940*, J.A Mangan and James Walvin (eds), Manchester University Press.

Mack, Edward C. (1971), *Public Schools and British Opinion Since 1860*, Greenwood Press, Connecticut.

Mack, John, E. (1976), *A Prince of our Disorder: The Life of T.E. Lawrence*, Weidenfield and Nicholson, London.

Mackail, Denis (1941), *The Story of J.M.B.*, Peter Davies, London.

Mangan, J.A. (1986), *The Games Ethic and Imperialism: Aspects of the Diffusion of an Ideal*, Viking, London.

(1987), 'Social Darwinism and upper-class education in late Victorian and Edwardian England' in *Manliness and Morality Middle-Class Masculinity in Britain and America, 1800-1940*, J.A Mangan and James Walvin (eds), Manchester University Press.

Mannoni, O. (1956), *Prospero and Caliban The Psychology of Colonization*, Methuen.

Marsh, Edward (1979), 'A Memoir' in *Rupert Brooke: The Collected Poems*, Sidgwick and Jackson.

Mason, Philip (1993), *The English Gentleman: The Rise and Fall of an Ideal*, Pimlico, London.

Maude, Angus and Powell, Enoch (1955), *Biography of a Nation*, Phoenix House Ltd.

Mayhew, T., ' "*Bwana DC*" *the rendering of a pro-consul Personal Narrative of a District Officer in Tanganyika*', SOAS Library.

McCutchan, Corinne (1992), 'Puck and Co. : Reading Puck of Pook's Hill and Rewards and Fairies as a Romance' in *Children's Literature*, Vol.20.

McLynn, Frank (1992), *Hearts of Darkness: The European Exploration of Africa*, Hutchinson, London.

Meyers, Jeffrey (1989), *The Wounded Spirit: T.E. Lawrence's Seven Pillars of Wisdom*, Macmillan, London.

(ed) (1989), *T.E. Lawrence: Soldier, Writer, Legend New Essays*, St Martin's Press, New York.

(1989), 'T.E.Lawrence in his Letters' in *Ibid*.

Millais, J.G (1975), *Life of Frederick Courtenay Selous, D.S.O.*, Pioneer Head, Salisbury, Rhodesia.

Morris, James (1979), *Pax Britannica: The Climax of an Empire*, Penguin.

Mosley, Nicholas (1991), *Rules of the Game/Beyond the Pale*, Dalkey Archive Press.

Mousa, Suleiman (1966), *T.E. Lawrence: An Arab View* trans. Albert Butros, Oxford University Press.

Nairn, Tom (1970), 'Enoch Powell: The New Right' in *New Left Review*, No.61.

Nelson, Claudia (1989), 'Sex and the Single Boy: Ideals of Manliness and Sexuality in Victorian Literature for Boys', in *Victorian Studies*, Vol.32, No.4.

Nimocks, W. (1968), *Milner's Young Men: the 'Kindergarten' in Edwardian Imperial Affairs*, Duke University Press.

Nutting, Anthony (1961), *Lawrence of Arabia: The Man and the Motive*, Hollis and Carter, London.

O'Day, Alan (1979), *The Edwardian Age: Conflict and Stability 1900-1914*, Macmillan.

Orlans, Harold (ed), *Lawrence of Arabia, Strange Man of Letters: The Literary Criticism and Correspondence of T.E. Lawrence*, Farleigh Dickinson University Press.

Pakenham, Thomas (1991), *The Scramble For Africa*, Weidenfield and Nicholson.

Pedraza, Howard (1986, *Winston Churchill and Enoch Powell*, London.

Plotz, Judith A (1992), 'The Empire of Youth: Crossing and Double-Crossing Cultural Barriers in Kipling's Kim' in *Children's Literature*, Vol.20.

Powell, Enoch (1965), *A Nation Not Afraid: The Thinking of Enoch Powell*, John Wood (ed), Hodder and Stoughton.

(1969), *Freedom and Reality*, B.T. Batford Ltd.

(1971), *Still To Decide*, John Wood (ed), Elliot Right Way Books.

(1977), *Joseph Chamberlain*, Thames and Hudson.

(1990), *Collected Poems*, Bellew Publishing.

Reade, Brian (ed) (1970), *Sexual Heretics: Male Homosexuality in English Literature from 1850 to 1900*, RKP.

Rich, P.J. (1991), *Chains of Empire English Public Schools, Masonic Cabalism, Historical Causality, and Imperial Clubdom*, Regency Press, London.

Richards, Jeffrey (1987), ' "Passing the love of women": manly love in Victorian society' in *Manliness and Morality Middle-Class Masculinity in Britain and America, 1800-1940*, J.A Mangan and James Walvin (eds), Manchester University Press.

Richards, Thomas (1993), *The Imperial Archive: Knowledge and the Fantasy of Empire*, Verso.

Richardson, Alan (1993), 'Reluctant Lords and Lame Princes: Engendering the Male Child in Nineteenth-Century Juvenile Fiction' in *Children's Literature*, Vol.21.

Ritchie, Richard (ed) (1978), *A Nation or No Nation: Enoch Powell Six Years in British Politics*, Elliot Right Way Books.

Roper, Michael and Tosh, John, (1991), *Manful Assertions Masculinities in Britain Since 1800*, Routledge, London.

Roth, Andrew (1970), *Enoch Powell Tory Tribune*, Macdonald.

Rowbotham, Sheila (1977), 'Edward Carpenter: Prophet of the New Life' in *Socialism and the New Life: The Personal and Sexual Politics of Edward Carpenter and Havelock Ellis*, Pluto Press.

Rutherford, Jonathan (1992), *Men's Silences: Predicaments in Masculinity*, Routledge.

Said, Edward (1991), *Orientalism*, Penguin.

Sartre, Jean-Paul (1986), *Being and Nothingness*, Methuen and Co.
    (1990), 'Preface' to *The Wretched of the Earth*, Penguin.

Schoen, Douglas E. (1977), *Enoch Powell and the Powellites*, Macmillan Press.

Scott, Robert Falcon (1900), 'Farewell Letters' in *Scott's Journals*, Peter Scott (ed), Methuen, London.

Sedgwick, Eve Kosofsky (1985), *Between Men: English Literature and Male Homosocial Desire*, Columbia University Press.
    (1992), 'Nationalisms and Sexualities in the Age of Wilde', in *Nationalisms and Sexualities*, Andrew Parker, Mary Russo, Doris Sommer and Patricia Yaeger (eds), Routledge.

Selous, F.C. (1893), 'Incidents of a Hunter's Life in South Africa', in the *Royal Colonial Institute Report of Proceedings 1892-93*, pp.347-363.
    (1881), *A Hunter's Wanderings*, London.
    (1970), Publisher's Introduction to *A Hunter's Wanderings*, Books of Rhodesia, Bulawayo.

Showalter, Elaine (1987), *The Female Malady: Women, Madness and English Culture, 1830-1980*, Virago.

Simmel, Georg, (1908), 'The Stranger' in *Georg Simmel on Individuality and Social Forms*, D. Levine (ed), London, 1971.

Simon, Brian and Bradley, Ian (eds) (1975), *The Victorian Public School*, Gill and Macmillan.

Skidelsky, Robert (1975), *Oswald Mosley*, Macmillan.

Smith, Janet Adam (1985), *John Buchan: A Biography*, Oxford University Press.

Smith, Stan (1986), *Edward Thomas*, Faber and Faber.

Springfield, John (1987), 'Building character in the British boy: the attempt to extend Christian manliness to working-class adolescents, 1880-1940' in *Manliness and Morality Middle-Class Masculinity in Britain and America, 1800-1940*, J.A Mangan and James Walvin (eds), Manchester University Press.

Stedman Jones, Gareth (1971), *Outcast London*, London.

Symonds, John Addington (1984), *Memoirs*, Grosskurth, Phyllis (ed), Hutchinson.

Thesiger, Wilfred (1984), *Arabian Sands*, Penguin.

Tidrick, Kathryn (1992), *Empire and the English Character*, I B Tauris and Co. Ltd., London.

Turner, E.S (1975), *Boys Will be Boys*, Michael Joseph.

Tyndale-Biscoe (1951), *Tyndale-Biscoe of Kashmir*, Seeley, Service and Co. Ltd., London.

Vance, Norman (1975), 'The Ideal of Manliness', in *The Victorian Public School*, Brian Simon and Ian Bradley (eds), Gill and Macmillan.
(1985), *The Sinews of the Spirit: The Ideal of Christian Manliness in Victorian Literature and Religious Thought*, Cambridge University Press.
Webber, C. (1984), 'Patterns of Membership and Support for the British Union of Fascists' in *Journal of Contemporary History*, Vol.19, No.4.
Welldon, J.E.C. (Rev.) (1895), 'The Imperial Aspects of Education', in the *Royal Colonial Institute Report of Proceedings 1894-95*, pp.322-346.
Wiener, Martin, J. (1981), *English Culture and the Decline of the Industrial Spirit, 1850 -1980*, Cambridge.
Wintle, Sarah (1987), 'Introduction' to *Puck of Pook's Hill*, Rudyard Kipling, Penguin.
Wood, John (ed) (1971), *Powell and the 1970 Election*, Elliot Right Way Books.
Worth, George, J. (1985), 'Of Muscles And Manliness: Some Reflections On Thomas Hughes' in *Victorian Literature and Society*, J.R Kincaid and Albert J. Kuhn (eds), Ohio State University Press.
Wright, Kenneth (1991), *Vision and Separation Between Mother and Baby*, Free Association Books, London.
Yardley, Michael (1985), *Backing into the Limelight: A Biography of T.E. Lawrence*, Harrap.
Young, Robert (1990), *White Mythologies: Writing History and the West*, Routledge.

176